M000189028

# THE WAY OF
# THE DRUM

## Tap Into the Rhythm of Life

We have not only a responsibility to ourselves to play and feel rhythm, but also a responsibility to the world and the Universe. By freeing ourselves through rhythm we become members of a greater whole—a whole that has been there all the time. Rhythm is life itself. By playing we connect to what is important.

The Universe is waiting for us to play. It needs us to play because the Gods like to dance. As individuals and in groups, we articulate the beat that is life, awakening the life force in all things. A sense of rhythm is a sense of life and rejuvenation that is essential to a well-balanced, integrated, successful partnership with life. And it's fun too—if you're not smiling, you're not doing it right.

## About the Author

Russell Buddy Helm is a multimedia artist and teacher who started classical music training at the age of eight. As a teenager he developed his skills in various musical styles: Rhythm and Blues, Rock, Country, Folk, and Spiritual. With his band, Bethlehem Asylum, he opened for the original Allman Brothers group, and went on to play with many great Blues performers such as Chuck Berry and Bo Diddley. He also played and/or recorded with Frank Zappa, Tim Buckley, Big Joe Turner, Pete Ivers, and many others. In addition to albums, his work appears in soundtracks for films. He also works in television and video production, both with live performance and with computer graphics. He was post-production supervisor for Lorimar on the *Falcon Crest, Knott's Landing, Hunter,* and *Dallas* series. A teacher as well as a performer, he gives individual lessons and workshops on drumming. Also an artist and sculptor, Helm's work is shown at several California galleries, as well as in Atlanta and Philadelphia.

**e-mail:** buddyrsh@ix.netcom.com **website:** BUDDYHELM.COM

## To Write to the Author

If you wish to contact the author or would like more information about this book, please write to the author in care of Llewellyn Worldwide and we will forward your request. Both the author and publisher appreciate hearing from you and learning of your enjoyment of this book and how it has helped you. Llewellyn Worldwide cannot guarantee that every letter written to the author can be answered, but all will be forwarded. Please write to:

Russell Buddy Helm
℅ Llewellyn Worldwide
P.O. Box 64383, Dept. 0-7387-0159-9
St. Paul, MN 55164-0383, U.S.A.

Please enclose a self-addressed stamped envelope for reply, or $1.00 to cover costs.
If outside U.S.A., enclose international postal reply coupon.

Many of Llewellyn's authors have websites with additional information
and resources. For more information, please visit our website at www.llewellyn.com.

# Russell Buddy Helm

# THE WAY OF THE DRUM

2001
Llewellyn Publications
St. Paul, Minnesota 55164-0383, U.S.A.

*The Way of the Drum* © 2001 by Russell Buddy Helm. All rights reserved. No part of this book may be used or reproduced in any manner whatsoever, including Internet usage, without written permission from Llewellyn Publications, except in the case of brief quotations embodied in critical articles and reviews.

FIRST EDITION
First Printing, 2001

Book design and editing by Connie Hill
Compact Disk label by Cory Qualey
Cover design by Gavin Dayton Duffy
Cover images by Photodisc
Interior photos by Cathleen Javier, Lynn Rank family archives, Chris Galfo,
    Marcia and David Galleher, Steve Karowe, and Ron Sill (see p. 243 for details)

Library of Congress Cataloging-in-Publication Data
Helm, Russell Buddy.
    The Way of the Drum / Russell Buddy Helm. — 1st ed.
        p.   cm.
    ISBN 0-7387-0159-9
        1. Music, Influence of.    2. Music—Psychological aspects.    3. Drum—
Methods. 4. Spiritual life.  I. Title.

ML3920.H422  2001
786.9'11—dc21                                                                          2001038568

Llewellyn Worldwide does not participate in, endorse, or have any authority or responsibility concerning private business transactions between our authors and the public.

  All mail addressed to the author is forwarded but the publisher cannot, unless specifically instructed by the author, give out an address or phone number.

Any internet references contained in this work are current at publication time, but the publisher cannot guarantee that a specific location will continue to be maintained. Please refer to the publisher's website for links to authors' websites and other sources.

Llewellyn Publications
A Division of Llewellyn Worldwide, Ltd.
P.O. Box 64383, Dept. 0-7387-0159-9
St. Paul, MN 55164-0383, U.S.A.
www.llewellyn.com

Printed in the United States of America

This book is dedicated to
Robert Christian Gandhi; Master Musician,
Magician, Sage, and Friend

and to all the people who don't think
that they have a sense of rhythm.
You do. We all do.

Thank you to Eilleen Trafford,
my first drum teacher,
and to Cathy Javier
for her unlimited help and support.

Also dedicated to Fred Neil,
one of the greatest singer/songwriters
and human beings.

## Also by the Author

*Drumming the Spirit to Life: Let the Goddess Dance*

# CONTENTS

Acknowledgments     xiii

Introduction: Notation, Theory, and the Miracle of Learning     xv

> Welcome to the world of drumming. A brief introduction about Rhythm Theory and our cornerstone, the downbeat. Careful about injuries and relaxation.

**Chapter 1    Hit the Drum**     1

> Releasing exertion and tension that interfere with our body's ability to drum. Release drumming to free us of anxiety. Flowing water soloing. Personality diagnostics with a drum. Following someone else's beat. Fast and slow magickal drumming. Macrobiotic breakthrough. Drumming as generator. Soundwaves. Electromagnetic torus. American Indian Ghost Dance. Dreamtime. Indonesian "Ketchak." Three-beat and four-beat songs. Meditation on the next moment.

**Chapter 2    Focus**     23

> Group intentions. Janis and nameless rock stars. Basic drum pattern. Downbeat, upbeat, Elizabeth's groove, spoons. Mother Earth Samba.

**Chapter 3    Grooves Are Footpaths of the Soul**     29

> Grooves are footpaths. Following the trail like a hunter. Pulsing in harmony with the planet. Impossibility of recapturing a groove. "Traditional" drumming challenges. Invoking the Drum God. Shakere parts. Drum pattern #1. Six-beat tonic. Subtracting notes. Rhythm theory. Releasing. Creative learning versus brainwashing. Inspirational content.

**Chapter 4    Shock 'n' Rock**     45

> Wolfman Jack saves the day at Halloween.

**Chapter 5    Music Lesson Trauma**     53

> Personal history of American grade-school band directors and their effects on sensitive kids. "Ruler on the knuckles" piano teaching. Gangsters and therapists learning on the same drum. Releasing our own music lesson trauma.

**Chapter 6    Tuning Up Your Ceremony**     61

> Gospel choir grooves. Tantric sex groove.

Contents

**Chapter 7     Grooves Happen**                                        67

Dynamics of invocational drumming. Tantric sex groove exercise #1.

**Chapter 8     The Courage to Stop Time**                              75

Courage to solo in life. We put unnecessary pressure on ourselves to perform.
The group supports the individual's solo attempt. It doesn't matter what you play.
Growth through terror.

**Chapter 9     Soul Surfing**                                         81

The drum as "browser." Internet as analogy for human and Universal
consciousness. Marshal Mcluhan and his vision of tomorrow's systems and how
they evolve from today's mindset.

**Chapter 10     Invocation**                                          95

A song on the CD to use for your own ceremony. Creating your own personal
magic each day.

**Chapter 11     Restraint**                                          103

Restraint gives us magical grooves. A bit of wisdom from Otis Redding's road
manager. A traditional "Soul music" drum beat.

**Chapter 12     The Tao of the Drum**                                109

Feeling the constant play of opposites in our drumming and in life as illustrated
in the Chinese philosophy of the Tao. Creating an exorcism to send a troubled
man away using a Ray Charles groove.

**Chapter 13     Conjure Drumming**                                   113

The sacred grooves were brought from Africa, hidden under Catholic imagery.
Today, they are played by people like Bo Diddley.

**Chapter 14     The Celtic Knot**                                    123

Following the maze leads to enlightenment. The Celtic rhythms are connected
to African.

**Chapter 15     The Myth of Improving**                              129

The unnecessary pressure we put on ourselves to always "improve" instead of just
doing something for fun. Life's lessons that force us to eventually slow down
enough to respect the spaces and the notes. Hitting the drum too hard to drown
out the inner voices that need attention. Women leading a drumming group.

**Chapter 16    Arriving by Accident**                                    135

Getting to the sacred chamber by accident. The hero's journey as interpreted by the "Two Guys from Film School," George Lucas and Steven Spielburg. Our lives as our own myths. A need for ritual that is connected to our own cultural roots. The Sex Pistols as a form of mythic ritual. Rock evolution.

**Chapter 17    Going Back to the Well**                                  153

My mystical, musical mentor, Christian. Martial art, and the changing mindset of our culture. The "clave" as a meditation.

**Chapter 18    Taboo Moves**                                            171

We have a need to do sensual body moves even though they have been deemed suggestive. The culture is slowly changing to allow women to participate in sacred dance moves without getting attacked by men. Our private language should be self-affirmations while we drum.

**Chapter 19    Personal Magick**                                        179

We must take responsibility for finding our own magic. Past-life regression gave me unexpected allies in this life. Rebecca's gift. The Egyptian and his life lessons for now.

**Chapter 20    New Way**                                                193

Two different ways to view the drum; as a musical instrument and as a healing tool. People can create music without any training. The Campbell's bottle orchestra. The richest guys in the world want to be in a band. The shared ritual magick of making up a tune together.

**Chapter 21    Artistic Connections to the Other Side**                 199

Hearing and feeling the artists from the other side trying to give us inspiration. Need to deal with lost partners and family members. "Card Precipitations" as communications from the other side. Messages to continue the drumming workshops from Chief Many Horns. Being careful with receiving artistic inspiration from the other side.

**Chapter 22    Keep Rolling**                                           219

"Keep it rolling" through the catastrophe at Rita's debut in West Hollywood. The Muscle Shoals musicians. Liberace's personal critique.

Contents

**Chapter 23     Why We're Here**                                             231
Mystical musical training.

**Chapter 24     Leaving Las Vegas**                                          239
Enlightenment comes from giving freely. First, the task of letting go of things we
don't need. Opening the heart with the drum, then giving and receiving from the
heart. Life changes for the Legendary Psychic Cowboy.

**Chapter 25     Our Body Talking to Us**                                     247
The ending of the Dark Ages on Earth and the beginning of civilization. Being
ready and willing to improvise during the next shift in consciousness. Sharing the
Gaia Beat.

**Appendix 1     Injuries**                                                   251
Simple remedies and cautions for drumming.

**Appendix 2     Tuning**                                                     253
Mali weaving.

**Illustration/Photo Credits**                                               255

**Contents of CD**                                                           263

# Acknowledgements

Thank you to Randy Prentice for the Palengue Jungle recordings and his scholarly advice on the history of music. And his wife Jean for her gracious hospitality and wisdom.

Thank you to my sister, Marcy Zinner, and my brilliant editor, Connie Hill, and all the people who have drummed with me around the country; it's been great!

## Editorial Note

Many of the photos illustrating this book are nonprofessional candid shots taken on site, and therefore reproduction quality varies. These are included for their relevance to the text.

## Introduction

# NOTATION, THEORY, AND THE MIRACLE OF LEARNING

**B**asically, we all play the drum the same way. If it is a frame drum, we hit it with a mallet. If it is a hand drum, we hit the drum using both hands, hitting back and forth: pata pata pata pata.

Doing this "pata pata" evenly, calmly, without a break in the rhythm is what most beginning drummers like to do. That is a great place to start. It begins to generate a pleasant sensation in our minds and bodies, as well as in our ears and in our souls.

Taking out some notes and leaving cool spaces is what good group drumming is all about.

"Pata Pata" back and forth, using both hands, can launch a deep meditation.

That space makes room for the dance. That is where the groove is born and we start to swing; in our lives and in our souls. Swinging, danceable rhythms are where we want to go from that beginning "pata pata pata" rhythm. But we might need to change some habits that get in the way. First, we need to change from the concept of *filling up space* to *opening up space*. This change is like night and day. It is our growth from a mechanical activity to a fluid, sensual celebration of the mystery of life.

I work with a rhythm theory that is based on this basic "pata pata" way of hitting the drum with both hands in a repetitive pattern. This doesn't exclude single-handed drumming. One-handed drumming is based on the same principles of rhythm. We can be great drummers, using one hand or two hands, if we respect the space and the groove. American Indian, Celtic, and Mediterranean frame drumming use one hand with great effect, but the theory underneath all rhythm is based on our ancient back-and-forth activity of hitting a drum with both hands. It is a brain/body language that we take for granted, but it is a powerful tool. We can access deep sources of inspiration and strength by simply subtracting notes from this "pata pata" rhythm. We can acquire magic and redemption. It is a mystery that is delightful and it has always fascinated me.

The notation I use in this book is an attempt to render rhythm into a readable and *feelable* format. Musical notation is a necessary part of performing certain types of music, but this kind of drumming is not just music in the traditional sense of the word. We are finding new (and ancient) ways to play the drum. It is not always musical. Many times it has nothing to do with music. It has more to do with feeling and healing.

Visual symbols can be vague, but hopefully intriguing enough for the student to contemplate the relationships of the different notes in the world of sound. If there is a desire, the student can learn to read the various conventional percussion notations that exist around the world. But let's remember to enjoy the learning as well as the playing.

Notation sometimes creates a restrictive effect on our learning abilities. The symbols are clues as to what can be played and felt. Many times students give up because they are intimidated about making *wrong notes*. People want to just play. The notation shouldn't intimidate them so much that it dampens their desire.

The act of learning anything is a miracle to me. I am trying to avoid some learning pitfalls that everyone, not just drummers, fall into. Stress is often learned with the technique instead of creative feel. In the anxiety of learning technique with our minds, we sometimes lose the connection to our Divine Creative Instincts. We also lose our connection to the groove. I have nothing against technique, but sometimes we forget to leave room for our hearts and bodies in the quest for knowledge.

There are a lot of drummers in the world, with all kinds of techniques. This can be intimidating to the novice and the advanced drummer, but the feel is more important than technique in this kind of drumming, especially at the beginning. "Feel" can be played by the novice or the advanced. If we learn tensely and intellectually, then we will play that way, which is not danceable, or even fun. There are plenty of technical methods for learning the drums. I encourage any motivated drum student to check them out. Our own sense of rhythm is what we are born with—that is our gift and that is what I see people trying to connect to.

*Gimme a Rhythm Lite, please.*

Smile, don't frown, when you're learning to drum. There are enough frowning drummers in the world. Smiling releases tension.

I approach the learning process from a physical and emotional perspective. That was part of the way I was taught and I believe it is good for a number of reasons. The main reason I value this feeling approach is that I am still drumming. After a lifetime of drumming and living, I still get spiritual and creative satisfaction from drumming. I have seen many technical players lose that joy along the way. Some never feel it at all.

The notations are for visual stimulation, if nothing else. The challenge of translating music into a written language is as old as sound itself. I like to use

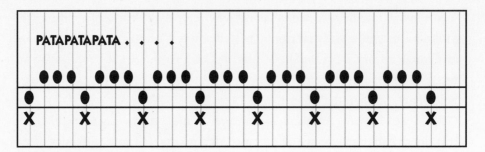

**PATAPATAPATA** ‣ · · ·

Notation example.

different approaches to musical notation that can become more like musical painting. Painting and drumming have a lot in common; they both use sticks, and there is rhythm in the activity. They both can be loud or soft.

To make things easy for us on the learning journey from our minds back into our bodies, I have simplified things.

I use notebook paper for the notation. This is not a casual choice, although it does remind me of bygone days of distracted doodling in school while the teacher was trying to educate us, but the main reason is that there are vertical

Use your whole hand for the downbeat. No fancy technique. Just hit it quickly. Get a deep ringing tone in the middle of the drum head.

The higher notes are at the edge. Hit them quickly. Get your hand up off the head to let the note ring.

lines that give us a breakdown of our own internal "pata pata pata" rhythm. Each vertical line can be a note played (or not played), by one hand (Pa), and then the other hand (Ta).

It doesn't matter which is right, which is left, which is right, or which is wrong. As we start to subtract notes, we see the relationship of the silence to the rhythm. This is a way to keep our inner clock going, but not get too intellectual. We want to stay in our bodies to learn and not get caught up in our minds. After all, we're trying to get funky here.

This music notation is less complicated than it looks. The top line has two different kinds of notes, above and below the line. The high

**The tambourine is an anchor, hitting the downbeats. It holds us together.**

note on the handdrum is above the line, The low note, in the center of the drum, is hanging below the line. That low note will also be our downbeat; our foundation note. It's the deep resonant note that you get when you hit the djembe, or any drum, in the middle of the drum head.

This downbeat is also the main note to be played on a frame drum, again in the middle of the drum head.

The downbeat is a beginning note in any drum pattern. It repeats. It's our anchor. We'll probably get lost, but find the downbeat and we're back on the groove again.

The higher notes, above the line, are the high notes on a djembe, played out close to the edge of the drumhead.

There is always a high note at the edge and a deep note in the center of just about any drum. That is all the technique that we need for this kind of rhythm theory.

The line of notes at the bottom of our musical notation is our time keeper. I use the tambourine, playing it with my foot. I hit it on the downbeats.

The downbeat is the beginning note for any pattern. It's our anchor and shared common note. We need to know where the downbeat is, even though we may not always play it.

Okay! End of lesson! Now just play and have fun!

## About this Book

This book is about many different things, but it all has to do with drumming: music, creativity, learning, healing, injuries, pride, fun, intuition, magick, inspiration, and Las Vegas.

This is a continuation of my first book, *Drumming the Spirit to Life.* It is an ongoing meditation and improvisation tool. There are new issues based on the wonderful drumming groups I have had the good fortune to have been a part of and we also will cover issues that I mentioned in the first book, but with more insight.

We all teach ourselves with our own inner language. The same ideas can be expressed in many different vocabularies by different teachers and students. The same rhythms can be expressed differently by different people. I am simplifying a lot of concepts so that we can all stay on the same groove.

There is a challenge in drumming groups; making them work for everyone. People want to drum but are worried sometimes that they are just beginners and can't play with real drummers. Those are the easy ones to drum with. I tell them, "Don't worry. Just play."

Another kind of drummer also has to be considered—specifically the drummer who feels more accomplished. That person wants a challenge.

The challenge is to play drums with everyone else.

Good, better, and *correct* are myths that have confused us. There is a lot of anxiety connected with examining one's performance. This book explains why it may be better to follow the flow of creativity as it happens around us, listening to what the outside world is teaching us rather than to get lost with inner voices that tend to isolate us from the world.

"Following the flow" is a mystical adventure.

## Drum Drama

Drum improvising gives us drama without too much risk. Injuries can occur though, usually because of our mental approach. Gentle drumming might seem to be a contradiction in terms, but a lot of people want to do just that. It can get hot and quick, but the overall volume and aggressive energy is at a minimum. There are fewer injuries. It is no surprise that subtle souls want to drum in this way, but they are struggling with people who are competitive and aggressive in everything they do, not just drumming.

Drummers can always improve. That is what keeps it fresh. Life lessons show up on the drum. My life had to change for me to improve as a drummer. The mystical side of drumming keeps it fresh for me. I feel important Universal energies at work when the drums are played in the right way—these powerful energies affect me. Life lessons have been made clear to me through the drum. Drum lessons become life lessons.

*The Way of the Drum* is an appropriate description for my life. I also see many people who are choosing the drum for personal and spiritual growth. I respect their instinctive connection to this ancient tool. I have followed paths in life that could be seen as various "Ways," and I've enjoyed different ways of creating, but I have always come back to the drum as an important conduit to the Universe. It is a personal connection and it has nothing to do with music or success.

My journey has always been about the drums. I've played drums since I was about eight years old: Classical, symphonic percussion, Drum and Bugle

Corps, Rock 'n' Roll, Rhythm and Blues, Delta Blues, Soul, Jazz, Folk, Reg-gae, Belly Dancing, Exotic Dancing (strippers), Flamenco, Second Line, Funk, Arena Rock, Country Blues, Salsa, Brazilian, Afro Cuban, Indonesian, Coun-try-Western, Free Jazz, Trance, Hip Hop, Punk, Gospel, Psychedelic, ritual magick, Christian Church, Yoga, healing, movie soundtracks, and perfor-

**The author playing an ashiko, an African standing drum, at Gaia Oasis.**

mance art. Basically, any kind of event that needed a drum. It's always been fun and it has given me a sense of belonging in this huge Universe.

## Las Vegas

Many years ago, I did a "Country-Western" gig in Las Vegas for a few weeks, across the street from Caesar's Palace.

But wait. . . .

There is something else I want to do first. . . .

I want to trick you into enjoying yourself. The drum is the Trickster. It can trick you into enjoying yourself faster than you can blink an eye—even if you don't want to enjoy yourself.

The drum can entice you into a healing, happy place. It is the greatest escape vehicle in the world, so put on some music and get into a feeling mode. That's where the fun is. Better yet, put on the drumming CD that comes along with this book and read while you're listening to the gentle grooves. Try not to worry about learning. Feeling relaxed is important too. We're trying to have a good time here!

# 1
# HIT THE DRUM

Many people are afraid of feeling their own rhythmic power. It's a simple and natural thing to feel. It makes sense out of the confusion that surrounds us. When you become a player your voice is heard by the Universe.

There are many things about drumming that can be explored. I bring them up spontaneously in drumming workshops. There is no specific learning order. I bring up the issues when I see them. There is no personal attack when I try to point out people's situations. We are all very much alike in some ways. We are not alone in our struggles to create.

## Fear

I try to counteract the fear some beginning players have by reminding them that there are no wrong notes in this kind of playing. This reduces stress. It makes learning relaxed and spontaneous. If we learn fearfully, we play fearfully. Learn relaxed, play relaxed. Learn with joy; people will feel joy when you play for them.

Musical notation for "joy" is not so simple. The notation in this book is somewhat generalized and elusive. That may be frustrating to the technical reader, but I am trying to focus on our bodies and souls as well as the intellect. It is a way to stay outside of our minds for a bit. We live in our minds so much that drumming can be a way out of that box. Learning to drum shouldn't put us back into that intellectual box.

It may be risky to say that that there are "no wrong notes," but I believe this concept frees us from the fear of playing, or fear of doing anything. There may be notes that are more appropriate, but that comes with experience, confidence, taste, and etiquette. What may sound "wrong" at the beginning, may sound great after your ears have become more experienced.

Drumming groups are a social contract where we can play, worship, and create together without the fear of wrong notes or aggressive competition. This is drumming with a coherent groove for the dance and creating magick in our souls. This "learning" is different than acquiring technique. It is scary for some of us; we have to learn to feel and share.

One drumming student is a retired electronics engineer who surfs and teaches skiing at Mammoth—a tough life. He said that there are four ways that people learn skiing or anything else in life: feeling, seeing, thinking, and doing. Drummers use them all.

The basic pattern that I start with is common to many cultures. It is based on the downbeat; the first note of the pattern. When we get going in a drumming group, that downbeat is our anchor. It is for the dancers as well as the drummers. The other little notes are important, but first we need a steady pulse to hang all of our fancy playing on. I play a tambourine with my foot, on the downbeat, so everyone can hear it.

## Tambourine

Here is the notation I use for the tambourine, which I play with my foot (top of p. 3). This is not traditional drumming—it is drumming for our culture. The tambourine cuts through the loudness and holds us together.

As we ponder symbols, our brains are stimulated and our bodies take a back seat to the learning experience. When we drum, we learn through our

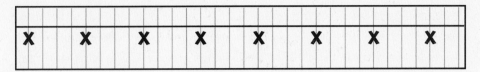

**Basic tambourine pattern.**

skin. This physical, liberating way to learn keeps our feelings alive. The enclosed CD has this basic tambourine pattern in all of the songs. You will hear it and get it without seeing it first. Our brains make things difficult sometimes when we are learning. Just tap your foot occasionally to give yourself a clock to keep track of the notes, but take a break if it gets to be too much work. Simply feeling the steady beat is the point here.

After we have a steady medium tempo going, let's set up the main downbeat. That is the first note of a pattern. That will be a big note in the middle of the drum head. Hit it quickly, but not hard. Get your hand up off the head so that the note can sing. Or hit the drum with a beater if you are using a frame drum and feel the steady pulse in your feet.

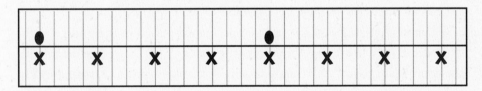

**Main downbeat.**

Remember, no muscle tension here—just a clean, relaxed, deep note.

Don't feel bad if it is no fun to do this. I just want you to understand the relationships of tapping your foot to the downbeat. Don't get worried about not doing it right. There is no right way. It's just symbols. It's not really playing the drums, it's just thinking. The fun part is in the playing.

Next we can add quicker notes that will give us a dance rhythm. The quicker notes can vary according to the country or region you want to emulate. For our purposes, I use a simplified Merengue pattern, but I avoid labeling it to keep us in our bodies and out of our brains—and also to remind us that these are *our* rhythms. They are part of our human culture—whichever culture that might be. They are not something from someplace else. Call it what you want. Basic Pattern #1 is pretty boring so call it something romantic that will conjure up an image. So when someone hears you play it, they'll say, "That's a (fill in the blank) rhythm!"

Now we introduce some little notes.

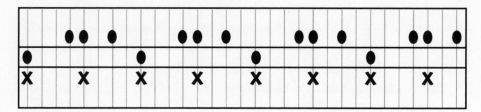

**Track 1: Downbeat.**

If you play the original continuous "PaTaPaTa" rhythm, then subtract notes where there are only vertical lines, you'll get an idea of how this might sound. Check out track one on the CD, "Downbeat."

The notes hanging down from the top line are played in the middle of the drumhead. It's a low note. Above-the-line notes can be played at the edge of the drumhead, giving a high note. Again, remember to hit the drum quickly, not hard, and get your hands up off the head to let the drumhead sing. Use both hands. But don't worry about which hand is the correct hand.

If you are playing a frame drum, hit that downbeat and don't worry about anything else. You can add a note or two if you can fit it into the groove.

This is based on the "PaTaPaTa" (all the notes), but with about 60 percent fewer notes. Low-fat drumming. Remember; no muscle, no tension. Breathe out and play relaxed.

In all rhythms, there are little notes in between the big downbeats. Most beginning drummers play continuously on top of the downbeats. That can get irritating if there is no space left for the dancers or the other drummers. Leave space to breath and dance and share.

4

Successful group drumming is based on *not* playing all the little notes. Play as few of those little notes as possible, remembering the downbeat. Play just enough notes to give you the magickal feel.

## Meditation

Leaving space for the groove is the meditation. Focus on this real moment and not on some removed intellectual concept of being in the present. Decide if your next immediate note is good for the groove.

## Competition

If drummers are competing, then you must make adjustments to the attitudes of the players—that is what I mean by a social contract. This has nothing to do with technique or talent. It has everything to do with sharing the space where the life force is generated; not from our brains but from our hearts and bodies as a group. The notes are unimportant. They are only clues to the magickal flow we are so hungry to share. It is a struggle to get through our intellect, ego, and fears. Life in general gets in the way, but the drum helps us get through it, when we play together and don't compete.

## Exertion

Sometimes people overexert themselves. Finding a balance in yourself, both physically and mentally, is a great part of drumming. Overexertion is a cultural habit and many times is inappropriate.

## Improvising

When a person tries to *cut loose*, he or she may exhibit tension in their face, arms, and shoulders. This slows them down and interferes with what they are trying to play. These reactions are common. Tension is a daily additive to our lives.

"Getting ready to do something," is a way to describe it.

There is a sense of building up to a point of excitement before actually playing the *hot lick*. Anticipation is a debilitating state of mind. I can point it out to people when they're beginning the process of improvising. They have usually gotten over the hump of just holding a steady beat and now they're ready to add something of their own to the groove, but an alarm goes off in their heads;

"WARNING! We are going into a performance mode! Let's panic! "

The adrenaline rushes, the muscles swell, tension locks up their mind and body. They get embarrassed, even angry, and the notes they play create anxiety in the people who hear them. Some people still force themselves to keep playing in this painful state and try to ignore the uncomfortable energy they are putting into the groove.

This is a state of affairs for a lot of people, not just beginning drummers. We tend to ignore discomfort until it is absolutely impossible to deal with anymore, then we go get it *fixed* at the doctor, therapist, shaman, or wherever. We need a subtle way to sense the comfort and discomfort in the flow of our lives. We habitually ignore the subtle voices of our own feelings. Rhythm helps us feel those voices, telling us when we are in tune with what is appropriate at that given moment in our lives.

Tenseness is not a workable state of being for a drummer. Life tends to trick us into accepting our daily dose of anxiety and tenseness as if it were required of us. Feeling anxious and "Going Critical" is habit forming. Eventually everything we do, even things we do for fun, go into a critical-performance-anxiety mode. That's not always the best way to have fun. It's a rough way to play the drums.

Anxiety and tension are habits. Breathing outward gets rid of them. Self-consciousness is a habit too, especially when we improvise. This is common in our culture. In any performance, there is an anticipation that can interfere. This is the inner critic deciding ahead of time if we can or cannot "do" correctly.

Great drummers aren't hindered by second-guessing of their intellect. When I see people getting worked up and ready to "let her rip," I try to laugh and get them to release the tension first. If they don't release the tension, the notes might stumble out, but then the improvised bit grinds to a halt and flubs around until the player just stops hitting the drum. That can get pretty discouraging after a few times. It is a reason a lot of people give up on drumming. They are bringing in their personal fears when they sit down to drum. The drum can help release those personal fears. Releasing is one of the drum's most valuable attributes. Subtracting notes from our playing is releasing.

*Call and Response drumming—where everyone gets a turn at improvising, no matter who they voted for.*

When that moment of truth arrives and you decide to hit some improvising notes, don't pay attention to them too critically. Just allow the creative energy to flow through your anxiety. It's just drumming. It's not a big deal. Just hit the downbeat, at least. That's all you really need anyway. That is enough to get you into the healing/releasing mode, which has very little to do with *performing* on the drum.

The most important note is the underlying downbeat anyway. Your overlaying notes should be in harmony with that underlying pulse. Your improvised notes can adorn that basic pattern. This seems to be what a lot of people want to do with drumming. It makes sense in a mystical way too. The interweaving of rhythms creates Tantric power if done in the right attitude. There is magick here. It must build gradually.

## Soloing

Soloing can come in smaller spurts that don't interfere with the dance groove, but it has to fit with the basic pattern. If it doesn't fit with the basic pattern, then the soloist creates anxiety and tension in the group and there is no healing or prayer or dance possible. If you decide to get tricky, be careful. The girls may stop dancing if your hot licks get too weird, dude.

At first, make a gradual addition to the basic drum pattern. You can be very tentative. Gradual soloing is good. Don't feel the need to compete with the hairy-chested blasters who start a solo "full out" with all the notes they can or can't hit. They solo many times without listening to what is already going on, anyway.

Rather, just slip into the solo with a short bit. Nothing too fancy. It's okay to be timid, then you can build up to something dramatic. Test the waters of the Universe before stepping in for a swim. A flowing, rhythmic pattern is like a stream of water. When we get into that flow, we have to abide by the currents around us. It would be silly to try to force the water to flow in the direction you want to swim. You need to allow for the flow when you drum. Don't try to dam it up.

Modern culture dams up the streams to harness the various energy flows to run our technologies. But what of the energy that we can't harness? That is the creative flow that is in all things; it is our source of magickal power. With the flow of our creative energy, we have a process for manifesting thoughts and forms.

A person who harnesses elemental forces such as hydroelectric or atomic energy is different than someone who follows the flow of elemental forces, but it takes at least two to tango in this world. The drum is a neutral place where different personalities can perceive how other people handle the flow of energies. "Call and Response" drumming is where the improvising goes around the group and everyone gets a turn—no matter who they voted for.

## Drumming As a Diagnostic Tool

People want to find the creative source in themselves. Sometimes we get confused by thinking and habits, and psychological states of mind may be apparent. If a person pushes the beat, then they need to relax and let go of tension, breathe out, smile, give themselves a break. If a person is locked up with their own self-critical dissatisfaction, then they need to see how lucky they are. Things could be worse; they could be playing a five-hour cocktail gig in Las Vegas.

For obsessive personalities, quiet drumming is good for releasing trauma. The player develops a vocabulary for their own state of mind connected to a sense of physical and spiritual honesty that is found uniquely in drumming.

One young woman started coming every week to our small drumming workshops at Seasons in Santa Monica, California, then stepped up to twice a week. She was ecstatic in her drumming. She smiled, she swooned, she let the rhythm take her. All the while, she played a simple pattern that was not too demanding or difficult. It was just enough of a beat to keep her in the group and feeling the groove. As she moved deeper into a state of trance, she didn't change her playing. It might waver a tiny bit, but it was always the three same notes, over and over again. She got such a great deal out of the group I saw no reason to make an observation about her playing. She was just fine, but there was something that made me wonder.

As a personal experiment, I decided to follow her beat instead of maintaining the beat myself. I had locked myself into the teacher/leader mode for a long time. I was in need of a vacation from carrying the groove, and needed another mindset to drum from. I suspected that I had become locked into perceiving reality in a very limited way as a drumming facilitator, so I became what I used to be in the music biz: the *Perfect Sideman*.

When I decided to follow her beat, I didn't announce it to the others in the group. I just listened very closely to what she was playing and played along with her, supporting her beat.

I had done this as a backup musician with many great singer/songwriters and performers. The drummer in a band has several duties to perform. One of them is to maintain a steady tempo so that the rest of the band can play together. Without that steady tempo, the music will fall apart. That was before drum machines.

The other, more subtle job of a drummer, before drum machines, was to support the creator, the singer/songwriter, in their interpretation of the mood of the song. Sometimes they will speed the tempo up for emotional effect. That is a difficult decision for a drummer to make. Must we keep the tempo rock solid or let the tempo follow the feel of the moment and speed up? James Brown plays all his hit songs twice as fast as the recordings during a live performance just to keep his music fresh.

Or maybe the singer would slow down a song for emotional effect. Some singers don't even know they are speeding up or slowing down. Sometimes, when you are on stage, the adrenaline pumps up and what was a nice five-minute song in private rehearsal speeds up into a tension convention, ending in two minutes and sounding horrible.

Old drumming habits die hard, then they come back to haunt you. My old "professional drummer" self-image was holding the beat steady. I realized that I was working entirely too hard, but following someone else's beat can be disastrous for a teacher. The blow-hards usually take over and things turn into a demolition derby. If the groove is lost, the dancers give up. Maintaining discipline unfortunately ends up being the main job in teaching or conducting a drumming workshop. No fun there. The job of the drum facilitator ends up not being artful or inspiring, but merely just to keep the groove steady. I decided to throw all that fear out the window and follow Elizabeth's swooning drum style, just for grins.

Elizabeth did not know that I was following her. She was lost in her rich trance of sound and feeling. She grew excited, the tempo sped up and I stayed with her. The rest of the group, unknowingly, followed my lead and stayed with me. We sped up to her personal tempo. She sped up again, she slowed down, she sped up, she slowed down, back and forth. It never stayed the same for more than a few moments. But all the time, she played the same three notes. We flowed up and down in tempo but held together as a group. It was a rollercoaster ride.

What fascinated me was the fact that those three notes *fit* with whatever I was playing around her. I could change patterns behind her, jump back and forth between time signatures, even double up and play twice as fast as she was going. It was quite a workout and we all had a great time.

After the drumming stopped, I explained to her we were playing *her* beat. She was amazed. She had no idea we were following her.

Bruk, one of the big guys in the group, is a professional athlete. He played on the American volleyball team in the Olympics. He's a big Dead Head. Drumming has been a source of release and a development of spiritual timing for him. He remarked that it was some of the best playing that he had ever heard from me. That was interesting. I had broken through some of my own assumptions about what was correct in a drumming group.

She definitely felt the emotional and psychic charge that we all generated. It woke up a curiosity in her to follow someone else. She suggested that we follow Cathy's lead. Cathy's pattern felt different, very cool and powerful. Elizabeth remarked that it was nice to *be* Cathy for awhile. This is personal, intimate, yet not intrusive drumming.

By following Elizabeth and then Cathy, away from my steady beat, I understood why a steady pulse works. The body follows the beat that is around it. When the beat stays steady, there is a deep sense of trust that emerges, based on the physical fact that the body is not trying to catch up with a frantic beat. When things are steady, the trance goes deeper.

When the pulse speeds up there is an adrenaline rush, a sense of the imperative. Survival instincts are actuated that can impede the playing. Trance is not that deep when drumming changes speed arbitrarily. Magickal power drumming starts slowly and then increases, generating a cone of power that can be focused when the groove finally locks in and stays steady.

There are scientific reasons why focused drumming can generate such powerful energies. In steady trance drumming, the body's electromagnetic fields lock up together to achieve a unified field. The speed of the drumming must not increase too quickly or the creative focus is broken.

# Slowing Down a Groove

Most drumming groups will not intentionally slow down a groove. The conventional drumming group mindset is to increase speed and volume until everyone *gets off*, or drops from exhaustion. Slowing a groove down intentionally has very important effects. It is first a habit breaker; forcing the drummer to see the world clearly instead of just going on automatic pilot. When the groove is slowed down or backed off in certain ways, trance deepens. Release comes from letting go of the need to keep up.

Some drumming groups slow down because they are too heavy. Sometimes the inertia of a large group of drummers slows the beat down until it goes to sleep. This feels like swimming in mud. It is a lethargic beat that results from a lot of drummers spacing out and forgetting about the steady state groove. Buddy Rich, the great Big Band Jazz drummer, was relentless with his musicians. If they started to slow down, he would yell at them to keep the tempo up while he pummeled his HiHat to drive them along. Small groups have the opposite tendency; they speed up. This has something to do with the number of players, whether it is Jazz or drumming.

Intentionally slowing a beat is not that common in drumming groups. People treat drumming like their sex life. They jump on, get excited, reach a climax, then jump off and check their beeper. Having a long, drawn-out affair has more sustained energy. Try slowing a groove down and discover the effect for yourself and your partners.

Enough about sex, let's get back to drumming.

Elizabeth came back the next session with a thoughtful insight. While she was cooking her usual macrobiotic mistresspiece, she realized that she was holding the knife with a tenacious grip; not just tightly, but, "Too tightly," she said. "My knuckles were white from the tension."

She then let go of the knife and felt an emotional release in her body and her mind. It was a release of tension. Tension had become her closest friend.

She realized that she had been tense most of her life; pushing everything. She had been tenaciously holding onto things in her heart and her mind that she didn't need. She feared that she had been playing the same three notes her whole life. It didn't frightened her. She was willing to explore this new insight. Those were her three notes. Now, she was aware of more possibilities in the Universe. She still played her notes, but they were much more relaxed.

When trauma, sadness, resentment, anger, and passions are released, space opens up in us for a new Universe.

I try to encourage people to express themselves through the drum because it is a peaceful dialogue where excitement and release can be experienced without danger. Call-and-response improvising happens when people aren't paralyzed with self-consciousness. Energy is created faster than it is used up. After a good drumming session, people are energized. They smile when they leave, even if they were not feeling too good when they entered the drumming group.

## The Drumming Group As Generator

Drumming groups create pulses of energy. This is energy like electricity or sound waves, but it is also very different than sound waves.

Scientists have visually described sound waves—their images are like hills and valleys. It could be a snake shape too. Uroburos, the World Snake, surrounds the planet and bites its own tail. The cult of the snake is very old indeed; drums made with snakeskin heads are powerful ceremonial tools in many cultures. Chinese Guchong uses a python skin for a vibrating membrane. I am all in favor of synthetic heads to save the animals of the world from becoming drumheads, but the deep tone is sometimes missing with synthetic heads.

The scientific visual image of a deep tone is first shown with an upward hill shape. Then the trough drops down before the next oscillation goes up the hill again. This imagery is nice as far as cartoons go. In reality this is not necessarily

Handcut/painted tin snake made by the author echoes the shape of sound waves. Drumheads made of snakeskin are powerful ceremonial tools.

what sound waves look like, because sound is invisible to us. This is just a cartoon to give us the properties of sound. It is important for us to remember that images and words are only simple sketches of the real thing. Drumming is different than learning to read notation. I discovered that after spending years learning to read music. Then I had to unlearn in order to just play.

We all have magnetic bioelectric fields in our bodies. There are millions of small "torus" or electromagnetic, donut-shaped vortices at our nerve endings—billions of them in our brain. Our body vibrates on many different wave frequencies. Our aura is made up of all these different energy fields, all pulsing at different rates. When all of these fields *entrain* or pulse together, then we have health. We also have power.

The body, mind, and electric fields become *in sync* with each other when we drum in a relaxed, steady groove. We can adjust bioelectrical pulsing by fine tuning our groove.

What do we do with this energy when it is in sync? That is up to the group or the individual. When we create energy, it goes somewhere. If we just let it dissipate, then we have a smiling, happy group of satisfied drummers who go home and have a good night's sleep. But what if the energy that is created were to be channeled?

Primitive tribes have been performing finely tuned grooves for countless centuries. It's what people want to do with drumming today in our "civilized" culture.

14

There is still the assumption that the primitive cultures are losers; that their cultures are not worth keeping because they have not survived the onslaught of capitalism or any other "ism." For all we know indigenous tribes may have been holding together the fabric of our existence by drumming. There is a basic connection between the drum, the earth, and our consciousness. Maybe as tribal drumming is threatened with extinction, modern people will pick up the beat for the earth to survive? Maybe we're saving the beat and the earth from extinction?

*Sound never dies completely. All sounds exist. Your sounds will always exist.*

The imaginings of drumming groups are rich and varied. Group hallucinations are not unusual. Group visualizations are what prayer and ritual magick are all about.

If a group decides to focus on an intent or an event, and they drum about it, there is a belief that something will happen. A *civilized* person would discount this but there is some kind of effect from focused drumming.

This kind of focus is used in Christian prayer groups when they're going after the Devil. It's also used in Pagan groups when they're defending themselves from the Christians. Rhythmic chanting is also used in Hollywood where actors chant for new cars and better scripts. I'm not kidding.

Drumming is associated with making rain. Why is that?

Alan Watts told a great story about Richard Wilhelm, the man who translated the *I Ching: The Chinese Book of Changes.*

A Chinese village was stricken with drought. No rain. They finally sent for a rainmaker. When the man arrived, he set up his living area in a house donated to him by the village. In a few days, rain fell from the sky. Wilhelm was in the village and witnessed this event. He humbly asked the rainmaker what he had done to make the rain.

"Where I live, we are balanced with the Tao. We have enough rain. When I arrived here, I put my life in balance with the Tao again, and it rained."

# Ghost Drumming

Ghost Dancing is an historically important Native American Indian Dance. Wavoca, a Paiute shaman, created the dance as a way for his people to gain spiritual sustenance and wisdom from their ancestors. It created hope if nothing else. Many tribes adopted the Ghost Dance as a gift from their ancestors. The dancers had conversations with passed tribal members. They gained strength and knowledge to survive. The Ghost Dance was feared by the American Government, and it was outlawed in the mid-1800s. Ghost Dancers were killed by the U.S. Cavalry.

The violent reaction by the U.S. Cavalry is a symptom of how our culture was deprived of a visionary mode of worship. Magickal drumming and dance are worldwide. We have come to the dead end, in a way, of our technological worship, and must now go back (or forward) to a method of sacred visualization that uses the drum and trance in a focused and protected manner. There are traditions of mystical warriors in the military of every culture. It is a part of human nature. Magickal imaginings, prayer, and drumming are tools for singing with the earth and our souls, for civilians, natives, and warriors.

# Rhythm in Visual Symbols

I like to discover abstract truths in drawings. Cave drawings hold that kind of fascination for me. African mud cloth paintings also have a symbology that hints at something ancient and magickal. Rhythm can be represented in mystical symbols. Relationships echo through different art forms. Creating rhythm with visual symbols can be beautiful and can weave a spell to the viewer as deeply as a drum beat.

The complicated symbols that Western culture uses to write music can be precise but lack feel for the music. I try to find visuals that convey rhythm without the intimidating intellectual confusion I experienced from Western musical notation. Precision is important but again, this kind of drumming is based on feel, which can be looser than the precision addicts are used to, although when everyone plays the same part accidentally, it is quite a charge of sympathetic magick. I enjoy accuracy, but not tension.

## Making Up a Song

Suppose that we were to create a song for our drumming group. Let's make up words for us to sing while we play a beat. This seems to be what a lot of people want when they drum. We need a spiritual experience where the participant can sing praises and send prayers to their own definition of the Divine Source. We could sing in a language that has this vocabulary already, such as Yoruba, Celtic, Santería, Arabic, Lakota, or any number of other cultures that have evolved songs to their ancestors and their Gods. Let's try something in our common language.

Let's make a phrase that we can repeat, together. How about "Mother Earth We Sing." Be patient, I'm going somewhere with this. Every time you say a syllable, hit the drum. Hit it at the same time as you speak or sing a syllable or a word.

Do this at a moderate speed. When you get the hang of it, try it at different speeds, but for now, just keep it comfortable. Each word or syllable has a drum note with it.

I wrote it out, using symbols. These kinds of symbols could be written on the embroidery of a maiden wrap. Or they could be painted on the side of a house to protect the family inside. They could be used to describe a mystery in a cave painting. Cultural symbols can be art, traditions, rituals, religion, or cartoons. There is an amazing commonality to rhythmic concepts, both visually and musically. It's called *synchronicity*. The same energy is being expressed in different forms and symbols.

Jackson Pollock's paintings have an intense amount of rhythm in them. He listened to a lot of music. Jazz was going through a tremendous evolution at the same time he was dripping and waling on canvas. It's the same creative energy we can use today, however we want to channel it.

Sting, the singer/bass player from that English band called The Police got the platinum-song idea, *Synchronicity,* from Carl Jung, the great therapist and cultural anthropologist. Carl Jung defined synchronicity in our mythic stories and in our everyday lives.

Let's make a dance song.

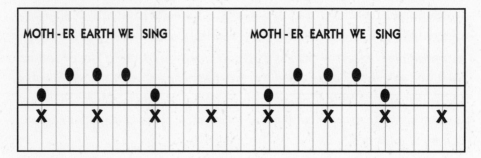

Track 2: Mother Earth Chant.

We will be hitting two notes on the word "Mother," which is a two-syllable word. You'll realize how easy it is once you hear it on track two on the CD.

Things can get technical if you use your brain too much. Drumming should be fun. You can just feel and not have to think when drumming.

The "x" marks our downbeats. Someone can play those slow repeating downbeats on a drum, a cowbell, a tambourine, a shaker, handclaps, water jug—whatever. Just keep it steady.

Rhythm is not proud; it wants to be played on whatever instruments are available. On the lesson CD I am playing those downbeat accents on a tambourine with my right foot. It is my secret weapon. It defines a downbeat for everyone to hear. I merely stick my foot into the tambourine and tap my foot on the beat; voilà! Suddenly there is whole rhythm section.

The tambourine can be a valuable key for holding together the drumming groups. The tambourine cuts through the confusion. Whichever instrument is used to keep the time, it has to be steady. It might take you some time to get the tambourine going on your foot, but it's great fun when you do. In the meantime, just feel those accent downbeats, or have someone else play that tambourine anchor part separately.

# Dreamtime

The aboriginal people of Australia have wonderful stories about their "Dreamtime." It is hard for us to understand the meaning in this culture, but generally it could be called the time before Time; before creation. They are the People of the Dreamtime. The Australian Aborigini people are the oldest race on the planet. Here is one of their stories about their music and their creation myths.

## Aborigini Creation Myth

The First Person decided to gather firewood for the coming night. The First Person sat down with an armful of branches and tossed them one by one onto the fire.

When the First Person picked up an Eucalyptus branch, he or she noticed that the inside of the branch had been hollowed out by termites. The First Person did not want to harm the termites, so they pointed the hollow, termite-filled branch up into the night sky. The First Person blew through the hollow branch and all the termites were safely blown out of the wooden tube. The termites flew up into the night sky and became the constellations. The sound that was made by the First Person blowing through the hollow eucalyptus branch was the Sound of Creation. That is the sound of the didjeridoo.

Let's go back to our song to Mother Earth and find a phrase that has the same sentiment, as well as the same number of beats. Then we can sing a different phrase with the same drumbeat and it will become a song. How about "Let the World Begin"?

This is in tribute to the Aboriginis who could do this sort of thing sitting around a campfire, hitting sticks on stones. They didn't need anything special, just the steady beat, to make the magick happen.

*Mother Earth we sing / Let the World begin /*
*Mother Earth we sing / Let the World begin.*

You can make your own words if you feel inspired. An interesting thing happens with rhythm regardless of what you sing. The words become powerful because the power of the rhythm reinforces the words.

We hit our first two downbeats on "Mother"; first on "Moth," then on "er" and it will also hit on "Earth," on "We," and it will hit on "Sing." Here is an image that might be usable; the first syllable of Mother is "Moth" (the moth is attracted to light).

This is a good animal image that is totally unrelated to any logical reasoning in the making up of a song, but that is the fun of making art; all things can be related if you want them to be. In our group consciousness, according to Carl Jung and many indigenous tribes, unrelated things such as a moth and a snake and Aboriginis and drums can be symbolically related. Don't expect a logical connection. This is inspirational so there doesn't have to be a logical, rational reason for your creative ideas. When an idea pops into your head, give it some respect; it could be art or a great mystical concept represented in symbols. That's what drumming is; sound symbols for another dimension.

An Australian Aborigini artist carved this didjeridoo from a hollow eucalyptus branch.

When we set up this underlying downbeat on those words, things start getting solid. The beat repeats and it becomes a pattern. It becomes a phrase and that becomes a song, all based on something as simple as finding words to sing. That is one way ritual has evolved. The magickal incantations are not just Latin, Celtic, Spanish, Yoruban, or Portuguese words, they are also rhythmic. The rhythm of the words creates the spell or prayer as much as the words themselves. Maybe more in some cases.

In many cultures, words are sung to invoke magickal states. The Monkey Chants of Indonesia are so compelling that I was frightened the first time I heard them. It is also called the *Ketchak*. The word "Ketchak" is the basic phrase that all the singers repeat over and over again. They vary the speed of the word and they vary the volume and the rhythmic combinations with others singing in a group, but there aren't any other words. It is an exorcism ritual and they have been doing it for hundreds of years. I feel that it does work.

The word "Ketchak" is a nonword in the Indonesian language. It may have some historical importance but that meaning doesn't exist anymore. It is a nonsense word from the technological view. A hundred people sit around, facing inward, circle within circle, singing toward the center where the oldest person in the village directs the chanting.

"Ketchak! Ketchak! Ketchak! Ketchak! KETCHAK! KETCHAK! KETCHAK! KETCHAK!"

They shout it over and over again, really fast and really loud, and something happens. If I were a monkey demon and I heard the monkey chant, I would stay away. It is overwhelming. It is only human sound and rhythm, but the power is undeniable. We have this potential, only we're so shy that yelling a nonsense syllable out loud, over and over again, is embarrassing—unless we're at a sports event or a rock concert. It's a challenge in our technological culture to let ourselves sing Cosmic songs.

# 2
# Focus

**F**ocus in drumming is where everyone is intent on the same idea. We start the groove with some kind of unifying concept. Bands back in the sixties would get together in the dressing room before the show and hug. It was like a huddle in football, only this was done with a lot of love and good vibes. It was many times better than what happened on stage. It was a way to feel psychically connected.

In one of my bands, Bethlehem Asylum, down in Georgia back in the late sixties, we all got together and sort of hugged the concept of being psychically connected, then went out on stage and acted like individual idiot rock stars.

When I worked in L.A. with Tim Buckley, he was an individual star, and could not really allow the idea of being immersed in a band. It bothered him that people called themselves by their band name instead of their own personal name.

Frank Zappa was a demanding band leader. The music charts were meticulously written out. The focus was on technical proficiency, not on psychic connections. That was different than hugging to get into a groove. His players hugged their paychecks.

At a pop festival in Palm Beach, Florida, in 1969, there were so many rock stars walking around the lobby of the Collanades Hotel that it was impossible to tell who was who. Janice Joplin did stand out, though. With her red hair flowing, she strode through the crowd like a tall ship under full sail. She was tremendously focused on her art and it showed in her certainty and power. Never mind what the critics say about Janis. They never felt her live.

But there were also lots of good blokes who just wanted to get together and jam, so they took over the hotel dinner club, which was filled with retired couples.

Introductions were kept to a minimum, so that they could get right to the good part, which was playing music together.

"Hi. Spookey Tooth," without giving you his name.

"Chambers Brothers," someone else might say.

"Hoople."

"Mountain."

"Janis."

"Butterfly."

You get the idea. There was this concept that the individual was not that remarkable, but together, a group—any group of people with focus—had a *sound* and some kind of magick. This group focus has always been my favorite way to play.

Kevin (left) played drums with Iron Butterfly. A great music video director, he still needs to drum!

Record companies prefer rock stars. They know how to control and market individuals. Bands were difficult because they were focused when a record label insisted on changes. An individual artist would cave into the demands of the record company, but a band could resist the intimidation. They would also argue about dumb stuff like who got top billing. There was a naive fantasy involved in how bands dealt with record companies, but the powerful psychic grouping of people with shared attitudes was very real. That was part of the era, but people have always done that.

The real magick that any group has, whether it be a band or just a group of friends, is their focus. It makes the group special and important. It's what I enjoy about drumming groups. The people focus with each other and we all get on the same groove. It is not hard work to play when we all pull together. Soon the energy is carrying us.

Here is a visual of a drum part that Elizabeth played. It works with almost any rhythm structure. Set up a steady feel though—that's the "x" marks. I play the tambourine on my foot. Hit one note in the middle of the drumhead, then pause, then hit two notes at the edge of the drumhead, pause, then hit one note again, another pause, then hit two notes. Keep repeating. It will work with an African beat or a Samba.

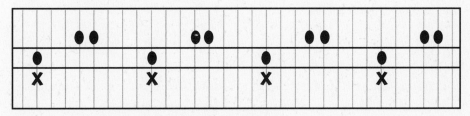

Track 3: Mother Earth Samba (Elizabeth's Groove).

If you put the downbeat on the single note, that will create one kind of feel. The downbeat or anchor for any drum pattern is usually the beginning note. It always repeats itself each time the pattern repeats. You can try to tap your foot on the downbeats (x) while you hit the notes, but stay relaxed. It's supposed to be fun.

# Samba Variations

If you put the downbeat accent on the double notes, then that will have a totally different feel. That is more like an "upbeat" kind of feel. It sounds like a Brazilian Samba. Sambas usually accent that upbeat with a big note in the middle of the drum head. So we'll change our hand patterns a little bit, hitting the high notes first, then end on that big note in the middle of the drum head. It's the third track on the CD.

At the beginning of the track I play the first part, then you hear the Samba whistle and we change the big note to the up beat. Then we create our Earth Song with words and music and everything. It swings pretty nice. Play along!

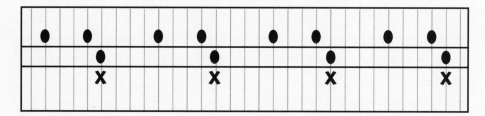

Track 3: Mother Earth Samba.

Don't get stuck in thinking one way is correct while something else is not correct. That creates tension. If you learn tense, you'll play tense. Different drum parts can be appropriate all at the same time. That is what is magickal about music. What you are playing right now is probably great.

If these notations are unintelligible, just use them to make images on a piece of cloth or on a box or the side of your house. The sense of rhythm is in everything. Rhythm is life. Visual images can sing to us. We can hear with our eyes and our hearts as well as our ears.

# Composing

I was a fresh kid drummer in L.A., about 1971. Van Dyke Parks is a genius composer and arranger. He was working on an album with Brian Wilson of the Beach Boys and also on charts for Randy Newman. I was lucky enough to be recording with him on a smaller project. I noticed that in his nice home, there was no piano. This seemed like an anomaly to me. He is a great pianist.

He was busy talking on the phone, doing a lot of things at the same time, then occasionally, he would pick up a pencil and write down some musical notation on a full orchestral score lying on the dining room table. Then he would go back to talking and being an interesting person. I could see that he was writing a string chart for a full orchestra—without actually hearing a single note!

"Wouldn't that be easier if you had a piano?" I asked innocently.

"That would only confuse matters," he stated simply.

So much for that Hollywood image of the struggling composer scribbling out notes while he painfully searches for them on the piano. That was a good lesson in composing for me. The music is in our souls and is struggling to come out. It is not necessarily in the musical instruments. Not even an entire orchestra can make music if no inspiration flows from the composer's heart and soul, and is then written down on the paper in front of them. Frank Zappa said sometimes the music sounded better in his head.

We're all receiving inspiration; the trick for us is to

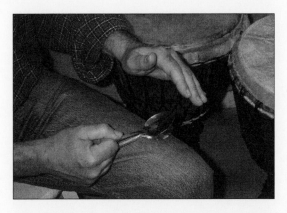

The author playing spoons. It's easy, just bend the spoons to get the correct angles, but don't let the waitress see you doing it.

allow the flow of inspiration and have our own personal form of expression, no matter what that form is—arranging for an orchestra or playing spoons. Real creativity just flows, but the editing and rewriting is where the art is, too. For now, let's just let it flow.

Now we are going to combine two things we just did: Elizabeth's Samba and our work in progress, "Mother Earth." You have a choice here. You can play either part, but have someone else play the other part. It might be very confusing. Don't be hard on yourself.

Just remember that you are a drummer, and that you have a part to play. Keep smiling, even if you don't mean it. Now, have a good time and play along with track three, *Mother Earth Samba.*

# 3
# Grooves Are Footpaths of the Soul

Grooves just are. They exist of and by themselves. We tap into them when we hit a drum in a steady, relaxed motion. Like an old footpath through the mountains, grooves have been followed for countless generations; like a deerpath that Native American hunters might have found, which becomes a trail that becomes a road, then becomes a highway; so grooves are highways of the soul.

It is ridiculous to try to put this into words, because the drum says things that words cannot. The drummer is the voice of a language without words and without intellectual restraints—if it's done in the right spirit.

We find a way that others have followed, like stone steps worn smooth from centuries of walking a familiar path.

In drumming, the grooves don't get worn down, they become polished. As we play less and less, more and more of the path reveals itself.

The temptation is to focus on the walking or the playing instead of the wondrous things around the footpath. Instead of keeping our heads down, focusing on where many feet have been, it might be more interesting to raise our heads up, look ahead, and feel the wind in our face.

Moving ahead, with good intentions, makes the energy in a groove build naturally, without anxiety.

Grooves just happen. They are discovered like the hunter parting a branch on a low bush and finding the evidence of a deer path. It is the kind of discovery where the hunter needs to keep quiet in their heart, so as not to disturb the deer. But the hunter can follow the deer trail and learn. The hunter becomes the deer in order to live off its gift of food, clothing, and wisdom. If we can stay quiet in our hearts, the grooves put us in a similar state of mind where we feel part of a great wholeness with life.

The wisdom obtained by following a groove is so subtle that there is no way to articulate it with words, except perhaps in poetry and song. The mystery is so immense that there would be no way to explain it with just words. That is what drumming ritual has always done. It defines the untamable.

The rhythms of our waking, workaday world tend to overpower the rhythms of our planet. That is the nature of the world we have created. We can still hear the pulses of the planet in our hearts, in our dreams and our souls. They may be from many different cultures, but they are still our rhythms. When we play to those cycles that are harmonious with the overall creative expression of life, we are getting in synch with the planet and the Universe, maybe on a deeper level than we have ever been as a species.

It is more than mindless and selfless communion with the Universal flow. We bring our intellect to this phenomenon too. Our intellect is a Divine Gift to the evolutionary song of humanity, but it can also be a curse. The gifts of our intellect are obvious, but the curse of our intellect is defined by many people as anxiety. Anxiety attacks to our brains are devouring our peace of mind. Drumming shuts down this automatic thinking activity, if we let it. There can be relief from the intense mental activity that never lets us sleep or relax. All the meditations of the world focus on relieving this out-of-control mental activity. Drumming also works for this condition. Play calmly, though.

Our intellect is now looking at the rhythms of our planet. We will soon define what these pulses do to us and how important they are to our survival, but don't let the intellect limit us. The brain can only take us so far. The path that has been walked for so long is not the destination. The notes are not the song.

Drumming low and slow is a way to give those cycles of the planet a voice. When we are feeling those pulses then we pulse in harmony with them. It is our nature to do so.

NASA has defined the pulse of the planet at somewhere around 8.7 cycles per second. Electromagnetic pulsing was installed in the space shuttles so that the astronauts could feel their home planet pulses while in space.

## Soul with Chops

We're all searching for the groove.

Once a drummer has tasted the magick of a certain groove he or she wants to go back to it. That is a real challenge because it is hard to recapture a magickal moment in time. It's good to learn to just let it go. There will be more. Still, some drummers try to recapture the power of a particular groove that they might have discovered last week or in the last minute. This is funny because it is almost impossible to recapture the same inspirational groove that you might have had just a moment ago. You can get close though. Sometimes it's better to enjoy the new groove at that moment instead of trying to force it to go somewhere else. A groove has its own identity each time it is born.

Traditional drumming techniques, whether they be African or any other kind of drumming, have been designed to recapture that magickal groove energy. This is the main reason that drum parts are memorized and handed down. Memorized drum grooves may be used for ritual and ceremony but the magickal feel of the groove is what makes the drumming piece really valuable as a spiritual tool. *Feel* is a subtle energy that is present only if the players are in the moment and they are not trying to recapture anything.

The memorized notes are really just a tool to get to that selfless plane again where the music lifts you to a different level of attention and awareness. When people try to learn and play traditional patterns, they are only getting halfway there. The magick comes through when they forget about playing a part and feel the spontaneous energy in each and every moment and in each and every note.

When people from a different culture try to learn an ethnic groove, some might assume that learning the notes and playing the notes is enough. That is just the beginning. It is an intellectual way to get to a nonintellectual state of grace.

Stressing the notes and traditional patterns is fine but it doesn't explain the most important magickal ingredient; the *feel*. That's in your heart, in the moment, in your body. That feel can be present in a person even if they have never hit a drum before. Beginning drummers many times have great feel but they don't trust themselves, so maybe they go *learn*, but there is a possibility that they could loose their natural feel and become only technically correct. The best drummers are both feeling and technically able to play. Soul with chops.

I sat in with a group of drummers who were playing traditional Yoruba drum songs. The usual leader was late and a wonderfully inspired man from Senegal was conducting the group in his place. He played hard and loud, and he sweated with his joyous effort. He was playing to his Gods.

There was a mixed bag of people from the American culture. Two Anglo men had huge djembes strapped on their chests and were prowling around the group, playing loudly. They interjected phrases over the African drummer's beautiful, solid groove. Their parts were okay but weren't as melodically appropriate as the master drummer's. This is understandable. They weren't from his culture, they hadn't eaten his food and walked his walk. They were playing what they had learned. From their point of view, they were right in what they played, but their licks were jarring and not appropriate to the flow.

Drum solos are a matter of taste, of course.

These two prowling drummers overwhelmed the groove. The sacred energy was struggling to come out instead of flowing out like water. As far as they were concerned, they were doing what was correct. They had acquired a few licks and they inserted those whenever they felt like it. They were playing aggressively, so I just stopped playing. I don't like to compete. The African master opened his eyes and noticed that I had stopped. For a brief flicker of a moment he let his own frustration show through. But then he went back to work and maintained the groove—smiling and forgiving and encouraging.

This kind of insensitivity on the drums is common. One visiting African drummer from Birgina Faso said it was shocking how all the drummers were talking but no one was listening.

As this traditional drumming group struggled along, I noticed a young man from India, probably a college student at UCLA, playing the djun djun, or bass drum.

He was not playing too steadily. His part was supposed to be the anchor for the rest of the group, but he didn't seem to realize how important his part was in the whole arrangement. I finally caught his eye and offered to take over his part on the djun djun. He gave me a relieved nod and we changed places.

*General Custer was standing on a hilltop with his Indian scout. They looked down at a huge war dance with hundreds of Indian Braves.*

*"I don't like the sound of those drums." General Custer said to his Indian scout. The Indian scout replied after listening a moment, "That's not their regular drummer."*

He didn't find the bass drum that interesting. He was more interested in playing the louder, faster parts on a djembe like the two power drummers. It didn't matter if their parts weren't in the same spirit as the master drummer's playing, it just seemed like more fun to really wail and make a lot of sound.

The Senegalese master drummer was working very hard, against the current. The two drummers weren't concerned that they were too dominating. In their ears, they were playing great. If the other drummers wanted to improvise over the groove, they would have to compete. They believed that they sounded pretty good. The master drummer was working hard to maintain the groove so they could noodle around on top. They could have helped him by playing the basic supporting part too, with some tasteful licks added; not just as an afterthought but as a full commitment to maintaining the strong current that everyone needed.

When I started to hit the djun djun with a steady, even tempo it locked into the master's drum beat, he opened his eyes and looked at me with new recognition. He smiled at me. It was a smile of discovery. He even sang a part to me and I played that part, as close as I could. He started to laugh and we took off. He started to sing the sacred words invoking Chango, the Drum God. The groove was finally beginning to feel right. The group energy was now focused toward what he had been struggling to get to all by himself.

As if a light had gone on in his heart, the master played with relief because someone was actually listening to him. I was supporting him by hitting the djun djun in a steady pulse. It was a very simple part. The whole group raised up a notch in spiritual focus. The doors of the Other Dimension began to open up. The master sang deeply from his heart and the blessing started to flow, taking us into the secret place. It was like a rushing river. The master sped up a bit to follow the immediate psychic charge of the invocation. I followed him.

The two guys were still bashing away, only dimly aware of the subtle change that was happening.

Then the master stopped suddenly and waved his hands to stop. Everyone sputtered to a halt, wondering why he had stopped the powerful flow that had started to take us to a higher plane.

"We can't go there, yet," was all he said.

The reason might have been that the leading master drummer had not yet arrived and no invocation was allowed without him. With tradition comes protocol.

Addressing the God of the Drum with an out-of-balance group could also be sort of embarrassing.

Our gracious drumming leader from Senegal changed the pattern and started from scratch again. The two drummers, again missing the dynamics laid down by the master, went off on their own. To me, they seemed like hunters, not respecting what they were trying to possess. At one point, the master sang a part to a woman who was playing (shaking) a shakere.

The *shakere* is a net of beads tied around a large gourd. When it is twisted and shaken, a loud wave of sound can set the tone for a whole groove. The master sang the part to the woman, but she couldn't hit the note he was singing to her, partly because the playing was too raucous. The woman tried to hit the

A shakere is a gourd wrapped in a net of beads or shells. Twist it or shake it.

right part, but she was embarrassed at not being able to get it right. Eventually, she gave up and just shook the gourd at a softer pitch and didn't really contribute as much as she or the master wanted her to.

When we finished, I showed her the part that was so hard to hear. She understood then, but it was too late to give it to the group, so I gave her a card and invited her to one of our drumming groups.

When I was leaving, the two men came up to me. They had a begrudging respect for the kind of smile I had exchanged with the master drummer, but they had to confront me. It was a guy thing. Drumming brings up confrontative energy. It can happen in the blink of an eye. I try to avoid that kind of playing.

"You were speeding up," one of them said accusingly.

I have been confronted in my life as a drummer in many different ways. One of my favorites was in a very crowded dark, night club. A large dark guy resembling a refrigerator confronted me and wanted to know what I was doing in *his* club.

I told him I was the drummer. That really offended him.

"I HEARD the drummer, man. You ain't the drummer."

Finally, someone came up and told him I was okay. That was a long time ago in a Galactic nightclub far, far away, somewhere back down on the Chitlin' Circuit.

So, a couple of CEOs in dashikis really didn't scare me too much. I decided to use a "Christian Gandhi" routine on them. If someone tried to confront Christian, he would turn the pressure around and put it back on them in a very Harlem/Zen kind of way.

"YOU were slowing down," I countered. "I was following the master."

They knew they weren't supposed to create animosity in the African drumming studio. Eventually they grudgingly stated, "That sounded pretty good, though."

It didn't seem to be a sincere compliment. They wanted me to tell them that they sounded good and looked good. They were wearing African clothing and African hats and they had African drums and they were playing African beats, but they seemed to be distracted away from the subtle, healing energy that is inside the big groove. I am just trying to keep a sense of humor about our cultural rhythmic quandary. I think we all feel rhythm just fine, but we've got such a bizarre sense of humor that we can't always let it show. It's like showing your knickers in public or something.

## Crossing the Street

On my first trip to San Francisco, many years ago, on my first streetcar ride, a young Anglo professional man got on and sat down across from me, next to a well-dressed older black man. He tried to talk jive with the old gentleman. The old guy nodded and tolerated the exchange as best he could. When the young guy got off the tram, the old guy said to the younger man driving the street car, "You can cross from one side of the street to the other, but you're still on the same street."

It's silly to feel more righteous or more *soulful* than some other person, but that is the kind of thing that goes through my head, so I'm betting other people go through the same little neurotic ego trips. I admit that I am sensitive about my soulfulness. I must have heard "You're funky for a white boy" too many times. Usually from white boys.

I am in need of truth and soul in my life, just like everyone else. The funny part is how we try to go get it. We are looking for the groove; it is the source of our missing inspiration and it doesn't necessarily come from what we know or are familiar with.

When we try to extend ourselves into another realm of soul it is important to respect and pay attention to the subtle gifts that are there. That is what we are hungry for; we just don't always know how it's listed on the menu.

Eventually the woman I had spoken with at the African drumming group came to our drumming group. It was quite a hike. She drove from Pasadena; it took over an hour to get to our shop. It was a grim testament to her desire. To me it was the same story of a gentle soul wanting to use the drum for healing and worship, but getting beat up by people using the drum for testicular glorification.

She was surprised by the number of women in our group and how assured they were. She seemed to be off balance—out of her element. Then it dawned on me; that had become her usual state of mind. The people she had been trying to learn from were making her really uptight about just playing the drum.

We started with the simple pattern that I usually start with: "Rhythm Lite" (see p. 38). It's a good warm-up.

The first note is on the downbeat, nice and heavy in the middle of the drum head. Go for a big resonant tone, no fancy stuff with your hand; just use the whole hand to pull the note up and out of the drum. Then three little notes at the edge.

Repeat the pattern steadily and at a moderate pace. No point in working hard. "Play lazy," meaning don't put too much thought or effort into it. Find

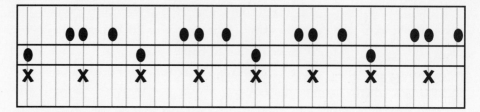

**The Rhythm Lite pattern. For the advanced drummer: accent the second note. It's a high upbeat note that is a Latin or Arabic accent.**

the fun and joy in it instead of slipping into the intellectual trap of judging your performance.

The "x" is where I played the tambourine with my foot on the downbeat as I coaxed everyone along. The woman hesitated, unable to just join in.

"Just hit the downbeat. Don't worry about the other notes," I suggested.

I usually offer this as a simplification. As you hit just the downbeat, you find it in your body. This usually brings a person out of their personal fears. It is always amazing to watch.

Slowly she came out of her shell and played timidly, but it was an affected method of playing. Her hands weren't playing, they were imitating what she had been taught. I coaxed her into forgetting all the the technique she had been burdened with. She had been attending drumming classes for a long time, hoping that someday she would enjoy it as much as her African friends.

I decided to approximate the rhythm that she had been trying to play with the master drummer the night that we had met. It can be a six-beat rhythm to our ears, with a downbeat every three notes. Tripolets. If you are playing a frame drum, hit the note hanging below the top line. Don't worry about the faster notes unless you want to.

My classical training sneaks in here and I say in my head "Trip-o-let" for each three-note pattern. That was the way I learned it from Mrs. Trafford when I was nine years old. In African Yoruba, the word could be "Bataka."

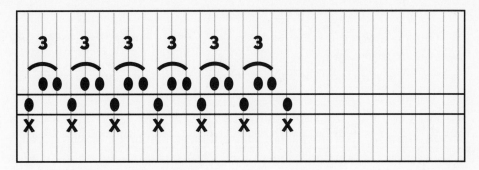

Tracks 4 and 5: Basic tripolet pattern.

The hands must alternate back and forth, with each hand getting a chance to hit the accent on the downbeat. It is a good tonic to wake up both sides of your brain and body. This is, of course, a simplification of a sophisticated beat. But the sophistication does not involve more notes. It means fewer notes.

I call this approach "Rhythm Theory." Rather than learning parts, you can learn how rhythm works and then teach yourself what you want to play. It gives you ways to improvise. You don't get locked down into playing only the part that you were taught. Your ability connects to your creativity, and you feel free enough to improvise, even if it is a very few extra notes. Improvising can be fewer notes too.

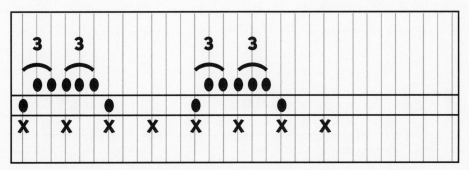

Track 6: Double tripolets; rest for the same length of time before starting the next Tripolet set.

The woman in our workshop was still puzzled even though we were working around a pattern that she already *knew*. That's why learning a *part* can be misleading.

I removed notes from the pattern that we were playing. Removing notes is very important. Drumming is like sculpture. The more unnecessary stone you cut away, the more the inspiration shows through. Taking away notes also breaks our habitual mindset about adding things and filling things up. That is a compulsive way to think and play or live. It's not being aware of the moment.

Instead of filling the space, we remove unnecessary notes and experience the quiet beauty inside the sound. This is a form of releasing. The player must release their belief that what they are playing is important. Don't get your ego involved. Releasing can be a good habit to have. Learning to release smaller bits of ego and trauma is easier than being forced to release a large amount of trauma/ego all at once later on. This is behavior modification by the players themselves. Releasing compulsive behavior makes us better drummers and maybe better humans.

I removed the middle note on the first three-note cluster. Then I left the end of the pattern completely quiet, so that we could get ready for the next repeated pattern (see below). Space is very important to get yourself "set up" for the next group of notes.

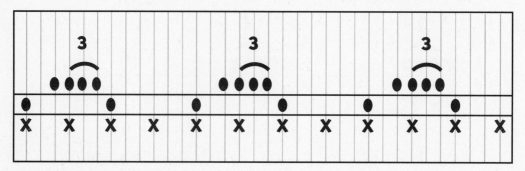

Track 7: Tripolets 3 and 4.

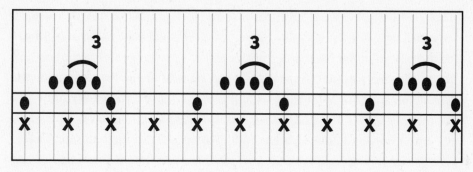

Track 7.

It almost sounded familiar to her, but she could not play along, even though she had already played this feel in the African group. We were approaching the traditional drum pattern from our cultural point of view, which is a mix of a lot of things. We played the part for a while, and she was able to get it.

Finally, I added the rest of the African pattern; two more tripolets but with notes taken out. Here is the traditional African rhythm written in our tripolet feel. See how it is a subtraction from "all" the tripolet notes in the first example.

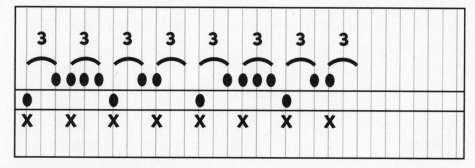

Track 7 (end): African Tripolet.

She still didn't believe that she was playing anything correctly. I asked her to play the African beat that she had learned so painstakingly at the African school. She did it like she had been programmed. Then I asked her to play

41

what we had just played. Both parts sounded the same. It started to make sense to her. Instead of just playing notes that she had been fed, she was hearing the notes and the "non-notes" in context of the whole rhythm foundation. The traditional pattern is a part of a larger pattern of rhythm. She made the connection and could play the part, but she still didn't trust herself.

I told her to feel free to improvise. It was hard for her to add one note or take out a note as a creative adventure. That is always tricky in this tripolet time pattern, and it is difficult for anybody if they are thinking too hard about it. She could only play the part that had been drummed into her head. That is not drumming. That is brainwashing. She tried to break loose and put her own touch into the pattern, but it was a struggle to create on her own. That is the state of affairs for most of us.

The learning mindset that we are in may fool us into thinking that we learned something, but it isn't a creative kind of knowledge. It locks us down, turning the most inspirational art form into drudgery.

The Senegal Master Drummer saw it in our culture but could not explain it to us in our language. He could not solve the problem. It wasn't his fault. It is our cultural context and it permeates all of our teaching of the arts. "Form over content" is a crude way to put it, but it really has more to do with recognizing inspiration when it is present—in a drummer, a child, or in any kind of creative endeavor.

## Content

Somebody looking for content? In this age of the internet, we have the same predicament of any other era of humanity. The amazing technology that is in place to provide the World Wide Web cannot create "content" for the internet. Content is inspiration that comes from the souls of people. We need to educate our souls to recognize and respect our own inspirational content. Inspiration solves problems and makes life worth living. It is a survival tool.

# Schools

If an innocent child is fed a steady diet of violence and then denied any kind of creative expression, the child's only recourse is to lash out in violent frustration at not being able to recycle life experiences in a gracious, creative, self-confident way. If music and the arts were a part of our school curriculum again, the children would find a vocabulary for their frustrations and let it out peacefully—adults might too.

Maybe we need to reexamine how the arts could be taught. Adults tell me often about their traumatic childhood music lessons. Are we passing down a mangled approach to music education to the next generation?

I did a lunchtime drumming event at a local "progressive" high school. I had been called in to conduct a drumming demonstration by one of the parents who had come to drum in our workshops. She said that they had drums at school but the teacher could not control some boys who dominated the group playing. No one wanted to play with them

When I arrived at the school for a lunchtime drumming event, none of the high school boys wanted to come forward. One large, angry Black student stood in front of me and spit with disgust. That might have bothered me at some point in my life, but not anymore. Discrimination comes in every color. Several of the high school girls finally got up enough courage to try

Then one boy came up and started playing. I recognized him. He was the problem child at the school. He started to play very loudly and without any regard for anyone else. I realized that this boy who was playing too loudly and too busily had been one of my private drum students from a year or two earlier. He had taken three private lessons and then stopped coming.

I might have given the boy some knowledge, but too little self-restraint. Or it could have been his diet: violent video games, brutal movies, and television. He seemed "normal" otherwise. It was impossible to get him to stop playing so much.

He couldn't relax. He played the loudest drum incessantly. I tried to appeal to his astute intellect, saying that no one liked him because he played too

43

much. If he wanted to have a girlfriend, he'd have to relax and leave some space, but it made little impression on him.

I like to pray with the drum now. Maybe I'm atoning for all those busy loud notes I must have played when I didn't know better.

On my first book-signing tour for *Drumming the Spirit to Life* (Llewellyn, 2000), I had the distinct honor of sitting in on a Jazz band class at Bisbee HIgh School in Bisbee, Arizona. The same issues apply in either a drumming group or a Jazz band—share the downbeat and keep it steady.

Mrs. O'Connell's Jazz band class in Bisbee, Arizona. Finding the downbeat with the high school Jazz band, using basic rhythm tools: drum and tambourine. Mrs. O'Connell is on the sax, to the author's left.

The drummer as timekeeper. Solid, steady, with a few licks to keep the groove moving along.

# 4
# SHOCK 'N' ROCK

Every Halloween Wolfman Jack, the legendary DJ, would host the "Shock 'n' Rock Review" at a famous theme park in Anaheim, California. He always had a big band behind him, complete with horn section, grand piano, drum set, guitars, bass, and percussion. I was lucky enough to do a Halloween show with Wolfman Jack, as the percussionist in his big band.

Everyone knows him as the DJ in the movie *American Graffiti*. In real life he was even larger than his own legend and more amazing. He was a generous man with endless stories about the music that he loved. He brought Rock 'n' Roll to the radio airwaves of Southern California and was the top DJ for more years than anyone else in the world. He had a big heart and lots of friends and a great family.

His Halloween shows every year were geared for the families who loved good old Rock 'n' Roll. The whole theme park went full out with lots of costumes.

We performed "Wolfman Jack's Shock 'n' Rock Review" in a beautiful theater with a large stage. The last weeks of rehearsal were grueling. The elaborate show was tightly choreographed. The three backup singers were dressed like Vampirellas and had to learn slinky dance moves while they were singing.

There were always last-minute changes in the show. Our music scores were a mess of scribbles and last-minute notations, based on what star showed up to perform. Lots of great artists showed up to play in the band. Junior Walker, Johnny Rivers—every musician who had ever had his record played on the radio loved the Wolfman.

Wolfman Jack always wanted to sing, but his voice was so gravelly that all he could do was talk the words, but he knew his musical history and he really loved the music in his bones and his heart. Wolfman had his trademark manicured beard and thick black hair. He was the hippest. For the Halloween show, he wore a long black velvet robe with mystical symbols embroidered in silver threads. He had a live hawk perched on his arm. The Wolfman was happening.

The set was huge. It arched over us. From the audience, it looked like we were playing in a graveyard inside the front of an old-time radio. The tuning

Poster announcing Wolfman Jack's Halloween show. (Photo courtesy of Knott's Berry Farm.)

bar glowed orange above us. There were three tiers to the band stand. The horn section stood up on the top riser. Jim Helmer was at the drum set, opposite the horn section that had some veterans from Elvis' band. Down on the floor in the center of the graveyard was John Herron, Wolf's musical director and piano player.

I faced John from a riser off to the side. I was playing a set of Conga drums, surrounded by shakers, gourd rattles, and all the percussion goodies in my collection. It was a first-class event.

Around John, me, and the rest of the band, was a cemetery graveyard, complete with dry ice fog creeping around the tilted headstones and dug-up graves. There were gnarled old trees with creepy things hanging from the dead branches.

The dead branches were tumbleweeds from outside the back door of the theater, which connected to the park's Western Town. The dried tumbleweeds from the cowboy shoot-out set now looked great as scary old treetops in our cemetery set.

Around the graveyard set, perched quietly on the headstones, were several large birds of prey. They were professional acting birds. There were several bird wranglers backstage ready to move at a moment's notice to contain the birds. These beautiful animals got the best of treatment.

There was a raven as big and black as any Edgar Allan Poe nightmare. There was a majestic and mysterious white owl with a wingspan of over six feet. Several other birds were tethered to the painted, Styrofoam headstones.

To make the scene even more scary, the special effects department had rigged up flashpots that would spew up plumes of smoke as the backup singers glided through their choreographed moves around the headstones.

Wolfman had the big hawk tied on his gloved arm with a leather rope. The hawk was hooded until show time. His claws were real. They were still capable of tearing flesh from bone. His eyes blazed fiercely when the trainer removed the leather hood. She cooed to the big bird and it settled down. It was a professional bird. It had been in front of many crowds. Wolfman was great with animals and loved the bird very much, but it was still very scary. Wolfman held it high as he entered the stage and we cranked into the first song.

Depending on which musician's memory you want to trust, the opening song was either *Monster Mash*, the Rock 'n' Roll classic written by Bobbie Picket and originally sung by Boris Karlof, or as John Herron insisted, the first song was *Fire,* by Arthur Brown. He's probably right. But we all remembered exactly what happened next.

The backup singers did their skulking, sexy thing, singing the background refrain as Wolfman Jack came strolling down through the cemetery. John was facing me, standing up and playing the nine-foot grand piano like Little Richard. He had on a top hat and a tuxedo T-shirt. He was grinning and directing the band, and stomping his foot in time to the beat. The birds seemed to like it, too.

The audience loved it. I could hear "Ooohhs and Aaaahhhs" from the audience as the stage lighting came up, making all the scary details apparent to the adoring crowd. It was a packed house.

Low creeping fog slithered around the headstones and the raven even seemed to "caw" on cue. The flashpots started to go off. I was playing hard. The music was pulsing through everyone. The show was working great.

The three vampire girls sang as Wolfman hit his mark at the footlights. He was moving to the beat in his black and silver robe, and jiving the kids down front. The hawk was digging the scene. It lifted its wings and showed off. The crowd loved it and cheered for more.

There's no business like show business.

Some of the flashpots ignited too brightly. Sparks began to fly. Some of the pots had probably been loaded with too much flash powder (which is basically gunpowder.) Each time a new flashpot went off, the sparks flew higher into the set. One flashpot went off under the grand piano, emitting smoke and sparks that looked more like a grenade than a special effect. It scared John, but he didn't drop a beat. He was a pro and the "Show must go on." He just looked at me and shook his head as if to ask, "We do this for a living?"

The three vampires cruised over to sing the next verse of the song. Wolfman was down front, working the crowd. As the smoke cleared at the top of the set, behind the teaser curtain where no one from the audience could see, I noticed sparks drift up into the old trees. The sparks settled onto the dried tumble weeds. It only took a moment and the tumbleweeds started to burn.

The music was loud. John was conducting the horn section and didn't see or hear me. It was suddenly turning into a real nightmare and no one saw it. I kept playing. I turned to look up at Jim, but he was drenched in sweat, intently reading his charts while thrashing away on his drum set. I continued to play the congas. I wanted to yell again at John, then I realized that I shouldn't do that. Panic was the last thing that the kids in the packed theater needed to see. I looked for the exits. The doors were closed tight.

I focused on John. I put all my thoughts into getting him to look at me. He was intently absorbed, reading the whole score for the orchestra in front of him, conducting with one free hand and playing the grand piano with his other hand. Bandleaders seldom look at the percussionist. It is usually at the bottom of their list of priorities.

The backup singers hit their parts on cue but sparks fell down and landed close to them. They saw the sparks, looked up, and stopped singing in mid-phrase. The spell the band had been weaving was broken. John finally looked up at me. I nodded with my head as I played even harder. He followed my head cue and looked up. He dropped his big grin when he saw the flames consuming the tumbleweeds and spreading to the curtains.

He looked at me with questioning eyes as he continued to play, but we both knew what we had to do. We had to keep playing.

The music was loud. The horn section noticed the flames next and their parts faltered. Wolfman turned around to see what the problem was. Mistakes were to be expected on the opening night, but that was a bit rude.

He followed their worried glance and saw the fire building up momentum over our heads. The hawk also saw it. The raven also saw it. The white snow owl also saw the flames and spread its huge six-foot wingspan.

The birds and Elvis' horn section all decided to leave the building.

Each bird took to the air amid the smoke and noise, but they were tethered to the headstones and could not get airborne. The hawk on Wolf's arm did get airborne and was so frightened that it almost lifted Wolfman Jack off the stage with it. The audience sensed something was wrong.

The band faltered. John nodded at them to keep playing. The tune picked up again but there was a new mood of uncertainty. Now the wranglers were coming out to grab the birds. The fire was growing. Sparks were falling around my congas. We kept playing.

I kept up the pattern and Jim kept the beat on the drum set. The rest of the band picked it up. It was an immediate, intuitive group decision by all of us to make the right thing happen. Wolfman was almost being dragged by the hawk. The wrangler got to him and removed the bird and covered its head. Wolf got back into his character and right away regained control of the situation.

I could hear voices in the audience saying the most terrifying words that you could ever possibly hear in a dark, crowded theater with all the doors closed tightly;

"I smell smoke."

Then, someone said the "F" word, "Fire!"

I never thought I would be playing drums in that classic situation.

Wolfman was the ultimate pro. He had been in so many situations where music was the only thing that saved him from an early grave that he instinctively knew what to do. He raised his hands in a gesture of peace and calmness.

"Now I want everybody to just relax and have a good time." He looked over his shoulder at us.

"That's right, you guys, Just keep that beat going. Everybody just feel the beat. That's right. There's a little problem back here but it's okay. We got it under control. Now I want everybody to get up and clap your hands. Just clap your hands to the beat. That's right. Now I want you to start moving to the beat. That's right. Just move on up the aisles to the doors. Keep clapping, everybody. Just feel that beat. That's good. Now don't hurry. Just feel the beat. That sounds good, you guys. Just keep it going."

The doors opened at the back of the large auditorium and the attendants watched with amazement as the the people moved calmly up the aisles and out of the doors, all the while clapping their hands. They were scared but everyone was united by the beat. We kept playing as hundreds of children and their parents streamed out of the theater.

The fire department arrived shortly, while we were still playing. They had the whole thing under control in a short time. The birds were safe in their cages. Wolfman was sitting in a wheelchair. He had tripped and broken his ankle on a hidden pipe while leaving the stage. The top part of the set was scorched, but it was not visible to the audience. It almost looked planned.

So. . . . We got ready to do the next show. The contract was for *two* shows a night for three nights. Wolfman did the second show in a wheelchair. I had a large glass of water next to me. The fire department hung around just for fun. It turned into a great evening for everyone.

I know the power of the beat. I've seen it in action. It is more amazing than most people ever realize. Lessons here could be many, but one that comes to mind is . . . oh never mind.

There is magick in the rhythm.

# 5
# Music Lesson Trauma

A lot of people have been traumatized by music lessons. Often as children we are forced into music lessons that we don't like; typically doing repetitive exercises under the watchful glare of a disciplinarian. We are forbidden to feel the joy in music and had to focus only on learning to read music and play it correctly.

Now we see what abusing the gift of music can do. Our public schools no longer have much music education. If the people who decide funding for school music programs had favorable memories of playing music as a child in public schools then there might be funding for it. Maybe we see it as a "Conservative vs. Liberal" argument but let's try to get outside that mindset and take a look at why we grew up with that kind of musical regimen.

Our particular society after World War II felt the relief and exhilaration of having been saved by modern technology, as well as blood and guts. The promise of a Utopian society was near and technology would get us there in style. Hence, fins on automobiles; the amazing fascination with the surface of things; usually shiny things.

The depths of the culture were being examined in the arts and poetry. "Beatniks" were playing bongos and sitting around in real coffee houses drinking plain coffee, discussing Zen, playing chess, arguing about what

Allen Ginsberg really meant, laughing at Lenny Bruce and grooving on Charlie Parker, and saying things like, "Did anyone see where Jack Kerouac went with my twenty bucks?"

The music was homogenized in the public schools. It seemed like a healthy thing to do; get kids to sing together. I remember singing in my third-grade classroom, with the rest of the students, songs like *Red River Valley* and *Cielito Lindo*. These were songs that had melodies and verses. It was great fun, primarily because of the elementary school teacher. They are the unsung heroes of our culture.

My grade-school band director was a young college graduate, teaching music fundamentals to a few fifth and sixth graders. There were a few drummers. They were an irritant to the band director, but they are necessary in a band and orchestra.

I had been taking private drum lessons in the fifth grade as well as attending this public-school band class. I carried a notebook with a drawing of my ideal drum set on the front; a big white Slingerland drumset with my initials on the front head of the bass drum—just like Gene Krupa's drumset. I kept my weekly private drum lessons in this notebook with several books of percussion music that was relatively advanced. I practiced at least an hour every day, but along the way, I had a little fun too. I started to write drum music. I had a secret notebook section with my own compositions. It was my personal, private music notebook. I would hear a rhythm in my head and I would write it out to remember it.

It wasn't written in correct tablature (musical handwriting). It was my own mix of notes and symbols.

One day I entered the band class and set my notebook down next to my snare drum as the other students got seated. The young teacher noticed my notebook with a drawing of a drumset on the cover.

"What is that?" he asked with a dour look. I learned later that many music teachers were bitter because they preferred having a gig over teaching. They felt trapped by teaching in a classroom instead of playing music in Carnegie Hall.

"It's my drumming notebook," I said defensively.

"Let me see it," he said.

I reluctantly opened it up. He thumbed through the various percussion pieces that I had been assigned by my private teacher. Then he went where I didn't want him to go; he opened my personal notebook.

"What is this?" he said, with a sarcastic snort.

"It's my music," I said. "I wrote it."

"That's not music," he sneered. He laughed rudely and let the book drop shut. He turned to his crowd of kids and said something about playing some real music now.

I stopped writing music.

I might have quit playing music altogether, but I sensed that nine years old was too early to quit show bizness. I just tucked my own ideas into the back of my mind and played the music that was put in front of me. The reason that I had taken to the drums was partly based on a schoolmate's cool status with the girls because he could play the drums. The other reason was based on an earlier incident.

My sister and I both had gotten hit on the knuckles with a ruler by our first piano teacher. I started to play drums after that because I wanted sticks to hit back with. My sister evolved past the music trauma and eventually became a psychic instead of playing piano. I am still trying to play music. I am grateful to have been exposed to music at such an early stage. It's just amazing that I can still enjoy music at all.

We inherited a brutal form of music education. There is tenseness in the music when it's learned with this kind of discipline and competition.

When music is shared, it is a community effort and there is no overriding sense of right and wrong. People listen to each other and talk to each other with instruments and make a surprising variety of interesting sounds. They respect each other as people. There is no competition.

I'm trying to define music in nonmusical terms. People who are traumatized by "Music" can then get through that block by playing something that isn't "Music." This is a talent that we are born with. Talking to God is one way to look at it, but it is also talking to other people and yourself; softly, gently, forgiving, nurturing, trusting, joyous, healing. This has nothing to do with "Music."

If there is a drum sitting in front of you, don't react as if you cannot play it. You don't have to play "Music" with it. If you're lucky, you'll play something more powerful than just music. You'll use the drum to connect to something more profound.

One of the regular drummers in our weekly drumming workshops had been growing in confidence and ability. He was excited about playing the drums. He studied with various African drum teachers, but he said he always came back to our group to "just play," which I took as a great compliment. He informed me that he was going to begin conga drum lessons with a respected teacher. I wished him all the luck. Congas can be tough when you have a dedicated teacher.

Months passed and when he came in to drum again, I asked him if he had done the conga lessons. His usually enthusiastic demeanor drooped into a sorrowful slump.

"I can't play the conga drums," he said, looking at the pair I had sitting in the front corner of the store (in the skills corner from the Feng Shui point of view).

I couldn't believe my ears. Here it was all over again.

"Why?" I asked, already knowing the answer.

"It's too hard. The teacher was great. He was amazing to watch. But it takes too much work. I'll never be as good as him. I just can't play the congas."

He was ready to walk out of the store, a beaten man.

"Don't leave," I said. "Don't you dare leave with that attitude. After all the fun you've had playing drums don't let the *teacher* spoil it for you. Of course you can play the conga drums."

I pulled out the dusty, used set of congas and also an old one that belonged to a former student, a great martial arts teacher. The drum was imbued with his energy and I just couldn't part with it. My current student reluctantly sat in front of the old conga drum.

"I don't know how," he complained. "I never hit a conga drum."

"Didn't you play a conga drum in your class?" I asked incredulously.

"No. He wouldn't let me. I had to learn technique first."

"Just hit the drum," I said and started up a beat that was too inviting for him to turn down. He grinned sheepishly and started to hit the conga drum, but then he examined what he was doing and promptly stopped playing.

"Don't stop!" I yelled at him. "Just keep playing."

I say that a lot in my life.

Now the rhythm I was playing on the set of congas was not a "real" conga part. It was a simplification. So I didn't worry about hitting the wrong notes. We can just find the voices in the drums that we are capable of getting out of the drum. Make those sounds work for you. Never mind what someone else can do. This is your sound. If the groove is working, then whatever you play will sound great, if it's part of the groove. Learn the harder parts once you are more sure of yourself. We tend to take the fun out of playing if we think we should be learning.

*Just keep playing!*

We played for an hour. He came back the next week and wanted to play the old conga drum again. He had developed a good sense of rhythm so he found new and exciting things to play, all on his own. Maybe someday, someone might say that what he is playing is *correct,* but so what.

The ironic thing is that this man is a gifted group therapist. The drumming is personally healing for him and it has nothing to do with music training. Yet he was psychologically impaired by his own need to have someone in authority show him how to do something *correctly.* We have a self-negating need to put our inspiration in the hands of some *expert* and then we become disillusioned with a teacher that is too human.

The story doesn't end here. The energy we generated on the congas stayed in the drums. Two men came into the shop late in the evening after having a nice dinner on Montana Avenue. One man wanted to buy the set of congas that had been sitting in the corner quietly gathering dust until the week before. I told him the price and he haggled. I told him I didn't really need to sell them because now we were using them in the drumming group. I was teaching on them. He realized that he couldn't get me down on the price, so he decided to buy them anyway. He had to have those drums. He sensed something about them. I think he sensed the energy that we had generated in them.

In the process he bought six beaded curtains and a load of other things. Price wasn't really an issue with this high roller.

My book *Drumming the Spirit to Life* had just arrived in the mail and he wanted to buy it, but it was the first copy from my editor, Connie, and I wanted to keep it.

"You have stuff out, but it's not for sale," he complained, trying to get in synch with the store's attitude. He was apparently some kind of tough guy; very strong; brash, and sure of himself in every way. The men were very nice guys in a pushy sort of way and could possibly be mobsters. Rich ones. I decided to show him how to *play* the drums since he was buying them.

I figured them both to be Italian. They weren't wearing any socks with their expensive Italian loafers. Plus he had on a shirt that said "Italia" on the front of it. That is the only way I can tell Italians anymore.

Bo Diddley once said, "You can't judge a book by looking at the cover."

After we had played a minute, the tough guy leaned close over the congas.

"I'm Cuban," he confided softly. "But I never . . . you know. Learned how to drum," he confessed. "But it's in my blood!" he added defensively.

"I'll never tell," I said. "All kinds of guys come in to learn the drums. No one will ever know that they learned drums from . . . you know, a guy like me."

"You're just a white guy," he said with a sly grin.

"He's a white guy with a book," said Renata, a friend of Cathy's from Czechoslovakia. She had just strolled into the shop. We all had a good laugh.

But the point was that the drums had a big emotional charge in them from when the therapist had broken through his own drum teacher trauma.

This total stranger had a different problem. He was *supposed* to be able to play the congas, only he had never done it. He felt shame and embarrassment. All I do is tell them they can do it. It's something anyone can do.

He did feel the energy in the drums though, and he responded to that. He loaded the funky congas into his brand-new Mercedes sedan. He put those old drums right on the new, gray leather seats. He didn't care. He was taking *his* conga drums home. The energy lives on. He was laughing as he drove away, a happy guy.

The therapist came in the next week.

"See what happens when you put energy into the drums?" I asked him. I indicated the empty corner where the set of conga drums had been sitting for so many months, untouched.

"Where are the conga drums?" he asked desperately. "I was going to play them."

"They're sold," I said.

"But why?" he asked, very upset. He thought he needed those particular drums.

"Some other guy needed them. He felt the energy you put in them and he had to have them."

The therapist played the last old funky conga drum and was grateful and happy; no more trauma about the conga drums. He was laughing again.

The energy that we generated in the drums was profoundly interesting to that guy who bought them. That energy can happen in any kind of drum. I had bought those particular conga drums from a strong, interesting woman who had just moved from Hawaii. She had very little technique, but had enjoyed them anyway. Now, they belonged to a gangster and perhaps they will work their magick on him, too. The life of a drum is an amazing thing. It has a calling and it goes where it is needed; music training or no music training—high-quality or low-quality instrument. Low talent or no talent.

Each drum is important. It has nothing to do with how much money it costs. Making magick with what we have at our fingertips is our only option. We can't wait to be trained or to have a special instrument or a special teacher. We need the magick now.

# 6
# TUNING UP YOUR CEREMONY

An invocation is a way to introduce yourself to the Universe. It is a way to humbly request an audience with celestial beings. All celestial beings like drums. It is a known fact. Every culture in the history of the world has used drums to beseech and bring forth their Divine helpers. It is making a joyful noise unto the Lord and the Goddess, but it is also a very exacting science of the soul. The invocation beat sets the tone for any ritual, whether it be Pagan or televangelist. Look at what is behind Jimmy Swaggert the next time you're channel surfing. It's a drumset. That drumset is a support tool. When the congregation goes to sleep, the drums wake them up again. It also wakes up the angels.

A drumming workshop session at the Unitarian Church in Tucson, Arizona, hosted by the Desert Crones.

You might want to start by welcoming the four corners with a slow, steady beat. It is a knock on the door of the other dimension, so do it with respect. In drum-based religions, these invocation rhythms seem simple, but they have the seeds of the complex patterns that happen later in the rituals. Start simply and softly so that you have somewhere to go with dramatic volume. Emotions are enhanced by the drum beats. To get into a state of magickal power, the emotions must be focused. Most music can be emotional, but it does not usually have sacred intentions. Starting softly is more inviting. We create a safe, sacred space with nonaggressive drumming.

By drumming forth a sacred place, the drummer has a goal and the power is focused. The more musical power focused into that concept of opening a door, then the more power in the accompanying ritual.

The feel in the groove carries the power of the ritual.

Certain forms of Christianity mistrust the drum, but that is changing. Maybe it was perceived as making people want to have sex and celebrate their animal instincts too much. The Church has always tried to deal with those dynamics of human nature in a socially acceptable way. The need for us to celebrate those animal grooves is obvious. Without our connection to those inspirational animal grooves, our souls turn gray. Drumming is a safe way to feel these animal powers. It is a safety valve.

Feeling a powerful groove puts us in a mythic state of horniness and personal power. We sense Universal mystery and unnameable magick. It gets our juices flowing and we feel alive. Without the groove there are only hollow ritual sounds and no real magick.

A Gospel church can groove forever on just a tambourine. They aren't singing about Christian soldiers, they're singing about Divine love, living a righteous life, and rejoicing in the gifts we have. Those subjects might come more from family and heritage rather than currently approved church doctrine. The grooves in Gospel church are African grooves. They had to sing about Christian subjects because they were forced to. If we all had our own heritages intact, we could be hearing Gospel songs about Chango, Yemeya, Babalu, Birgit, Cernunnos, and Pan, among other deities.

As it is, the sacred African grooves are disguised inside of the Gospel choir grooves, as well as other kinds of soul music.

The grooves have to be played. They are part of life. If they are denied, then we can turn bitter. Everybody seems happier when they play, maybe because they are feeling the primordial swamp in their butts. It's a funky thing and we all have a right to feel it. All of us.

The slavery of the technological mind is not as obvious as other types of slavery. Technological slavery is cross-cultural, cutting the individual off from the creative grooves of the Universe. We are just now waking up to the fact that we have been slaves to a life-threatening dead beat that has covered great portions of the planet with concrete.

Our colorful, healthy upbeat grooves are hiding in secret places like the rain forest, the deserts, mountaintops, swamps, ghettos, Gospel churches, homes, and in our hearts.

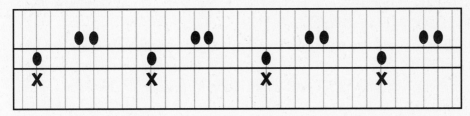

**Tantric Sex Groove, exercise #1.**

Face your partner. You may wear clothes or you may take your clothes off. If you are in a public place, don't push your luck. It might be wiser to keep at least some of your clothes on, unless you're on a nude beach.

This works even if you have one drum that you both can play simultaneously. It doesn't have to be a big drum, just large enough that you can face each other. Put the drum between you so that each of you can hit a note close to the center, then at the edge. You should be facing each other.

Don't worry about hitting it loud. Softer is better. There may be a "pop" if you both hit the middle of the drum head at exactly the same moment. Don't worry about it, just keep the groove going. You may find that playing slightly off center will enable both of you to get a good deep note. Standing or sitting is fine.

If you prefer, each of you can be playing a separate drum or a rhythm instrument. The point is to create a feel between both of you.

In each and every relationship there is a dominant and a passive personality. Let the *less*-dominant personality start the tempo. They can hit a simple downbeat at a steady rate or play a basic pattern. The other person (the dominant) can then start to play along with that basic beat, supporting it, modestly improvising around it, adorning it, playing with it as if it were part of your love making—but never overwhelming it.

If it is not possible for the less-dominant personality to start the groove, then the dominant person can start the groove, but at some point they must relinquish control of the groove to the less-dominant partner. They must let go of their control secretly and not tell their partner. The less-dominant person must take over control instinctively.

It is important to remember that the person now setting the downbeat (the less dominant), is in control. The other person is just decorating the basic beat that the first person has set up. I know this may be hard for control freaks, but just give it a try.

The person in control can speed the beat up and slow the beat down. This then means that the second drummer must follow the speed and intensity of their partner's changes. The second drummer "goes into" the first drummer more and more, in a supportive, nondominant way. If the second person is very alpha, this may be a challenge, but the effort is worth it. You might know your mate in a new way.

The first person maintains a beat for a long period of time—keeping it steady. The second person plays around that beat, not making it go faster or slower or get louder or softer. The second person just follows the first person's every move and subtle change of emotion in their drumming as closely as possible. It is as if the second drummer were reading the first drummer's mind and soul through their drumming.

The second drummer *becomes* the first drummer.

The melding together of the two spirits creates a music that neither person can play alone. The combination of both people's energies makes a whole sound, but it is being decided by the first person's energy.

You may find yourselves gazing into each other's eyes. Do not worry if your partner's eyes become glazed-over or appear intensely focused in some other Universe—you might look the same way.

The mingling of energies can go on indefinitely. Timing this event is not what is important. The feel of the two people focused on each other is very intimate. The heights of passion or depth of contemplation will be whatever the two make of it. That is not to be decided by anyone else.

There will be some experimentation but remember to keep a groove going. Speed up and slow down, but at some point maintain a long, sustained, steady groove. Make it longer than you want to. Don't get bored and stop. Stay with it and watch what happens. The Tantric energy that is being generated will cycle up and through both people, then back down into the drum, then cycle back up and through the two players. It generates a strong Eros energy. Ideally, both people will feel the juices flowing.

Eventually, the one being that is created by playing together must split back into two separate beings again.

The parting of the two energies must be gradual and gentle, and conducted by the person controlling the beat. To separate is like birth and dying at the same time. Do it gradually and without tension. The first drummer makes signals for a change. By now, the second person is sensing what the other is feeling and wanting.

As the parting process continues, both players make peace with what has happened. When it is finished, there should be no talking. Let the sound die away without interruption.

Try it again. Reverse roles. The dominant personality might control the beat quite differently, but a similar mingling of spirits takes place.

The challenge for the alpha personality is to subordinate themselves, at least for a few moments, to something else—something greater than their ego. That sensation of *release* of their control structure by the dominant personality is really important in this process. Releasing control makes room for other sensations and a deeper quality of a shared experience. It also gives us a clue as to how to drop emotional baggage that is no longer needed or wanted. Generally, we hold on to old psychological states like keeping a scrapbook of old pictures.

Drumming keeps the releasing process fun and relaxed.

The lesson for the less-dominant personality can be terrifying and exhilarating. They actually get to decide the tempo for the couple. It has to do with taking responsibility for your own creative energy. That is the Tantric energy. That is the life force at work. This little exercise is a way for us to put our finger on our own source of creative power and develop it with the help of another person.

This can also be done with total strangers.

Clothing might be an issue there.

# 7
# GROOVES HAPPEN

**W**hen you least expect it, grooves happen. It is a pleasant surprise. Most people notice when it happens, sharing the discovery with a grin at each other. It is a sense of knowing that we are all feeling the same thing. There is a sensation that something just connected in our playing. It suddenly opens up and becomes effortless. It gets funky. It connects to a greater source of energy. Suddenly you feel like you are being pulled along in a rhythmic tractor beam.

Grooves can happen based on traditional rhythm patterns, or grooves can happen in improvised drumming groups. It is a place of happy accidents. People play together as one drum. The groove cannot always be gotten to by forcing your will onto the music. It cannot be had or possessed. It is a quicksilver event that is electric and ephemeral, but everyone knows when it happens. That is the real mystery.

We have weekly drumming workshops in our store on Montana Avenue in Santa Monica, California. For several weeks the attendance had been low; just one or two people. That is when it can get very interesting—not so many distractions. The players can tune into the grooves easily, and work the subtleties without being overpowered by a lot of different egos.

Sue, a veteran workshop member, had just recovered from a long series of operations on her hands and arms. She was looking forward to feeling the deep healing sounds that she could play, after playing for months with casts on her arms. She is an amazing woman, a retired doctor. There were also two young Englishmen, about the age of twenty. They played hard and fast with lots of notes, and they rushed the tempo. They had a great time, but they had no interest in feeling the subtle grooves. Sue tried to hold her own by hitting the big standing drum with a mallet, but she wasn't enjoying herself as much as she usually did. She told me later that the two boys just wouldn't listen and play *with* us. They had to compete. She felt drained after that drumming session, whereas before, in other drumming sessions, she left smiling and temporarily free of her physical pains.

They were nice guys. I was aware they were overplaying. I suggested that they play less. They tried. Their smug smiles dropped for a moment and they struggled with playing funky and with less notes. They both said it was much more difficult, but they really liked it. It gave them food for thought, at least.

Mystic Isle's drumming event in Isla Morada, Florida Keys, in the Coral Rock Quarry State Park. Staying in the groove kept us all warm in a chilly January night.

English Rock 'n' Rollers have borrowed music from American Blues, making money off it by sounding like American black artists. The good effect of that appropriation is that they learn a little about Soul. The laid-back grooves aren't always geared toward world dominion, but they get a crowd up and dancing. I hope those guys remember to leave some space for the other folks when they drum back in Jolly Old England.

I am trying to make a distinction between these two different kinds of drumming. The bashing that the young boys got into was fine. I was guilty of making it easy for them to take off and sound great; I was making a solid backbeat for them to solo over. They had no idea why they sounded so good. It was the rhythm section behind them that made their night.

There needs to be an explanation sometimes of how this particular drumming method pays off. It is not in the number of notes played. It is the amount of silence that is let through the wall of sound. Let more silence through while maintaining a groove and you have healing magick. Only the most inspired players can play a lot of notes and still let the silence through.

Many folks studying "African" are not letting the feel come through the drumming. They cut loose with the six or seven Yoruba drum licks they learned from an Olatunji video and think that they are drumming. That is difficult for the African teachers. They have no words for the kind of self-centered noodling that most technological drummers do. It is like a cocktail party where no one is listening to anyone else and they are all talking about themselves.

I supported other musicians for years, making them sound good, even if I didn't think the music was that hot. It's a habit that is hard to break. There is a part of me that wants to make every musical moment as good as it can be. That professional attitude makes it hard on me sometimes. I end up playing too strenuously, hurting myself and sometimes even disliking the music that I am working so hard at playing. It is a disappointment, because I feel that I am contributing magick to their music and the person doesn't realize the magick is there.

Welcome to the music bizness.

They want magick but they don't want to pay for it. And they don't want magick that misbehaves and doesn't do what they tell it to do. Real magick is the Trickster, the Coyote, Kokopeli. The unexpected energy in the grooves is the Trickster energy. It is a constantly pleasant surprise to the player as well as the dancers. That unexpected kind of energy makes record producers nervous but it is what real music is made of. It is what Rock 'n' Roll is built on. That's the beat that drives kids wild. It is a combination of knowing where the groove is and how to "play against it" just right.

*Did you hear the one about the famous drummer at a cocktail party celebrating his new CD release? A young girl is hanging on every word he says but eventually she gets bored with him. He tries to regain her attention by changing the subject of the one-sided conversation.*
*"Well, enough about me," he smiles charmingly, "What do YOU think about my drumming?"*

Little Richard, Chuck Berry, Jerry Lee Lewis, Huey Piano Smith, Professor Long Hair, Doctor John, Alan Tousaint, Fats Domino, Chick Corea, Herbie Hancock, Miles Davis, the list goes on. They have something in common. They know the secrets of the groove and how to play "behind the beat." If you were to write it out, there would be no way to explain it. It might happen in a rhythm section when one person is playing a swing pattern, then someone else plays a steady driving pattern against it. Normally these two different patterns are like oil and water; they don't mix. But when they are layered over each other, a mystical oscillation occurs and Rock 'n' Roll is born. The marriage of opposites equals drama.

The Trickster is at work. That same phenomenon can be heard in Los Munequitos de Mantazas, the sacred drummers of Cuba, who are gracious drummers. They are too good to have big egos. No one hogs, everyone listens for the groove. If it is not there, the music is hard work. When it is there, the music is easy. Los Munequitos de Mantazas had their first hit in Cuba in 1953, and they are still playing together. Now, that is a classy band.

Let's take a look at a trip-o-let variation. This is also on the CD, in the Tripo-let Variations, toward the middle of the piece. I decided to present these ideas in a musical, improvised format rather than formal lessons to keep it interesting—also to implant the ideas into your creative memory, not just your technical data bank, so you can play around the concepts instead of just mimicking a part.

I call this one "Elephant Walk." It will lope along. The two big notes at the beginning of the phrase will set up a swinging pulse, like the Count Basie Orchestra had.

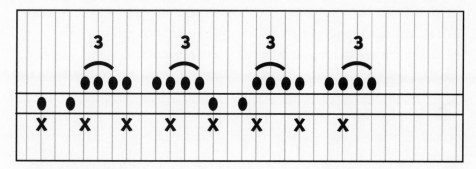

**Track 8: Elephant Walk.**

Okay. Stop working at your desk—right now. Put your hands on the edge of your workstation and play those notes over and over again. Try to tap your foot. The simultaneous activity of hand movement and tapping your foot is very powerful medicine. You may happen to process trauma. There can be a relocating of memory as a positive experience because you are grooving in a New Way. This is self-healing by playing a groove, tapping your foot, and even nodding your head while releasing trauma memory. You have to swing, though. It's a body activity. The brain has to get out of the way.

If this is no fun, maybe you love your job too much—I don't know. Maybe you shouldn't do this part at work—wait until you get home. All these rhythmic body movements can change your mind, your memories, and your environment.

The phenomenon of doing two things at the same time is intoxicating, or it can blow your fuses. Don't get frustrated. Laugh. Slow down. Slow WAY down.

Go away from it. Come back after earning a million dollars on the Internet. Try it again. Go very slowly, making each note or combination of notes an individual event. One note at a time. It is not music. This is a meditation and a riddle.

This "Elephant Walk" is a contagious pattern; when it is played at the right speed will get everyone to sway like a willow tree in the breeze or bound like a gazelle. This rhythm is used in Zulu dances.

Our next level of integration is more sophisticated, and I'll include it here (below), but don't expect to get this one right away. When this kind of thing works, you are functioning on different planes of awareness at the same time. This happens because each of your body parts is playing in a different *time signature*. This is track nine on the CD.

Tap your foot on (1) and on (3) and also on (5), while still going back and forth with your hands playing tripolets. Some musicians call this a six-against-four pattern.

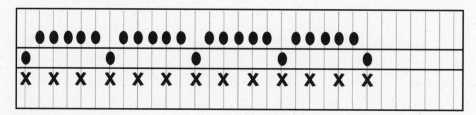

Track 9: Six against four.

The simultaneous events of tapping your foot in a different pattern than your hands is a multitiered activity; There are different things going on: first, you are hitting the drum evenly, back and forth. Then you are hitting a deep note; our repeated downbeats. That in itself is tricky. That is two operations going on at the same time. When you do this, don't fixate on any one thing.

That will draw your attention away from the other things that you need to quietly keep track of. Just keep moving your attention around to the different parts of your body. Keep your mind moving and relaxed. Then, finally, when you have that basic pattern going, you can add the tapping foot (I use a tambourine on my foot). The addition of the foot tapping is the icing on the cake. It puts an entirely different pattern over the other events which launches it out into a larger rhythmic universe. Don't expect to get this concept right away. It took me years to grasp it. But it triggers amazing events in your brain. Chemicals are secreted. You feel first a tenseness, then a pulse of enjoyment when you *accidentally* get it right; that is really your body getting control of the moment away from your nagging intellect that keeps telling you to stop doing this sort of thing.

Let your body take over and send the inner critic out for a walk. We can do many things at the same time. We just don't trust ourselves to do them. This rhythmic multitasking is a survival skill, a profound meditation, and a powerful magickal tool. Plus, it swings. You can hear it with Elvin Jones playing with John Coltrane, or you can hear it with the great John Bonham, the drummer who made Led Zeppelin swing. You can hear it with Ravi Shankar and Ali Akbar Kahn performing classical Ragas from India. The combinations of grooves has a deep trance effect, no matter what culture you're in. Your brain is listening to one groove, then another groove slips in to interest it, then that becomes a new journey, but the original grooves are still going on. The weaving of rhythms becomes as rich as a Persian rug. The relative relationships are the same.

*Turn that old rut into a new strut. Some kind of soul-surfing samba, baby.*

73

# 8

# THE COURAGE TO
# STOP TIME

There is a moment of truth for some people when they try to improvise on the drum. *Soloing* can be an adrenaline sport; we get excited and bash away. But it is also a "head game," to take a phrase from the basketball court. Some people carry a lot of psychological baggage into the drumming workshop. It is a good idea to drop that stuff off first. Old emotional baggage gets in the way when improvising—whether on the drum or in life.

Sometimes an artist or an athlete must improvise because things aren't going well, according to their plan. They have to change their game plan and improvise. That is a spur of the moment thing. It requires faith in one's own abilities. It is the key to making good moves on and off the court as well as in art, music, life, magick, and especially with drumming for the dance.

Allowing yourself to improvise is actually a survival skill. Trusting your own split-second decisions could save your life, or your job, or a loved one from being hurt by an unkind word. The world can change in a split second. Being able to change appropriately and flow with unexpected surprises makes the path a little easier to walk.

You've heard this drumming pattern a million times. We've done it before. The pattern itself is easy. Anyone can do it if they hear it. Reading it first is something else, but many of us have to filter it through our brains before we can play it. It's worth the effort. People who can read music have good math skills. Read music, make money. Play music, have fun.

Play this phrase at a brisk speed. Not too fast. Make it comfortably quick, not frantic. This is a meditation, not a competition.

There is a big note on the first note of the phrase. That's the downbeat. Keep that downbeat solid and low, hitting the middle of the drumhead quickly so that the head vibrates and the sound comes up. Don't lift your hand up too high. That's a waste of energy; you end up hitting the drumhead too late and you miss the wonderful vibration coming up off the drumhead. I leave my hands close to the head, so that I feel those vibrations, but I don't muffle them. The vibrations wake up the acupuncture meridians in the palms.

The *hole* after that first big downbeat is where you let the drum do its healing work. Vibrations fill the space after the first note. Then you can add the last three notes as a spice to keep the groove popping along.

Once the groove is set (when it feels fairly stable), then we try something that is very exciting; we do the Stop Time.

Someone decides to count it down and everyone joins in. The first person yells loudly so that everyone can hear them. They yell on the downbeats: "One—    Two—    Ready—    Stop!"

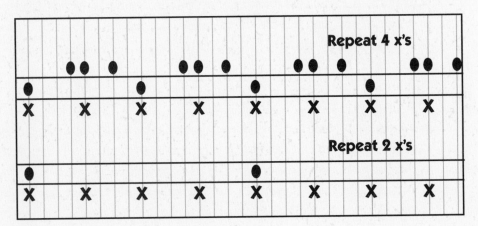

Track 10: Stop Time.

Everyone then stops and hits *only* the downbeat for four phrases. This leaves a lot of empty silence in between the downbeats. That is the moment of truth. The first person takes a solo in that empty space in between the downbeats. Everyone else must support the person's soloing by keeping the downbeat going. Then after four phrases, everyone comes back in again and picks up the original pattern. Usually the groove is a little shaky so it takes a few minutes for the group to reestablish the solid groove again. Then someone else, or the leader, can yell, "One— Two— Ready— Stop!" and someone else takes a solo.

Everyone again just hits the downbeat for four phrases and someone else will solo. Then everyone will join back in with the original pattern. This has to go all around the group. *Everyone* should have a few chances at soloing at the stop time. It is important that everyone support each other as they try to solo. That's why everyone hits the downbeat and leaves the rest of the space open for the soloist.

What happens when everybody joins back in playing the groove together is what is important. What the person plays in the soloing section is not important.

Some people will see that stop time section as a terrifying confrontation to their anonymity in the drumming group, but it is actually very much fun. Some people get so worked up that all they can do is laugh or cry when it comes their turn to solo during the Stop Time.

Some people may rush the beat. That is because we put so much pressure on ourselves to perform. Hey—it's just a drumming exercise, so every time you feel that pressure build up, just let it go. Laugh, then take a solo. Soon you will not have the fear anymore. It will just be another opportunity in life to express yourself calmly. This exercise is a way to realize just how much pressure we put on ourselves when we have to perform in life. We can learn to relax at critical moments and just play for fun.

The social skills involved with this meditation are important too. Everyone is supporting each member as they try to create something out of thin air. It is an act of magickal courage. Everyone usually cheers after each person's solo effort. It gets very supportive.

The existential dilemma of what to play in your given stop time is daunting. That represents your life. You can make a note and live with it, or you can not make a note. You can make a mess, or you can show off.

You can also just play through your stop time like it didn't matter what you played. That is fun. You can play what you always play, or you can try something new, but the relaxed attitude is what counts. If someone were to just throw it out there—let the notes fall where they may and not be embarrassed—they could be very surprised at their own accomplishments. Casual creativity is a good thing to shoot for.

The best way to feel a sense of accomplishment is to not have unrealistic expectations going into the endeavor. This also keeps you calm and cool so that you don't flub up by tensely judging yourself. Stay cool, let it rip, don't worry about it, and share the groove. Even the most spastic drummers get better when this cycle goes around the group a few times. It creates a great deal of sympathetic courage in all who witness this effort too. It shows people how to deal with crisis situations in a calm, creative manner.

The crisis is created in the mind of the person who is about to solo in the Stop Time. They get tenser and tenser as the moment of truth approaches, then when everyone stops and the silence is all theirs to deal with, they'll hit a note, then stop, freeze up, and not be able to do anything. The mental confusion of performance anxiety, embarrassment, self-consciousness, and terror are all present in that split second, and it is only about hitting a drum. It is nothing important at all and yet people go into shock sometimes when they have to do this.

Give yourself a break and laugh at yourself and with the others. It helps when you laugh it off. In a moment all the fear is gone. The Stop Time is past and you feel a sense of completion. It doesn't matter what you play. Just don't stop and don't give up. The next time it won't be quite as bad. The third time around the group, you are starting to get some ideas, and the fourth time around the drumming group, you look forward to taking a solo.

It is growth through terror, but there is no real risk involved. Sometimes humans are slow learners, until they are put in a terrifying situation where they either learn or die. With the drumming stop times, we can simulate a life-threatening event without actually getting into a dangerous situation. This gentle kind of terror develops our survival skills and we don't even have to strap on bungee cords or surf the North Shore of Oahu.

When we actually do something that requires instant courage then we have a feeling for it after we've experienced something like this kind of safe drumming exercise.

Earth Day weekend, April 22, 2001, at Club Kilimanjaro in Bisbee, Arizona. Total strangers support each other's groove while they each take a Stop Time solo. It's terrifying and very much fun, as well as magickally healing.

# 9
# SOUL SURFING

**M**arshal McLuhan was one of the first media gurus in the sixties. He had a larger point of view than most people immersed in our culture. Our communication systems were evolving and it was affecting us in subtle ways. When he discussed this jump in consciousness to the general public, much of what he explained was abstract and hard to comprehend then, but now we take his concepts as obvious. Reality changes. Our perceptions change after we realize things are different.

McLuhan saw the way a new system would grow up and surround the old system, enveloping it, taking what it needed for nourishment from the old system. The old system would then dissolve away from the inside and the new system would then be the dominant system and everyone would forget about the old system. We have forgotten a lot of old systems and old ways of feeling the world.

It may be hard today for young people to understand the strict American mindset that was the dominant system during the Eisenhower years; the fifties. As the sixties transformed the culture, the new system was regarded as dangerous, un-American, pagan, sinful, anarchistic, even insane—but we absorbed it anyway.

Some of that new system of the sixties has now become the old system. So we must get ready for the next new system. New systems of thinking and behaving can't always be seen clearly or even anticipated. We use new or old cultural ideas because we need them, not because they are good or bad. What was bad in the fifties, such as hot rods, blue jeans, leather jackets, and "DA" haircuts are now cultural icons. They have become respectable.

Today, the ability to feel rhythm in a healing way is a new phenomenon in technological culture. We need this primal, physical experience of the world. It is a method of grounding as we rush into the future.

McLuhan said that a new system always borrowed something from the old systems and updated it to use. He mentioned the example of his students listening to his lectures on media while some of them read Tarot cards. The new with a bit of the old gives us a well-rounded perspective. Playing a drum can connect us to ancient methods of wisdom that we will need in the future.

I once bought a rare deck of Egyptian Tarot cards in a small dusty bookstore off Trafalgar Square, in London, while on tour back in the early seventies. Mcluhan was a voice in my head, telling me to look to the past to make sense out of my very intense and confusing future. I also purchased a book on Atlantis, published by Madame Blavatsky's Theosophical Society. Living in Coconut Grove, Miami, had put me close to the Atlantian energy lurking beneath the Bermuda Triangle.

These books were my newfound treasures, from a breakneck tour that included Van Morrison, the Allman Brothers, Tim Buckley, Mahavishnu Orchestra, and many others. We played outdoors in Amsterdam where the clouds billowed upward like a Dutch Master's painting. John Luc tore at his violin like a demon while Mahavishnu John ripped out transcendental guitar licks at a deafening volume. Going on after music of that volume is intimidating, but the show must go on and it was great.

The festival outside of London was at an idyllic private estate with wild deer and thousands of kids. The Allmans had brought Mrs. Hudson from Macon, Georgia, to cook soul food. I thought I was hallucinating when I smelled it. I was getting homesick. Tim Buckley was interviewed for the influential *New Musical Express* by a brash female rock journalist named Chrissie Hynde. They chose Tim Buckley as best male vocalist of the year. No tour was free of pranks. We all ended up in the lobby of the Kensington Hotel on Hyde Park in the middle of the night after someone tripped the fire alarm. The London Fire Department was not amused.

I sensed something demonic along with all the good vibes of that trip. There is always a bit of the dark inside the light. That is why there is a little black dot inside the white energy of the Tao symbol, as well as a white dot inside the dark side of that swirling ancient Oriental symbol. Something seemed to be lurking in the shadows. I just couldn't put my finger on it. But I could feel it in the music.

The tour finally ended in central California.

Palo Alto and Santa Cruz have always been a center for good Blues. Big Mama Thornton and Howling Wolf were living there in the seventies.

We performed at Stanford University, opening for Loggins and Messina at a great outdoor concert. C. C. Collins, who played congas with Stevie Wonder, sat in with us that afternoon. He was a proponent of Black Pride as well as a great percussionist. He cut an imposing figure wearing a beret and Black Panther insignia. A great-looking girl in tie-died harem pants and blond curly hair floated up to Carter.

"Are you Buddy Helm?" she asked him.

For a moment, he was almost offended, then he just pointed to the skinny white kid standing next to him. We all had a good laugh. I had recently met a new friend, Katherine, a great painter, who lived in the area. She hadn't mentioned what I looked like to her friend, Carmen, who was now standing in front of me and Mr. Collins. She was just looking for "the drummer."

*"Ugly buildings, women of the night and drummers all gain respectability with age."*

*—partially attributed to film director John Huston*

Assumptions about the way way things are supposed to be are the way most people get through life. I was getting tired of people's assumptions about me and what I was supposed to do. Being a rock star seemed like a dead-end job to me. I know that sounds idiotic, but I was burned out. I wanted something else. Maybe just a little peace of mind, maybe some solitude, but primarily I was hungry for the magick that I had always gotten from a certain kind of music. Music that wasn't necessarily what sold gold records.

This gig was scheduled to be my last with Tim, I was moving out of L.A. and away from the music biz for a while. It was no longer that fulfilling to me. The spiritual and mystical aspects of music were calling to me. I loved the music I was playing with Tim, but I had made a decision to take a step back from the show so that I could find some honesty in my own music again.

Katherine's friend Carmen had come to welcome me to Palo Alto.

That evening, after the concert, the guys in the band couldn't believe me when I got out of the limo and boarded a Trailways bus that took me down to the ranch that Katherine and I had rented outside of Santa Cruz. All the players' mouths hung open with amazement. Art, the rock star guitarist, had played with everyone from Paul Horn to Ricky Nelson. He grinned.

"Write when you get work," he said with mock sarcasm.

The limo door slammed shut. I waved goodbye to the road. It was worth it just to see their collective faces drop off as I left life in the fast lane. I was feeling the forces of spiritual evolution and it wasn't taking me down the road to stardom. It seemed to be taking me somewhere else entirely.

A new chapter in my life was opening. Tim understood but the guys in the band were dumbstruck. They could not comprehend my career suicide. I was leaving a very lucrative gig, but I felt free. I was excited about new possibilities in art and music.

Carmen invited me to meet her partner, a great guy who worked at a research facility in what was starting to be called Silicon Valley. Jim was really into the Blues. We jammed at his house, while a computer in the corner of his living room spat out paper that turned black after a few minutes. I had never seen a computer in someone's home before—this was 1974. At that time, computers were used only in banks, college research facilities, the military, and the intelligence biz.

After we jammed, Jim wanted to show me what he did. He opened a book and pointed to a paragraph that mentioned a small item: a roller ball connected to the cursor on the computer screen. It didn't seem like much at the time. We got back to picking some off-brand Blues Shuffles on his two old Martin guitars. Little did I know that in twenty years the whole world would be singing the "Mouse Blues."

He let me get a taste of his world at his job. They ran a security check on me, and luckily, being a drummer wasn't considered too dangerous. Jim sat me down at a computer terminal and showed me some basics. I got online for the first time and felt a rush of evolutionary energy that was stronger than a standing encore at Madison Square Garden. It pulsed through me like some exotic drug from another dimension.

Jim watched my reaction. He knew what the future was going to be, and I was maybe a guinea pig. He fed me more information, then let me run wild by myself on technology that was then restricted to only a handful of people in the world and his elite team of researchers at Stanford Research Institute. I was hooked. He knew that's what would happen to me—to almost everybody who got exposed to it. He was a wizard and he placed me in his spell without any effort. He showed me the the future—the Next System. I was pulled into the next evolutionary stage of my life just like a tractor beam pulled in a space ship on the *Star Trek* TV show.

Jim was a person who really didn't have much in common with my life as a musician, but music has a way of making friends out of total strangers. I am thankful for musical magick that brings different people together to create new worlds—a world that I couldn't imagine before suddenly coming face to face with it. But there is always something old with the new, just as Marshal McLuhan had said. In this case it was the Blues. The Blues will always be a part of humanity. It is a part of the Universal energy flow that courses through all of us. We all get the Blues sometimes.

The Blues Shuffle is a tripolet feel with the middle note taken out; the "O" is missing. There is usually a "fill" at the end of a long phrase, then it repeats. Play a medium to slow tempo; don't push the beat! Lay it back, man!

The Blues Shuffle is an American rhythm, but it is based on the tripolet feel of the Bataka from Africa. It has evolved a lot as a rhythm. Playing it on a handdrum is different than hearing it on a drumset, but it can still swing, because the hand drum is where it came from originally. The trick is to accent the upbeats to keep it moving along. The upbeats are the notes without the "x" marks.

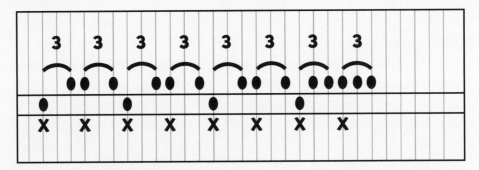

**Track 11: Blues Shuffle? Could be.**

Visionaries like Jim created a network back in the early seventies that has now evolved into the World Wide Web. That vision is based on the evolution of human consciousness. In the sixties, there was a revolution of the mind. People realized they were part of a community of higher consciousness. It was brought on by technology, by nutrition, by philosophy, by the arts, by ancient spiritual endeavors that held a seed for the future. It was about time. Now we take those various "crazy ideas" as acceptable.

For example: acupuncture is now an accepted tool of health care. Meditation is now an accepted part of religion and healing. Organic food is more available. Our perspectives have widened. A short time ago, these ideas were not tolerated very well. The next evolving consciousness may seem just as outlandish to some of us.

The World Wide Web is a technological approximation of our consciousness. Technology imitates life. The "browser" is a concept that most people have a basic understanding of now. It is like a vehicle that you get into and cruise around the Web. This is all just a new version of Universal Consciousness.

The original browser is, of course—you guessed it—the drum.

Plugging into a deep trance rhythm is like going online. You go where you want to go, but you also go where you weren't expecting to go. There is a non-verbal kind of wisdom acquired in drumming adventures. Entering a magickal realm with the drum opens universal portals into other realms where anything is possible if you can only perceive it.

This is all heady talk for philosophy students, but what about John Q. Public who is trying to find a real way to make magick? The drum will carry you there, to a place of intense magickal realism, if you have the courage to let go of your fears, insecurities, and dependence on old systems of thinking. This ancient browser runs on love and confidence. Our fears are what the culture uses to keep things in order. It's not the worst way to manage things, but it is a bit crude and old-fashioned.

Maybe we could create a new working system where people got along by feeling a deeper source of wisdom in their decision making. Would it change the stock market? I doubt it. What will most definitely change in the future will be the way we experience the world.

When we find a groove, our perceptions change. We lose track of time, our own self-consciousness disappears, we become explorers. When we return to this ordinary realm we have a heightened awareness. We bring back wisdom from other worlds.

Evolution can happen with rhythm just like the World Wide Web is changing consciousness through our phone lines. Let the grooves into your soul in a manageable smooth way and you'll go online with the Universe. It may be easier than getting your e-mail at rush hour on the infomercial highway.

# Soul Surfing

Soul surfing is visiting other souls, other lives, other sources of wisdom. It is a way to learn. Visiting the souls of departed loved ones and friends or geniuses or great teachers is like hitting their Web sites. The drum has always done this.

Soul surfing in a drumming group gives everyone access to each other's souls. Conversation between drummers is based on soul sharing of all the players. The strongest, loudest players have the most to learn from the softest players—and vice versa, of course.

When a drumming group is focused on traveling to the deeper realms of consciousness, there is a common sense of mission that binds everyone together and gives everyone equal status. There are many analogies between technology and our ever-expanding consciousness because our inventions are extensions of our consciousness. The drum illustrates life analogies because it has always been an extension of our psyches. It was one of the first pieces of technology.

I was an advanced drummer at one time, now I'm a beginner again. When I decided to *follow* the most humble drummer in the group, I learned a lot. First of all, I learned that I had put myself into the role of authority and had been focusing the group in ways that I thought were proper. I was being a control freak. By being aware of someone else in the group, I sensed possibilities that I hadn't considered before.

We all tend to play rhythms that are familiar to us. It takes listening and studying to learn someone else's rhythms, but it is rewarding. We can *become* another person when we support their rhythms. We can visit other souls when we can let go of our own sense of self-importance long enough to connect to the greater cosmic picture.

Marshal McLuhan's most famous quotation was, "The medium is the message." This has always been true for the drum. The drum is our medium of expression and it is also the message itself. It is a direct experience that we decide ourselves. It is self-evolution.

My hiatus from the music bizness didn't last long. Tim put a new band together in L.A. and booked himself at San Jose State University for only one gig. I sat in the audience feeling anonymous and secure in my new role as artist/writer/teacher and computer nerd. Tim's new band was great. I enjoyed the new energy, even though the drummer was a bit lackluster. Tim was singing in tongues, trying for an ecstatic trance, but the drummer didn't know about that kind of drumming. After the standing ovation and a few encores, Tim came down off the stage, out through the audience until he stood at the row that I was sitting in with my new friends and art teachers. He was dripping wet and glowing with the intense energy he had just generated. He was also very miffed at me. He gestured to me. I shrugged and got up. The art student sitting next to me was awed.

"Do you know Tim Buckley?" he asked me incredulously.

"Yeah," I said simply and excused myself as I pushed past a dozen or so perplexed college students and teachers. I followed him back to the dressing room. Tim slammed the door after I was inside. He turned to their current drummer and pointed to me.

"*This* is Buddy Helm," he said with bitter satisfaction.

I nodded to the drummer. He was sick. He was tired and was not enjoying the gig at all.

Tim glared at me. "Are you still playing the drums?" he asked bluntly.

I nodded. "Of course."

"We've gone through every drummer in L.A.—even Dylan's drummers—everyone. No one can play the parts that *you* came up with."

I felt a certain amount of pride, but I felt his angry frustration too.

"I broke the management contract," Tim said decisively. "You and I can write together now. Publishing will belong to us. No more agents. No more crooks. You want to go on tour?"

I looked at the tired, beaten drummer they were using. He looked sorry. I went over and sat next to him.

"Did they treat you this bad?" he asked morosely.

"No," I answered simply. I felt bad for him. He was a really good drummer, but he was having a hard time meeting their expectations. He let the pressure get to him.

I agreed to go back on tour. They would book the shows in short spurts so that I could finish my classes. The album would begin immediately. I finally had the best of both worlds; I could do art, magick, and drumming all together now. I felt whole for the first time in my life. I also felt loved by a very great and talented person. Tim was bending over backward to get me to do what he knew I should be doing; playing the drums.

Later, I laid out the Tarot cards by candlelight. Something was still lurking. Katherine watched me nervously.

"What's wrong?" she asked. "Everything is going great."

"Something bad is going to happen," I said.

"Don't say that. You'll make it happen," she said with a shiver.

The candle flickered as I pondered the symbols.

"No. I've been here before. I know the feeling."

About three months later, we finished a victorious tour with fantastic reviews, stating that our playing was paving the way for the next evolution of music combining Rock, Folk, Jazz, Reggae, and Soul music in a driving blend of hypnotic, trance-inducing rhythm and exotic melodies. Our encores were comprised of only Tim's ecstatic vocals and my pounding shamanic drumming. The crowds were loving it. The new album was being recorded at Wally Hieder's high-tech studio in Hollywood in between my classes back up at San Jose State. I was functioning on all levels of my creativity and I was feeling appreciated. The bloodthirsty vampires that run the music industry were watching though. Tim had old enemies.

After returning from a Texas tour, Tim Buckley was murdered by a trusted *friend* and it was made to look like a drug overdose. His publishing was taken over, and his widow was deprived of royalties. Old business partners collected on hidden insurance policies. We put one of the culprits in jail, but nothing we did could bring Timmy back. The money from the last tour went into dispersing Tim's ashes over Santa Monica Bay.

I was devastated, but I had felt it coming. I had seen it in the cards. The feelings were very strong. That didn't help my broken heart, though. The darkness of pain and loss enveloped me. There is only the Blues at times like these. Music was the only thing that could keep me from crawling into my own hole and forgetting the world. It was the only thing that kept me from dying of a broken heart. Only I could not play a note. I was blocked and I could not understand why. My own dark path was just unfolding before me. There was another death that had been hidden, waiting for me to face it: the death of my own father when I was a child. The hard work of recovering from death and loss was my primary job now. Everything else would have to wait.

We've investigated the tripolet, which gets us into thinking in three-note patterns; now let's slide back into a straight-ahead kind of four-beat rhythm and find a nice, danceable groove there. When we look at the notation, we will see that there is a line in between each downbeat instead of the two lines when we were playing tripolets.

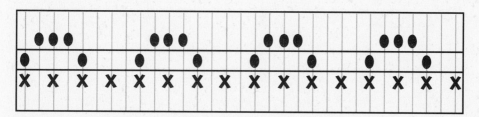

Track 12: Five minus one.

When we have the blues, dancing is the only thing that can help us get out of our personal predicament. As I've mentioned, dancing is a healing activity. It loosens the spine, which holds onto sadness. Move in a healing and joyous way and things are released. Let's dance to get rid of our blues.

Here is a subtraction exercise: Play five notes, then rest for a beat. Then play five notes, then rest.

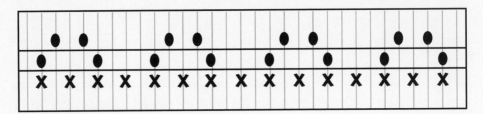

**Track 12: Five minus one.**

Next, leave out the middle note (the third note). It becomes a belly dancing beat if you play it on a Dombeq, a Mediterranean drum that is smaller than the djembes from Africa. If you are playing a frame drum, hit the downbeats hanging below the top line. You can also use your fingers on a frame drum too.

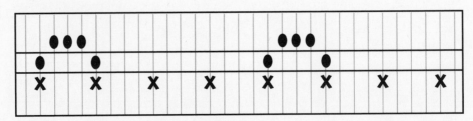

**Track 13: Five minus one, stretched out.**

We can also play the same beginning five notes, but this time we change the tambourine downbeats underneath. When we change the pulse to a slower four-beat, and leave more room, the groove gets funkier. It's a little closer to home.

Take out the third note and this time, it might become a Samba.

Play this new first part a few times, then play the second part a few times then go back and play the first part again. Just go back and forth to get the feel of changing a pattern then getting back to it.

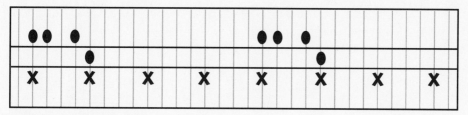

**Track 13: Samba rhythm.**

Playing this rhythm can take us to Brazil Karnivale or Egypt's sacred belly dances in the King's Chamber. The dance's grooves connect us to the constellations, long-lost friends, or our own dancing feet. It also gets us up out of our own ruts.

There are variations on the general idea. The ability to move tastefully between different variations is a form of improvisation. It is important to remember that the downbeat pulses must be steady, so keep the space as open as possible, but don't let the tempo get frantic—the groove should be relaxed. Play behind the metronome; hit the downbeat a little later than you think it should be. Your brain tries to be on time and puts anxiety into the groove. Lay it back, man. That doesn't mean play it slowly, though. Go ahead and cook.

This is an Egyptian dombeq, with a fish skin head. It is a belly dancing drum, but we can use it to dance with other parts of our bodies as well.

# 10
# INVOCATION

The CD that accompanies this book contains a piece called "Invocation." It is a meditation and a ritual piece. The length of the music is long enough to complete a beginning ceremony, such as blessing the four corners or lighting candles on a church altar.

I admit it. I was an altar boy for the Methodist Church.

I remember walking down the aisle with the other altar boy, struggling to keep the flame of my candle lit. Sometimes I would have to light it again when the two of us got down front to the pulpit. The organ and the choir kept everyone entertained during that longest of treks from the vestibule to the stage. The church organ was essential to maintaining the pace of the event. I knew that, even at ten years old, but couldn't there be a less embarrassing thing for a ten-year-old boy to do in church?

One holiday season when I was eleven years old, I was asked to play *Silent Night* on the marimba for the Christmas pageant. I love the marimba. It is a seven-foot-long, dark, warm-sounding xylophone. Long resonator tubes hang below the Brazilian mahogany keyboard. I was getting the hang of playing with three mallets but I ended on a wrong harmony. Paralyzed with guilt and shame, I stayed on that last twisted chord, trilling the three wrong notes for a perverse amount of time before finally letting the dissonance fade up into the candlelit vestibule. There was a sigh of relief from the Indiana congregation, but I loved the sound of those rich notes echoing away.

At eleven years old I became avant garde by accident. Charles Ives would have been pleased. Charles Ives was a modern American Classical composer who experimented with nonharmonic combinations of notes. Some people might say they were wrong notes, but now it is easier for us to appreciate odd sounds. Our ears have become more worldly.

Music sets the mood for ceremony. It can be stately, mysterious, haunting, righteous, or joyous—whatever is needed. The emotional mood of drumming can determine the emotional content of a ceremony. It is important to keep anxiety and tension out of the drumming because we go into a very receptive state.

The rhythmic pattern in this particular invocation is simple and slow, but has a workable feel to it. The feel carries through for a long time without withering and dying. Grooves are a good place to start when making an invocation. Your group or religious institution could try this pattern. It could conceivably be called an African pattern if you hear it that way. It is also a traditional pattern in Egypt. It is also the Blues and Celtic.

The beginning pulse for "Invocation" was based on a *walkable* tempo; such as walking a circle, or a labyrinth, or a walk to the altar.

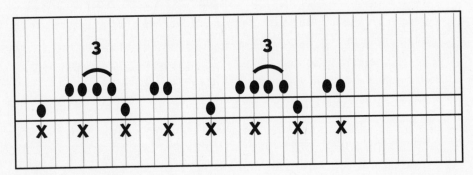

Track 14: Invocation.

Sometimes you might try a melody or chords with ceremonial drum rhythms. This will change the character of the drumming. Our brains will go to the melody as if it is the most important thing. This may lessen the power of the trance. There is a big difference between the effects of melody and rhythm on our souls and bodies. Simple, body-friendly rhythms may be better than intellectually distracting melody, tempo, and chord changes. I was recently asked to drum with a church organist who habitually changed the tempo in order to be evocative in a Classical sense. It was an odd sensation after doing drumming prayers with a steady beat. Traditional church organ players are not really into keeping a groove, but many times it wouldn't hurt. We must satisfy our basic human ritual needs by what is available in our culture; a stick, wire, and gourd like the Amazon Birambau, or a choir in a cathedral.

I wanted music for this invocation, so I messed around with various melodies until this one came up; it is not too intrusive. I wanted something to be just coloring behind whatever ceremony was being held. *Messing around* is what musicians must do in order to discover musical ideas. The hardest part of playing sometimes is just messing around because it is a state of freedom that most trained musicians might have trouble with. It is a psychologically free state where accidental musical notes come together into an idea that can be turned into a song. This is the closest a trained musician can get to the primordial innocence of a child, but they still have the technique to make sense out of the messing around.

With a drum, we can mess around with less self-consciousness because we aren't trying to be so technical, but the song can still get created, the prayer can still be woven, even if we are messing around without any technical knowledge. That is because the drummer creates *feel*.

I also had to *find* a drum part. I just played whatever felt good. I ended up playing an ancient ritual beat that is used worldwide. That was a good sign that I was on the right track for making a good invocational song. It was coincidentally the same beat that is used in many ritual rhythms in Africa and the Caribbean. It is also a powerful rhythm in America with its roots in Rhythm and Blues.

If we were to learn this rhythm in Africa, we wouldn't necessarily have to read the notes. We would just hear it and do it, but because our minds have been so bound up with seemingly important information for so long, we can no longer just feel, hear, and play. We must learn first.

Then we must unlearn to just play.

This tripolet feel wakes up your sleeping hand and the sleeping side of your brain to which it is connected. It makes both hands active and steady. It makes the brain fire on both sides.

*Some musicians may still think that being a drummer and being smart is a contradiction in terms but things are better than they used to be.*

It is a wake-up call to deeper feelings of spiritual power, partly because of the simple physical things it does to integrate the both sides of your mind and body. There is a chemical reaction in your brain that increases communication between the lobes. You get smarter. Yes, Martha . . . drummers can be smart. I come from a generation that treated drummers like they were subhuman. Some musicians may still think that being a drummer and being smart is a contradiction in terms, but things are better than they used to be.

It's because we drool.

Just because drummers drool when they are really in the groove doesn't mean they are stupid. Don't feel dumb if you realize you are drooling. It happens. Even the best drummers have drooled. It's a sign that something is happening to you that is more important than the way the world sees you. That's what a religious experience is supposed to be.

What do drummers get on their SAT tests?

Drool.

African drummers teach this basic pattern and do not encourage the novice to improvise for a good reason. Beginners disrupt the flow of magickal energy when they improvise because they play from ego, fear, and pain. When the drummer can play from relaxation and humbleness, then the real power of the rhythm will take you to a sacred place. It is built into the rhythm, but you must play it with the right attitude before it will work.

The reason I write this out is not to get you to play the *correct* notes. This is a basic pattern that will change as you play it. I wrote this out is to show you that taking out notes is a key to improvising.

I have seen many earnest drumming students study African drumming. They attend the culturally rich classes and they diligently learn that rhythm, but then, when they play it, they cannot improvise around that part. They are locked into that part as if it were a prison. They'll sit and play that part forever. Then they lose interest in drumming because it is just as boring as the other parts of their lives that they want to get away from. That isn't fun playing; they have become slaves to their own learning system.

When I have shown people this traditional drum part, I try to show them an overview so that they can feel free to create within the rhythm. The way to create is personal, but if you get into the habit of seeing spaces and notes as interchangeable, then you can subtract and add notes at will and it will be compatible with the group. This is a different way to improvise. Most people try to add as many notes as they can, but taking away is easier and more pleasing to the dancers and other drummers—as long as your creation is based on the feel; that mysterious source of inspiration.

Traditional parts are very necessary. I am encouraging people to stay free enough so that after they have learned the great traditional drum patterns, they are still able to feel creative in the right feel.

We don't need more robot drummers. We need drummers who feel the flow with the group—not just by themselves.

In most drumming groups, I end up playing a very simple part that is comprised of only the most important accents in a rhythm. Then there is room for the other players to experiment and improvise. It could be boring for me, but playing the simple parts is my meditation. Every once in a while I'll throw in a lick to perk it up and give the others a clue as to possibilities which can stimulate the drummers to move to a deeper level of trance. This kind of playing has a minimum of soloing. It is a maintaining of the groove. It is a simple kind of playing and it is the most important. Without this foundation, the more aggressive players would dissolve into confusion. It is the source of the trance—not the fast hot-shot licks.

*Caution: Drum driving tickets can be very expensive in some states.*

I can enjoy this because I am listening to the group groove, not just what I am playing. The creative energy actually comes through stronger when I let it, not when I am forcing it to my will by playing too much.

*Just enough* playing is the key.

In terms of playing an invocation, the space between the notes is necessary as a part of the invitation to the sacred energies that we want to participate with us on this plane. The space in the groove gives them room to enter our sphere.

These energies are like personalities. They are beings that mingle with us in creative endeavors. The Greeks referred to them as "the Muses." They are sources of inspiration for anyone, not just the artists. In Santeria they are

Montana Avenue Street Fair, May 15, 2000, in Santa Monica, California. These Seasons drumming workshop participants have been playing together since 1987. Among the group are clothing designers, a classical music academic instructor, an actor, writer, comedian, a theses writer, active clothing production manager, a retired biomedical research physician, business consultant, and some university musical fraternity members. One of them had just gotten a parking ticket, but the trance was so deep they didn't even get upset.

Orisha. In the Christian Church they are saints and angels. They are Pagan Elementals. They are Hindu Gods and Muslim sages. Every religion uses these forces. We can invoke them for help and guidance. A common bond of all religions are the drumbeats for invoking these helpful energies.

We are starting to rediscover an ancient *tunneling* process with drums that access these creative energies. There is a sensation that an opening occurs. In trance drumming, we bore a hole through our reality, which is usually perceived to be as substantial as rock, but drumming helps us break through. It is like coming out of a cave into the light. The "Doors of Perception" open and we can talk to the other side; the outside.

The spaces in the rhythm are openings; a humble way to entice these entities into our realm. It is different than the wild bashing of some drumming groups. That kind of over-the-top playing conjures a different energy that might be exhilarating for the moment, but lacks a deeper effect, and could leave a psychic stain. Conjuring the right spirit is based upon playing the right rhythms in the right attitude. You really don't want to get the wrong number.

We all make magick, every day. The more we do it consciously, the better our effect on the Universe. We all affect the Universe with our magick. Drumming your fingers on the steering wheel is a source of magick. It's the groove that carries you—not how much you paid for the drum or the car.

# 11
# RESTRAINT

Restraint is necessary. Loud, angry banging will ruin any magickal groove. I understand why some people play from a place of pain; they hit the drum to release personal hurt. Restrained drumming lets the hurt out gradually. Healing, creative energy can then come through us in a manageable form. It is a good tool to learn in life. The high voltage of our pain, as well as our Divine inspiration, is stepped down to a usable voltage when we use the drum like an electrical power transformer.

It is the inclusion of both sides of the Tao of the drum. There is the side that is creative and lets the energy flow; there is also the side that needs to be restrained in order to make sense and beauty out of the Universe. There will always be opposites at play with each other. That is what the Tao, or "the way" talks about. Keeping opposites in balance is the dance of life. Balance and drumming go together.

Martial arts students develop a sense of restraint in order to exert just as much force as is necessary. Some people don't have a sense of restraint in their lives so they end up doing something all the way. They think that is the only way to play drums. One person said that if they "got into the drums" they would want to focus on it completely and master it, otherwise they wouldn't bother. That's a complicated way to deprive yourself of fun and enlightenment.

Music is all about restraint. Without restraint there would just be confusion and noise in our world.

In a drumming group the challenge for the drummer, sometimes, is to restrain his or her own exuberance in order to allow the energy to come through the group and not just the individual. Restraint adds longevity too, even in drumming.

Let's get funky now.

Hit two big notes in the middle of the drum head, then one note out at the edge. Wait, then hit the two big notes again followed by the high note. Medium tempo should get you one of the most traditional American beats: Soul music.

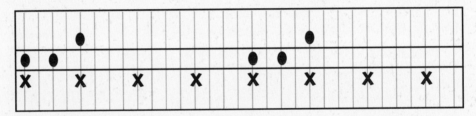

**Track 15: Soul.**

Otis Redding had a song called *So Hard to Handle* with this sort of beat. Try putting a shaker with it to keep the groove going. Or "shake your own thang."

Playing a hand drum in this way is like playing a drum set; the big note in the middle of the drum is your bass drum and the high note at the edge is your snare drum. The shaker will then function like your HiHat or Ride cymbal. Traditional African hand drumming is nice, but we know this kind of beat in our culture. It is an evolution from the traditional African into a modern rhythm that we all relate to. We can use this. It's part of our traditional beats.

No book is complete without a CIA story.

I traveled to Florida to do a weekend drumming retreat with a men's group. I was the guest drummer. There were approximately two dozen men. There were some very good-hearted souls in the group. There was a great amount of work and support by the organizers.

I realized when I arrived at the campsite that I was going to have to deal with men who were not particularly open to working at drumming. They had a sense of something needing to be fixed in themselves, or something that they needed to connect with that was greater than themselves, but they weren't interested in working at anything. I don't blame anyone for that attitude. That's why I don't teach. It's work.

The three days were filled with exercises to open up the men, and also some of their sons, to their more sensitive sides. They wore face paint, crawled through a rebirthing tunnel, ate communally, and slept in cabins labeled "Beaver clan" or "Duck clan." It was a nice summer campground for children; this weekend it was filled with big guys in cut-off jeans.

There was an American Indian man there who took the men through the rebirthing. He also got them to sing songs around the campfire. We drummed together. He seemed to approve of how I was trying to get the guys to loosen up and play. But it was difficult. The guys were stuck in their own self-images and would not take a chance out of that character cage. I worked very hard for three days to find a groove in this group of attorneys, real-estate agents, and businessmen. It was like pulling teeth.

The first thing I told them probably put them off.

"Drumming is great, but we are playing rhythms that belong to tribes and cultures that we thought were unimportant. We need to atone for that."

"A ho," the American Indian said in agreement. That was all he had to say.

These guys didn't want to bare their souls, or atone for anything. They were only willing to wear shorts and eat something that they had to fix themselves

*Terry, Otis Redding's road manager, told me a story a long time ago down in Macon, Georgia:*

*A young bull was grazing with an old bull at the bottom of a steep hill. The young bull looked up to the top of that hill and saw a herd of grazing cows.*

*The young bull turned to the old bull and said, "Let's run up this hill and mate with one of them cows."*

*The old bull shook his head and said, "No. Let's WALK up this hill and mate with ALL them cows."*

over the weekend. They weren't intending to work too hard at anything. I didn't blame them one bit.

It turned into a great weekend anyway. The campfire drumming was prolonged and transformational, but I worked for a long time before we finally hit the groove. When the groove finally lit up I got excited. I yelled at the firelit faces around the big fire.

"There it is! Do you feel that?"

Some of them did. Most looked almost sheepish but willing to try to feel. Some grinned and tapped their foot. One man danced. That was some consolation, but I was working very hard, and I almost fell back into my old music biz attitude: "What a bunch of stiffs. They're as bad as record company executives."

It's hard for guys to loosen up their psychic armor and then have to get it back up for their job. Nonetheless, there was still a great deal of opening up with these men, and I was very glad to be there for the weekend retreat.

On my flight back to L.A. I was sitting with my feet jammed up against the bulkhead. My sore wrists and elbows were wrapped in support bandages. A bothersome mood had descended on me since the weekend with the men's group. I had taken on something. It felt like I was carrying extra Karmic baggage back to L.A. All the guys around the campfire had just kicked back and thought of roasting marshmallows while I was banging away trying to get them into a meditative dance groove. I was in an older mindset that I was familiar with. It was a cross between the disgruntled road musician and the underappreciated diva/shaman. It was my problem, not theirs.

"Are we gonna make it?" A guy asked as he sat down next to me. He gestured to my mummified wrists. He had on a white shirt and tie, dark slacks, and high-shine wingtips. Spook.

He had that kind of good-natured inquisitiveness.

He drew me out with a lot of casual conversation and we talked about music. He mentioned several obscure bands and we sort of bonded, having grown up in the same general era. We talked about why he had become a Navy Seal and how the discipline and focus was meaningful for him. He had considered his youth to be somewhat wild, even anarchistic, but the military straightened all that out for him. He informed me in that special casual soft voice that he now worked for the government.

"I figured that," I said.

"Why?" He said.

"The way you dress."

"My tie and clipped mustache?" he said demurely.

"No. Your shoes. They're too shiny to be worn by anyone other than a CIA agent. Too expensive and shiny for a local cop."

He nodded quietly in tentative appreciation. That cooled him out for a while, but he had to keep talking and gathering information. He was geared for that. So, I decided to talk about how healing the drumming was. How it could free a person from all sorts of mental and physical restraints and problems if they let themselves feel this process.

"It sounds like you love what you're doing," he remarked with appreciation.

I would have agreed with him at any other moment but I was hurting and feeling cranky. I was still puzzled about the weekend.

I mentioned that a martial arts instructor for the Special Forces had studied drumming with me and that he used the concepts in his seminars. He knew of the man. But I finally ended up talking about how rough the weekend had been. The guys were a hard nut to crack. I wasn't currently in love with what I was doing.

"I wanted them to drop their armor," I told him.

"But those men have spent their whole lives developing their armor," he countered with a pragmatic tone. He was defending his own.

I tried to keep it simple. "But after a certain amount of time, that armor doesn't work any more."

He finally stopped smiling at me and sat there thinking for a while.

"You're right," he finally said, very quietly. I invited him to come and drum.

# 12

# THE TAO OF THE DRUM

In our technological minds we see the world as concrete—solid and stable. The Tao looks at the world as a fluid, constantly changing event. Drumming is a way to feel the Tao as it really exists. Every note and space is a balancing act between the emptiness of the void and the business of reality.

The act of playing gives us the power to decide our own realities in this seemingly contradictory event called life.

When we are flowing with a groove, the play of opposites is a constantly changing orchestra that is fresh and improvised at every moment. The flow of the Tao energy through the drummers when they play with this fluid openness is healthy and invigorating. When the flow is trapped, there is discomfort.

We have no real working systems to show us the way the Tao flows through all things. We are getting an inkling of it through Oriental studies like Feng Shui and the I Ching. As we develop an understanding of these principles, we'll have our own words to describe this fluid state. For the moment, "grooves" might work.

Interpreting the Tao in every moment of our lives is a way to be awake and in control without feeling anxious. Playing with the Tao on a drum is a way to channel Chi into an area of one's life that needs energizing.

# Exorcism

A woman came into the workshop after having been away for several months. She had gotten married, then things got complicated, and she was in the process of separating from her spouse. She came in to drum to regain a sense of her self.

We played a few different grooves, then we settled into one that seemed right for her. It seemed to be a groove to send the trouble man away. There is absolutely no reason why you can't make up your own exorcism grooves.

I realized we were close to the groove that Ray Charles used for *Hit the Road, Jack*. The Universe is always grooving along and we are in synch with it. We may not know it, but the hints are there. It's our choice to notice the connections between our groove and the Universal Groove.

This particular groove is brisk. Take that slow Blues Shuffle we did earlier and speed it way up. It becomes a tap dancing groove that is more of a Swing. This is much more fun, even though it is still based on the Blues. "Shuffle" is an old American Jazz term. "Swing" is what happened to the slow Blues shuffle when it got played by a big band like Count Basie, Duke Ellington, or Paul Whiteman. It is based on the tripolet rhythm that we have done before. This time it goes faster.

The feel skips along. Playing it fast can get tiring and busy, so take out notes. Take out most of the middle notes of the tripolets to keep the skipping feel, which is based on feeling all those tripolet notes but not playing all of them.

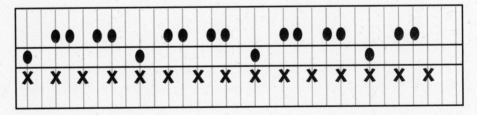

Track 33.

On a Drum Set this can be played along with a "Ride" rhythm that you play on the Ride cymbal. A "Ride" feel is when the Swing groove bops along smoothly. Pretty soon you may hear the Raylettes singing the background parts: "Don'tcha come back no more."

This seemed to be a good exorcism rhythm for the woman. She appeared to gain power as she played it. She was still making subtle body moves that were connected to her mental state of self-criticism. She would get into the groove and sound really good, then she would jerk her head to the side and stop playing. I mentioned it.

"I was abused as a child," she said calmly. "It's hard for me to believe that I can do anything correctly. I stop playing because I think I'm doing it wrong."

"You are playing the best just before you stop yourself," I said truthfully.

Her eyes lit up with a new point of view. She suddenly found the power to stay with it for a longer span of time. When we finally finished she was flushed with excitement and a sense of accomplishment. Something had changed in her own self-perception. She knew the stumbling block was there, but now she found a way to get over it by using the drum as a tool to pass through an old habitual state of mind into a fresh outlook.

Don't expect these exact notes to *work* as an exorcism. It's the feel that works. The notes may change. Don't get stuck in thinking "right notes." They are just symbols.

You'll know it when you feel it.

This rhythm is also part of a traditional rhythm called Kassa, from Guinea, where it is used for planting and harvesting. We need rhythms for certain things in our lives too. It's just a little different—instead of drumming for planting and harvesting, we need to drum for detoxing after rush hour, computer overload, coffee nerves, or even getting rid of unwanted company.

# Downloading Inspiration

Facing the creative source is a Tantric meditation. It is also a way to drum. By enjoying each note that you hit, you can handle the download of inspiration from the Divine Creative Source without blowing a fuse.

The Book of Changes, the I Ching, is a literary masterpiece that is a tool for divination and oracular insight and magick. It is a tool for downloading inspiration. The I Ching has many references to drums and drumming. The drum is a tool for celebration, for magick, and for sacred ritual. It is also an analogy for life situations.

When you throw the three coins a total of six times, the I Ching tells you where you are at that given moment. The combinations of heads and tails gives you an observation about that specific moment in your life. It explains the energies that are rising and the energies that are declining and how they interact with each other. There are also recommendations for one's attitude at that given moment. This is based on thousands of years of observation and insight into human nature and the nature of the Tao.

Substitute the word "groove" for the word "Tao," and you'll have an approximation in our language of what the Tao is: streams of energies that are going in many directions, interplaying with each other. Gee, that could also be a drum group.

The I Ching or Book of Changes nails down one moment in that flow and tells you what it might be. Similarly, there are moments in the drumming meditation where you become aware of what you are playing—only it's too late to really enjoy it because it is already gone. If you try to recapture it, then you fall out of the flow of the groove.

Maybe this is getting too intellectual. Let's just settle back into the groove and feel better. The Tao is always moving. When we get an insight into just one moment of cool licks, we loose our *oversoul* connection to the flow of life. Rhythmic movement is life—trying to hold on to one moment is human.

# 13
# CONJURE DRUMMING

**R**emember the earlier "Stop Time" exercise? The "stop time" kind of drumming exercise is a beginning way to improvise and gain confidence. Why do this? It can be terrifying, so what's the point?

When you take that little solo and everyone is just hitting the downbeat to support you, you are conjuring. You are making something from nothing. It is magick of the first order. Sometimes we become self-conscious and it turns into just noodling, but the potential is there.

New Orleans comes to mind when the word "conjure" is used. There is a history of magick in this country. It has always had a home in New Orleans as well as other places. But New Orleans has it's own style that is a blend of French, Spanish, free African, Caribe, Akadian, and many Indians of mixed origin. The Wild Touchapoulis was a band that articulated the magic as well as any band, and better than most. They dressed up in colorful feathered headpieces and strutted their stuff during Mardi Gras. The grooves are elusive to play unless you are raised there and eat the food.

Sacred texts have always been written in code. Mystical teachings have been hidden. Mystery Schools have always existed throughout history. America was founded on a Mystery School. All of the presidents were high initiates in the Masonic Lodge. John Kennedy was the first president who was not a member of the Sacred Order of the Masons—he changed the system.

A change in our consciousness creates a change in our social systems. We expand beyond the limitations of our previous order. We are giving birth to a new order once again in our world. I am not referring to the worldwide capitalist marketplace. It is more subtle than that. It is part of a greater history of secret spiritual teachings. It has always been secret because the writers, practitioners, and initiates had to survive in an unsympathetic world. Intolerance is a quality of human nature that doesn't seem to change too quickly.

There are always people who want to keep things the same, especially if they're making money at it There are always people who want a change, for good reasons or just because they are not making money. If only life were really that simple.

When Africans were forcefully brought over on slave ships four hundred years ago, they brought their Mysteries with them. These secret codes of ritual religion evolved in the Caribbean slave community. They had to be hidden behind a facade of Catholic imagery to placate the slave owners who didn't want to see any demon-worshipping. The ancient sacred religions born in Africa were hidden under approved Catholic images.

Magickal rhythms are sacred and eternal. They are older than any race on the planet except maybe the Aborigini people of Australia. The rituals that go along with the sacred rhythms from Africa had to be modified to fit into the New World that was being born four hundred years ago. They took on the superficial appearance of the prevailing order based in Rome, but underneath there was still the power of the real inspirational source of magic and life from the African people. The names of the Gods changed to the names of saints, but the drum beat was still invoking the eternal deities of the earth, sky, water, fire, and metal. This might seem primitive to the technological mind, but the need was always there in people's hearts to worship the elemental forces of creation. We are feeling that need today.

The worship of the earth and the elements was the first science. In this culture, one way of expressing the sacred hidden knowledge is with music. Everyone knows a song that sends goosebumps up and down their spine when they hear it. That is magick. The rhythms are powerful, even if they sing about silly things. That's why Rock 'n' Roll was such an amazing discovery for people caught up in the miracle of progress in the great society of America in the fifties. It reminded us that we are magickal beings. Hovering near the radio speaker late at night, listening to our favorite song, was a way to save our souls. We needed to hear "That Song." It was as if that song was written for us and no one else. There was a feeling that the song held a mystery that applied to only our lives and no one else's. It was a secret that was ours alone. And hopefully a million other kids felt the same way and bought the record. That mysterious feeling is in the rhythm of the song as well as the lyrics and melody. The secret beats.

*We need to hear "That Song," that song written just for us and no one else, that song that holds a mystery that applies only to us, our secret beat.*

The sacred beats were reborn in New Orleans and called Jazz or Rhythm and Blues, or Second Line or Funk, or Swamp Boogie, or Chanka Chanka, or Soul music. What it's called doesn't matter. The beat is what is saving us and connecting us to the sources of truth that we need now to make important decisions about our planet.

Take a shaker and shake it.

Here is the symbol I'm using for the shaker: ( ■ )

If you shake the maracas or shaker at a medium tempo, nice and even, you'll get a lot of notes in between the downbeats. Four notes in between each downbeat is what we are hearing for this beat. There is still that PaTa PaTa rhythm going on underneath, only now, we will count nonsense words for the different little beats. We do this, counting in order to hit the right upbeats (see notation, p. 110). The cool accents fall on important upbeats.

"**One** de an da **Two** de an da **Three** de an da **Four** de an da"

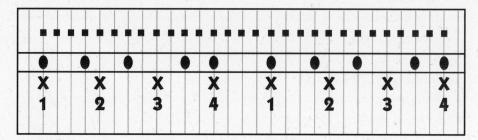

**Track 16: Bo Diddley.**

This is track number sixteen. It is the Bo Diddley beat—the Mississippi Delta Blues Rock 'n' Roll rhythm that everybody knows. The subtle thing about this is the second note. That note has to hit on the last note before (2). Say, one-de-an-da and hit on (**one**) and then on (**da**). This accent is also in the "Clave" of the Latin beats. It is one of those often-used accents that we can't always hit correctly. Our ears get lazy and that subtle upbeat slides into the next downbeat and the groove goes to sleep. Our ears are very lazy. It is important to feel the four notes in between the downbeats, but it isn't good to play them all. They function as your inner clock so you can stay on the beat and hit those cool upbeats in the exact spot to get it to swing.

In New Orleans the tempo of the songs is slower than the rest of the world. They have developed a special way to play *behind the beat*. That means it is slower than the metronome. Listen to the Neville Brothers and let that "Second Line" groove sink into your soul. It is important to relax when playing drums. That is why New Orleans music feels so mysterious and good; the players are relaxed. But New Orleans has it's own style and not all musicians can play it believably. It can feel forced and tense and too fast. That is why I prefer playing *back in the pocket,* so the medicine of the relaxed groove can work. It is important for any real magickal event too. If the tempo is tense, then any kind of conjuring will be weak. The groove with the most open feel will carry a ritual better than something frantic. All this is foolish to try to articulate in words, but it's kind of fun to try. The real reason I keep hitting on the relaxed thing is because tension ruins drumming. Most people are tense. They decide to drum to relieve their tension. They play the drum tensely and they get tenser. Then everybody else trying to play with them gets tense. Everyone ends up tense.

Let's intentionally try to relax the beat when we play that Bo Diddley beat. Most people play it too fast. When you discover the pocket you'll never want to play any other way. Play slower than you think you should be playing.

Bo Diddley is one of the most inspiring musicians I ever worked with. He plays a square-shaped guitar and everyone knows his Delta Blues dance songs. Just for a goof, one night, in front of thousands of kids, he sang a bit of an aria from an opera. It was very beautiful. He had also been classically trained. His big grin shone out from under his black, gunslinger cowboy hat and thick glasses when he saw how that surprised everyone. I saw him then as a young boy studying the violin, not the Gut-bucket Bluesman that made everybody dance. Then he went back into his own Delta Blues music. He knew Classical music but it was his own music that got you so deep down in the lowest chakra of your soul, it made you feel the swamp between your toes. You can taste the soul in his music.

## Pushing the Beat

In a groove, if someone is *pushing the beat* the whole thing can turn into a mess. The energy gets tense and the tempo speeds up. Nobody enjoys that, and there is no magic.

But if there is the *illusion* of pushing the beat, then you have excitement and a heightening of the magical groove. This is a subtle trick that great players can mess with.

Marvin Gaye comes to mind. *What's Goin' On* is a great piece of music. The album is full of secret beats.

That three-beat rhythm that we did earlier is on this album: *Flying High in the Friendly Skies*. Check it out. It is a God-inspired album, driven by love and patience. Marvin Gaye was a proponent of that sacred drum magic that went back hundreds of years to another place in time. He was a drummer at Motown before he was a singer.

The beat that I think is the most intense is at the end of the album: *Inner City Blues*. It's also called *Make me want to hollar, throw up both my hands.*

It starts with two big notes, then a great big hole before the next two big beats. It settles into a groove that is laid-back but really intense. The holes make the groove cook right away. It ain't the notes, brother. There aren't any. The energy that this track generates has survived over the years. It is a classic. It is a great lesson in the finer points of relaxed drumming. It lets the holes breath and live. No tension.

A good exercise is to hit those two beginning notes with the song. Leave the space. Then hit those two notes every time they come around. Waiting through the space until your next two notes comes around again can be hard. You'll notice that you probably push the beat in your head and hit the two notes too soon sometimes. That is your impatience coming through. That is your nervous brain trying to get in control of the situation. Just relax, let your body have the authority it needs, and hit just those two beats with the song, each time they come around. You'll have to slow down in your head to hit them just right. But it is a good meditation because you really want to hit those two notes "right on the money" because it is such a great song, and you want to be a part of it.

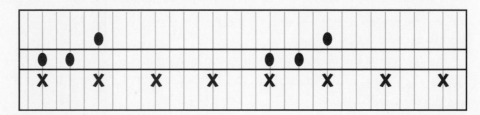

Track 17: Marvin.

The section where Gaye sings still sends shivers up and down my spine. He has a great deal to say in the words but it never comes out angry. The music gives him the power and authority to say what needs to be said without loosing his temper. That is beauty and magic.

His rhythm section *pushes the beat* in such a way that it gives the song urgency without speeding up. One reason this kind of thing works is that they hit just those two strong beats at the beginning of the phrase. It is a relaxed tempo, not too fast, but those two strong beats at the beginning of each phrase set up a forceful meditation. It is a power prayer that is sung with gentle conviction. He could be singing in any language and it would still be inspirational. This is like the earlier *Soul Beat*, but very back, way behind the beat.

This beat has been used in a million hit songs, but what Marvin Gaye does to it is special. It's the heartbeat of American rhythms. We all feel this. Just play the first two beats and nothing else. You'll need the rest of the space to relax and slow down for the next two big beats. We tend to rush everything. This track is a good example for learning to relax the beat and our lives.

We can use these beats in our modern rituals whether we know them correctly or not. What it could turn into next is what keeps it fresh for me. The beat always resurrects itself in a new, yet old, way. Write your own song and sing it while you hit the drum.

Club Kilimanjaro in Bisbee, Arizona. I hope Bob Marley approves.

# Independence

Take that beat we just did, with the two big beats at the beginning, and tap your foot on the "x". When you can do both parts at the same time, you have *independence*. This is where your mind and body are doing different things at the same time. It can be frustrating and nerve-wracking, but if you relax, it can be an exciting, deep meditation and a source for magickal power.

The ability to detach a part of our awareness and not lose our place with some other activity is what independence is all about on the drums. You get above the confusion of desperately paying attention to all the details, and instead become a sublimely removed spectator while you play a number of different parts, all at the same time.

Juggling all the elements of your life in a gracious manner is a good life skill to acquire. It can ease the stress. The combining and blending of separate creative energies is important for focused ritual, whether it be a High Holiday or a low-down Saturday night.

Some drummers will intently watch my hands, trying to imitate what they think I am playing. They get thrown off if I change the part because of their total focus on my hands. That can get very strenuous for the novice, but it is one way to learn.

Sometimes, a player will lock onto what I am playing, in an effort to play the same part. When they are locked onto *my part*, they get lost if I change what I am playing. Independence can give your mind the ability to do what it wants to do, while other things are going on around you, without getting distracted by someone else's playing. Staying on *your part* is important in a drumming group and in life.

When the drumming group gets busy, each player becomes immersed in their own sound, but also in the sound of the other drummers, so it is a good meditation to stay on your own *part*, even though the rest of the group may be going nuts. They will love you for not getting distracted by their playing because they are depending on your basic pattern.

The novice is very important in a group because when they focus on their own simple part, the group works on a higher level of magick, even if the novice can't comprehend what that level is yet. That is a key in Santeria drumming, where the three drummers play specific parts. The beginning drummer plays the simplest part and must not waver.

Independence is the first step in getting strong on your own, whether it be drumming or living. Independence of your own attention is where you choose what will interest you, rather than being distracted in a world of confusion.

*Delta Blues music, so deep down it makes you feel the swamp between your toes.*

We have played beats that are more gentle. There are also more forceful magickal rhythms. Drumming beats have changed the world. We continue to discover the power of the different beats as we develop, *improve,* and improvise.

# 14

# THE CELTIC KNOT

The mysterious Celtic knots are a form of meditation and prayer, a secret knowledge encoded into the myriad twisting of the cords as they wind and turn on themselves. This is a form of hidden knowledge in a way that is not what people think. If you follow the maze of knots, then you unravel the mystery of your own journey. It is the act of knowing the tangle and making a path of wisdom out of it that is the secret teaching. The act of unraveling is an inspirational act—not necessarily the knots themselves. Walking a maze or labyrinth is also a meditation in unraveling.

Drumming is like unraveling the Celtic knot shown here. The rhythms intertwine and create confusion unless you are willing to follow the pulse and find your way back out of the maze intact, but with new inspiration.

The bodrain is the Celtic drum. It is a very old design and the way it is played is unlike any other drum in the world (see photograph, p. 124). It is propped up vertically on your knee

**Unraveling the mystery of our journey is an inspirational act.**

123

The author playing a bodrain. Even his dog Lily enjoys Celtic music.

and you strike it with a "tipper" that you hold like a pencil. You hit the drum head with both ends of the tipper. The tipper technique is marvelous to watch and a challenge to learn. The sound is mysterious, yet it is really driving and strong. The bodrain is the drum of choice in Druid ceremonies. The songs of Ireland have been sung to the beat of the bodrain for a long time and they have a unique rhythm that is related to the way the bodrain is played.

This is incredibly specialized music, but guess what? The three-beat (tripolet) that they are playing is that three-beat that we were working on earlier and the same three-beat pattern that Marvin Gaye used. It's also a traditional Yoruba beat. Small world isn't it?

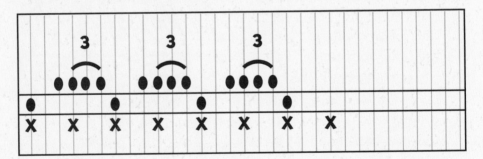

Track 18: Celtic.

This is a simplification of a Celtic beat, but it is based on the same three- and six-note patterns. If we learn the underlying rhythmic principles, we can acquire some ability to play it in one cultural setting or another—but it has to do with what we are able to hear. If we learn to improvise around the six-beat then we can approximate a lot of different kinds of world beats. It is a universal language.

If there are drummers out in the Universe, I'll bet they are playing this six-beat pattern.

A note about improvising in six-beat patterns. Since the underlying pulse is the tripolet, it is difficult to improvise the way we would throw in extra notes in a regular four-beat pattern. The six-beat locks the possibilities down to only a few added improvisational notes, so the best way to improvise is to take out notes and accent certain cool notes that are already in the pattern. This may sound like too much technical talk, but you may get the idea from the CD.

## Death and Drumming

The weight of a soul has been measured in hospital laboratories. At the moment of death, body weight decreases by a tiny amount. If you want the specific numbers, you're missing the point.

The drumming energy can be like a boat for the departed soul, as in Egyptian hieroglyphs. The sound carries the soul away to whatever is next in their cycle. The energy also gives the living a taste of something from beyond. It is an opportunity to give and take across the barrier between life and death in a meaningful way, and the drum is an important ceremonial tool to address the other side at this unique moment.

I'm sure anyone who was alive then remembers the JFK funeral march. The drums were draped in black and the somber slow beat was etched into our tribal memory. That beat is ominous and terrifying, especially with the riderless horse prancing nervously next to the caisson carrying the coffin as it rolled down Pennsylvania Avenue.

If there is a chance to drum for a departed soul, please take the opportunity to hit the drum for them. This is one of the most important uses of a drum. This is the beat that accompanies the fallen.

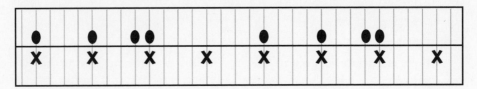

**Track 19: Funeral.**

The JFK funeral drummers played a nine-stroke roll at the end of each cluster of notes. I remember hearing it, then figuring it out on my own field snare drum. My drum was like theirs—but the military field snare drums were draped in black. It was a very sad moment, one of the most powerful drumming moments in the world.

It's a good idea to celebrate the crossing-over of a soul instead of just feeling our own loss. If we were in New Orleans, when we returned from the cemetery, that Death Dirge rhythm would be speeded up into a Second Line Strut.

On an upbeat note, Lynn Rank, a member of our drumming workshop at Gaia Oasis in the Sierras, sent me a photo of her great-grandfather, Moses Findley Campbell, who was a drummer in the Civil War, and also called back as a drummer in World War I (p. 127). That is an incredible change of consciousness in one lifetime, but it is also a testament to the eternal usefulness of the drum. By the time of this photo, Campbell had arthritis but he was still able to hold his hickory drumsticks and no doubt play very well. The gleam in his eyes is the most inspiring look I have seen in any photo. This man was very much alive and enjoying himself when this picture was taken. He was proud of being a drummer, a kind of pride I appreciate immensely. He felt the beat and it showed up in his eyes. He still had his jaunty stature and a spiritual readiness to play with the Universe.

**Moses Findley Campbell, 1841–1928.**

# 15

# THE MYTH OF IMPROVING

There is a need to feel we are improving at something in our lives; the drum, career, art, music, our stock portfolio, or exercise workout—whatever. People choose some pretty weird self-measuring devices to judge themselves by. That's all well and good, but what happens when our desire to be *better* interferes with our joy of living, playing, and sharing with other people? It becomes a destructive demonic energy. There are many Hollywood movies about artists, athletes, politicians, actors, and others who strove for excellence, yet ended up as tragic basket cases. Our own desire for improvement can turn on us.

I strove for excellence as a drummer—in more than one way. Initially, as a preteen, I worked at technique; sightreading, fast hand and foot sequences, obscure rhythm patterns. Speed and power were the watch words. When I grew older, stamina and flash were important. But the real meaning of excellence started to dawn on me when I could feel what others drummers could do with the groove and yet not be technically as *good* as I was. One of the first times was in Macon, Georgia, where some of the good old boys were recording some tunes in what had been Otis Redding's recording studio, in the back of a deserted storefront. When I heard what these local boys were laying down, I realized that my grooves were too intense, too busy, too intellectual. I didn't have a clue about the feel! I thought I was good. People had told me I was good, but suddenly I doubted everything that I had believed about what excellence really meant.

The mystical side of drumming became the most important aspect for me. The technique and flash were eventually burned away by the tough realities of life as a working drummer. I had to fight the disappointment of always being the bridesmaid, but never the groom. Finally the real excitement of drumming came down to talking to God. Feeling the inspired Universal energy coming through me was the only reason to play. That was not always commercial, but now, in my drumming workshops, all of that journey toward excellence seems to be worth it. I have become more of a human being as a side effect of my drumming quest.

*The real excitement of drumming comes down to talking to God.*

One workshop member is a very intellectual woman. Her words are her passion and her foray into the realm of rhythm was an attempt to *improve* her own poetry. Her drumming seemed somewhat cold and analytical, but okay. It was on the beat, it was steady, she could improvise easily, but she wasn't getting enough out of it. Whatever she wanted was eluding her, so she eventually stopped coming. I saw her later at the grocery store. She had stopped coming to the drumming because she didn't feel that she was getting any better. I knew that mindset. It can be a trap. It comes sometimes from how we are raised, trying to meet inappropriate standards of excellence. Or it could be what we have become as adults, habitually forcing ourselves to survive better than the guy next to us. Fear and competition. That's no fun.

I suggested that she could just come and play and not worry about getting better, but that was too much of a stretch for her. Drumming *just for fun* wasn't her goal. Doing anything for fun didn't seem to fit into her world, so I let her know that she was welcome and left it at that.

Another woman who had been coming for years became very sick and was admitted to the hospital with meningitis. She recovered, but was somewhat debilitated. She came back to the drumming as a form of physical and mental therapy. Previous to her illness, she could play quite a bit and improvise glibly from her Classical music background. Sometimes I would suggest that she *lay back* a little bit and not play so much—leave some room. This criticism shattered her at the beginning, but she came to understand that I was trying to get her to break through the superficial noodling that many intellectual people do. They don't hear what they are playing in relation to the feel of the group. They carry on conversations with themselves. I thought she would benefit if we got her to the simpler, more direct voice that is inside the groove and inside herself.

She expressed the same discontent after her illness as did the first woman I mentioned. She felt the need to improve. Drumming can show us that our lives are a steady state of improvement. The challenge is to give ourselves credit.

"Improving" on a drum is when you finally play less.

After a month in intensive care this woman could play only the simple patterns. She could not improvise around them. Her illness and the medication left her with little of her old self as a glib drummer. I stressed to her that this was an opportunity to play less and to really feel the subtlety of the groove without the distraction of intellectual noodling. I truly believe that she will be a better drummer than she was. She is finally accepting the healing space in between her busy notes.

Sometimes the workshops really cook because I am holding down the pattern. I'm playing simply and with open spaces so that people can feel the joy of improvising. Some people do not realize why they are sounding so good; it is because the backup band is working very hard to make them sound good.

When we realize that our job is to support the groove so that others can sound good, then we become strong drummers—strong in the sense that we can carry a whole group with our own simple pattern.

Many women want to become strong drummers. They want to lead a drumming group. My advice is to bring more of the woman into the drumming. Don't try to do the guy thing. There is a subtlety that women have on the drum that men need to hear. Men want to understand the way a woman is feeling rhythm, but sometimes they are so unsure of rhythm in themselves, that a rhythmic woman is an overwhelming experience for them. So be gentle, girls. Guys' egos are very delicate in this situation, even though they may not sound that way. The calling of the deep note opens their heart and sometimes that is a terrifying moment. Guys think they need armor.

I love it when there are both women and men in a drumming group. I don't have the slightest need to show off and compete anyway. Everybody is supporting the groove, and then just a few little solo notes pop up to stimulate the feel without too much distraction. We have nice dialogues at a moderate volume. Just guys in a group tends to turn it into a contest instead of a conversation.

I was told that I was "hard on guys" by a guy who came in only once, after reading *Drumming the Spirit to Life*. He said he only wanted to do transformational drumming, and that I qualified. He studied my technique. He finally mentioned that he was a drum facilitator. I knew that. Way back in high school, other competing Rock 'n' Roll bands would come and try to steal licks from our band, Those Five. That's a guy thing to do.

This facilitator unconsciously came to heal, and I hope that happens. But he also came to steal licks, *cop my style*, or steal anything else that he could use to make a buck in his drumming facilitator gig.

Look out! There are a lot of "drum facilitators" out there who will bum you out and take your money without the slightest hint of the honest magic that is available in the drumming experience. If you come away from a drumming group feeling dissatisfied, don't blame yourself. It's because the guys are making it difficult to pray with the drum.

The joke may be on him; he mentioned that his wife had bought my first book, *Drumming the Spirit to Life*, and asked him to read it. Maybe she was trying to tell him something.

Maybe she could see something about him that needed some honest attention. Here is a possible list: a sense of panic, greed, fear, psychological armor, shut-down feelings, no consideration for others, self-centered loathing, no fun at a party, he can't dance, lousy in bed, doesn't even care about anyone else's needs—the list goes on and on.

I'm not that hard on the guys—I am one. We make it hard on ourselves and everyone around us. We get insular with our feelings and fears. The drum is a way to open up a channel of communication where our inner voices come out and talk "with the world," not "at the world."

Allowing the deep, slow, heavy tone of the drum to open up our hearts is the hardest drum part for all of us to play, but some guys just make it harder still. Maybe they are in need of a heart to heart with their wives instead of a head to head with me. The drum shows that condition very clearly.

It could be called arrogance, but I think it is closer to a little kid in a big body. The drum can bring the man up to his full potential, but it is not about beating your chest and stomping around. The feminine side of men must come out in a safe way. The heavy, deep, easy tone of a drum is asking men to open their hearts and release anger, hatred, and fear; then fill them with healing love and compassion. Men bang the drum hard to avoid these feelings. They hit the drum too hard to justify themselves.

Children being teased by their classmates will stick their fingers in their ears and yell, "I'm not listening! I'm not listening! I'm not listening! I can't hear you! I can't hear you!"

Sometimes that image comes to me when some people don't listen in the group. They hit very hard and hold on to their old emotional baggage. Releasing it now, in a gentle way, might avoid exploding like a cheap watch someday. It's better not to do that all over your friends and loved ones.

Hit the drum slowly and give thanks, because you are a lucky, lucky guy.

The women can do their kind of thanksgiving too—maybe when the guys have stopped hitting so hard.

Drum carvers outside of Accra, Ghana, sharpen their blades often to keep the job moving as quickly as possible, yet still maintaining the traditional quality. Their creative joy becomes our own healing groove. We are all connected.

# 16

# ARRIVING BY ACCIDENT

There is a classic scene in many adventure movies where the hero steps into a secret chamber and sees something that is awesome. Many times he has arrived there by accident. The heavy tones of the drums are usually heard on the soundtrack. They cue us into the feelings of awesome power and mysterious forces at work. Movie drumming is a subtle art form. People are very easily influenced by rhythm, not only in movies, but in life. We go through our daily lives and are being told what tempo to talk to, buy to, eat to, live to, dance to, and make love to. If we were to decide these personal rhythms for ourselves we might have less anxiety in our day. In drumming many times we arrive at a perfect state of rhythmic feel by accident. That feeling should be respected.

In the first feature movie directed by Ron Howard I got to play loud drums over a lot of car crashes. Peter Ivers, a great underappreciated musician in L.A., put the music together and hired me to play on the soundtrack. Ron was a prince to work for. When the movie hit the theaters I had forgotten about it. I was reading the newspaper one day while a commercial was running on the TV. It was irritating me. I looked up and realized it was a movie trailer for *Grand Theft Auto*. I was being irritated by my own drumming. Is nothing sacred?

I worked in the television and film industry in a variety of positions. Don Kirshner's *Rock Concert* was the first live Rock show on television. We shot everyone from Chuck Berry to Phoebe Snow to the Bay City Rollers. I hadn't seen Chuck in a while and he thought it was not right that I wasn't drumming, but I was fascinated with how our music was being changed by television. Rock was getting self-conscious and artificial.

I cowrote a Rock opera about the same time, with a great keyboardist, John Herron. The producer was from Apple Records in London. *The Last Rock 'n Roll Show* was a puppet show, conceived by an art director we met with Wolfman Jack. I wrote the libretto, the story, and then composed a lot of the music and produced the recording sessions. I was totally involved with my creative energies. I felt like I was back on my path again after having been thrown off by the death of my last partner. John and I had met playing in Tim Buckley's band. We shared a respect for our lost music partner.

The director of the opera wanted to have Hollywood-style demonic energy. He decided to have a "Black Mass," so I did some research, then tentatively wrote some music with Latin phrases from the Catholic Mass. Before I realized it, the room temperature dropped and the candles flickered and that recognizable shiver ran up my spine. The portal opened. I scared myself so bad, I shut everything off. It was a bright southern California afternoon, John came back from playing tennis, dressed in white. He stopped at the door and refused to enter.

"What did you do?" he asked suspiciously.

"I wrote a Black Mass—by accident. I guess it worked. Sorry about that."

The energy eventually died down, but the place was never the same. I couldn't find the words that I had written down. The whole piece sort of disappeared. The show never got made, and I was glad. It is entirely too easy to conjure dark energy with or without a drum. From then on, I became very careful and only focused on positive energy when drumming. No aggression or anger, no revenge, no hatred. Waking up the demonic forces that are part of the human condition is just too easy, especially in Hollywood.

A neighbor hired me as a writer and I moved on to work for George Lucas during the *Star Wars* production saga in 1979. We were located on Lankershim Boulevard in Universal City, across the street from the ominous "Black Tower," which was the Universal Pictures offices. We were ensconced first in an array of mobile homes on a parking lot, then in a restored old building. There was one small brass plaque on the outside of the building that read "Egg Company." It looked like just an old red brick building, but inside the machinery of the movie business was going at full speed, cranking out the second movie in the original *Star Wars* saga, plus all of the spin-off products. It was exciting to be on the inside of that cultural phenomenon. I was there as a result of giving some free advice to my neighbor.

She played piano and wrote songs and worked at Motown Records as a secretary. When she finally left and looked for another job she was a traumatic basket case. She had never made such a dramatic change in her life and it scared her. When she got a job offer from Lucasfilm, it wasn't a big company yet. She asked me if she should take it. I told her, as well as myself, "Never pass up an opportunity to gain power."

She hadn't looked at it that way. She became an editor and ended up hiring me. Eventually she wrote and produced her own feature movies. She has gotten used to wielding power.

At Lucasfilm, I wrote eight-week *Star Wars* comic strip stories. Every day in over 350 newspapers around the country there was a four-panel cartoon of an ongoing story. Sunday was the big four-color splash panel comic strip. I wrote the stories, sketched out ideas, then handed the story off to various comic book artists who rendered the story onto paper.

I had disagreements with Russ Manning, one of the older artists. His idea of what a space suit should look like was based on his years as a Marvel Comics artist dating back to the fifties. I suggested a solar sailship as an escape pod for the good princess, but he balked. He didn't understand the concept of solar winds because his generation did not have the concept in their data banks.

I defended my ideas by telling him that astronaut Jim Lovell had told me about the idea way back in the early seventies. That might have intimidated the Marvel artist a bit more. Space travelers had been only fantasy to him. The future was catching up to his imagination. I could sense his feelings of dislocation; he was feeling out of his own time frame. "Future shock" was a term that was just being heard then.

Commander Lovell gave a lecture tour on his own time and money after Apollo 13. He had to talk about what had happened to him. We were introduced to each other at the University of Miami by Elvis Presley's cousin.

*From orbit, the lightning storm looked like flashbulbs going off under a blanket of cotton.*

*—Jim Lovell*

Jim Lovell was talking about seeing the Earth for the first time as a single unit: one whole thing. He was one of the first humans to get far enough away from Earth to see it with that perspective.

"It was no bigger than my fist," he said with amazement. "Everything I knew was hidden behind my hand. It wasn't sitting on a table, or hanging on a string. It was floating in the middle of nothing. It was beautiful, but it seemed very fragile."

He described a lightning storm from orbit as looking like flashbulbs going off under a blanket of cotton. He saw the effects of humanity on the planet; the rivers dumping pollution into the oceans of the world. He had experienced a tremendous shift in consciousness and he was struggling to find the words to describe these life-changing events.

He felt that his vocabulary was lacking. He said that he needed to learn more about being creative so that he could describe the incredible things he had witnessed in space. He was tired of saying, "It was a very interesting experience."

Here was a man, a hero, who had learned to fly by the seat of his pants as a young boy, in cropduster biplanes, then went on to become a voyager to another planet. Yet he did not trust his own vocabulary to describe his adventures. We all were the poorer for it. Eventually he told his story, of course.

His story could be a signal to our school systems to bring the humanities up to speed. If we embark on heroic journeys, we need to tell others in vivid detail what has happened to our souls. This is evolution and it needs to be articulated. The Spiritual as well as the space warrior need to have a vocabulary to explain their transcendental experiences, such as being lost in space in a tin can with no heat, low on air, no help on the way, and only one chance to land safely.

Drumming patterns are ways to take the journey as well as ways to tell about it. We are searching for our own mythic drum patterns to complement our lives.

Years later, back at Lucasfilm, Russ Manning, the old Marvel Comics artist, pulled rank quite a bit and refused to draw what I suggested, even though it was based on scientific fact. It was great fun to argue with him over styles of space suits. I knew I *had* this old Marvel Comics artist about the solar sailor though. He had to come to terms with what he thought was fantasy but was now reality. His artwork looked dated next to the real thing, but it was still great art. Comic book artists are a breed unto themselves. They deserve all the respect they seldom get.

The kitchen at the "Egg Company" was incredible. The two guys from film school, George and Steven, would hang out in the high-tech kitchen and bake cookies. No one was allowed to use it except them. I pushed through the stainless steel French doors one day and came face to face with George, Steven, and a few others discussing the next project.

I sensed a momentous opportunity in my life.

I wanted to say something that would change my fate. Here were the two most important people in Hollywood munching on warm chocolate chip cookies. George looked at the quiet kid standing next to me.

"What do you do for me?" George asked him pleasantly.

"I'm an accountant."

"Good," George said and nodded appreciatively.

I was leaning against the counter and I was next. Too late, I realized that I was too tall. He would have to look up at me and that is one thing any "king" does not do. I tried to shrink down but it was an awkward gesture. I seemed to be melting into the gray flagstone floor. I sensed that I had disturbed the Force. George did too. So did Steven. My mouth froze up and I was too panic stricken to say anything at all. I probably looked like I was ready to explode. George turned away from me and exited the kitchen.

I thought I had once again scared them. "Them" meaning the powers that be, the *kings*. It was my energy or something. My big chance, like a soft summer breeze, had drifted by me again. I sunk back into obscurity.

The next day, my old friend and editor gave me a script to read.

"Don't tell anyone you're reading this script," she said with toneless authority.

"I won't," I swore solemnly.

"Read it. Tell me what you think. Don't write anything down."

I brought it back the next day and she waited for my reply.

"It's like a Saturday matinee with cardboard cut-out characters. The woman isn't real. She's more like a guy in a dress. It's just a series of cliffhangers, like the old-time Saturday morning movie matinees. The only way to make it work is with a whole lot of special effects."

A cliffhanger is where the hero is in trouble and the bad guys are winning. There were usually a lot of drums on the soundtrack during cliffhanger scenes—that's why they always fascinated me. I was fascinated with rhythms that got people excited.

She nodded and took notes.

She got back to me in a few days and said, "Your breakdown was great. You were on the money with 'Raiders.' They're going to make it. Since you understand this one, what would be the next movie in a series if *Raiders of the Lost Ark* takes off?"

I thought for only a moment, "If you're going to do this one, with the magickal overtones, and the mysticism of the Ark, then the next step would be sword-and-sorcery movies."

She frowned at me. "What is sword-and-sorcery?"

I was shocked. "You don't know about sword-and-sorcery stories? Do you know Conan the Barbarian? The Hyperborian era?"

She still frowned. It was outside her area of literary investigation. The year was 1979.

Today, it is hard for us to imagine a world that did not know sword-and-sorcery movies or *Star Wars*. It is now a pervasive part of our lives, whether we want it to be or not. It has become part of our active cultural myth. The two guys from film school understood something all great moviemakers knew; the myths of humanity make great movies—the Hero's Journey—but they decided to pass on the *sword and sorcery* ideas.

Maybe because it hinted of a more intense, darker magick. I got the impression that they were interested in lighter fare. Dino Delaurentis ended up making the *Conan* movie with Arnold, which made sense. Europeans handle the dark mythic images differently than America, maybe because the European cultures are indigenous to their land and own the myths more than we do here. We, here in the U.S., do not have mythic stories related to our land—unless we use Native American Indian myths. Our modern culture feels the lack of a mythic tradition, but this has also been one of the dynamic qualities of our culture. Leaving the past behind opens up a new future, even if the transitions are brutal. The past may be something that we don't always need to hang on to. It can weigh us down, so we put our myths into the future.

Various rituals may take us back to our own racial and cultural myths, even though they are from a part of the world where we have never been. We still feel a connection to that history because it is the closest thing we've got to roots. We have a basic need to connect to religions and philosophies, even if they were created in other parts of the world, such as Christianity or Buddhism were.

> *What we need is a common story that connects us to Creation, that discovers the sacred, the magic in every moment. We need to evoke the deep sense of connection and relationships, the pattern that illuminates our place, our identity, direction and purpose. We need stories we can share as children of the earth, stories that bring us to a knowledge of ourselves as global beings and as participants in a vast and wondrous unfolding of Creation.*
>
> —*Joseph Campbell*

The two guys from film school felt that need in people and knew what to do with it. They were getting the real breakdown from the master of myths, Joseph Campbell. He wrote a lot of books: *Hero of a Thousand Faces* was his first big hit; another was *Man and His Myths*.

Bill Moyer did a wonderful series of interviews with Joseph Campbell about the myths of the world. They were shot at Skywalker Ranch in northern California. There are images of drawings, cave paintings, fetishes, and ceremonies from primitive cultures all over the world that strike a deep, familiar tone in our psyches. We need these things and Mr. Campbell graciously explains them to us in a vocabulary that we can understand. Suddenly the magick world is real.

I was told not to write about the Force. I understood why George did not want anyone else to write about the Force on his time. He was saving that for himself. He was also keeping it a mystery. That is what always happens when a new idea appears. It is a mystery. Eventually it is a common part of the culture, but first it is a mystery—even if it is an ancient concept to begin with.

We all know what "the Force" is these days, thanks to the vision of George Lucas and Joseph Campbell. The concept is an old one, before the movies, even.

The Force is in the drum. If you treat it with respect it has great power.

# Meanwhile: On the Other Side of Town

Punk music began in downtown L.A. and underground Hollywood at the same time. The old sacred cows of Rock had grown fat. Room was needed for the next hungry breed of rockers. The Rock 'n' Roll culture was shedding its snakeskin once again.

Writing was a retreat from the crazy world that Rock 'n' Roll had become. I had grown dissatisfied with the music biz. My friend and partner, Tim Buckley, had been killed and I watched his legacy get chopped up by lawyers and managers until nothing was left. The dangerous side of the music bizness showed itself and I realized that being a Rock star was not the smartest thing to be. My friends from the old days were still making songs that sounded boringly nice and *pop*. There was no juice left in them. They had gotten smug in their concept of what music was. They had gotten downright snobbish. I don't blame them. They were making money at it. I was the one with the crises of faith. Rock 'n' Roll wasn't saving my soul any more.

One day, I walked into a rehearsal in a friend's living room. They were working on four-part harmonies for a show at the Troubadour (a Hollywood Rock club). They were also working on good hair moves. I had been listening to a tape a friend had gotten from Ringo of a rocking Gospel group, The O'Neil Twins. It was the only thing that moved me, but I was also fascinated with the high energy and lack of pretense of some new music from England. My old friends were sounding a little boring to me.

"What record did you buy?" one of the Rock stars asked me. I was trying to get to my room without letting them see my purchase.

"You wouldn't like it," I said.

He got curious and offended, "Oh yeah? What is it?"

I held the tawdry yellow and pink album cover up for them see. It had rude torn blackmail lettering.

"Never Mind the Bollocks, Here's the Sex Pistols" it said.

They looked with revulsion at the crappy artwork.

"Put it on," Big John said. He was always ready to take a good idea and use it.

I hesitated; he took it from me and put it on the turntable. He had played keyboards with many great acts, from the Electric Prunes to the Beach Boys. His opinion was always respected. I winced when the first chords of *God Save the Queen* ripped across the antique furniture and shredded the vintage Rock posters on the wall. The flowers wilted. So did the Rockers' hair.

There was a look of revulsion and fear in their eyes. They sensed that their time was over; they knew that they were the dinosaurs—they were obsolete. It horrified them and they struck out at it. They shut it off without letting the song end.

"If I had a gun," Big John said, "I'd shoot that record."

"You guys sound like your parents," I told them. I was watching evolution in action. They now viewed me with distrust. I was not surprised. They had not yet made the transition to the next era.

There was an amazing commonality between the Gospel tape that Ringo had made of the inspiring O'Neil Twins and the new Punk music: the fast upbeat tempos. Our spirits are energized when that tempo gets going real fast. It has to be steady, though. It can't just keep speeding up. It has to lock in at a solid tempo at about 140 beats per minute and stay there. The tambourine is the key in Gospel music. It can be heard over the wailing. I use a tambourine in our drumming groups because it can be heard above a lot of random noise—it also gives us a cue to feel the Holy Spirit coursing through us. Iron-ically, Punk music discovered this same effect, probably out of frustration with the boring status quo of Pop music. The result is very similar to uptempo Gospel music. The kids went wild.

Our Spirits are hungry for that inspiring uptempo groove and it doesn't matter what the fashion trends are. Just keep it steady and avoid the easy trap of generating anger. Generate a thankful attitude and you'll feel pretty good.

The trick is to play the tambourine on the upbeat. Up to now, I have stressed the tambourine be played on the downbeat, but there are no hard and fast rules here. We use what works. Just play the basic pattern that we have done before, but this time, put the tambourine on the upbeats. If you have a group, have someone hit the tambourine separately on the upbeats. If we count it out, say the words, ONE de an da TWO de an da THREE de an da FOUR de an da, the tambourine will hit on the upbeat "an". We still *know* where our downbeats are, but now we are getting so good that we can accentuate the upbeats. Upbeats are dance beats.

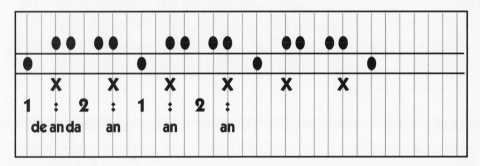

Track 20: Gospel.

I tried working in Gospel many years earlier at the LeFevre Gospel Studio in Atlanta, Georgia, but I didn't fit in. I was looking for something more musically avant garde, but with an inspirational feel. When I finally worked with Tim Buckley, his singing and my drumming were ecstatic and shamanic before anyone used those terms. I couldn't find anyone else doing it. Most musicians were not that interested in the spiritual aspects of music. Success overrides a personal quest for inspiration sometimes, but our souls still have the hunger, even if the pool is cleaned once a week and the gourmet food is being delivered. Our souls need to be fed too. Mine was very hungry. I started to play with artists instead of musicians. They didn't have the same egotistical attitudes. They had their own version though. I played with New Wave bands like The Resistors and Diana Harris and The Tuff Tones. These are obscure bands that were popular, but never received a record deal or recognition. It was closer to an honest sense of power, but it still didn't have the spiritual energy I was seeking. The time was still not right. I ended up spending more time at places like the Theosophical Library than at the Troubadour nightclub. I researched obscure music like the African Gospel songs of Zanzibar, where tribes had been converted to Christianity at the turn of the last century, but kept their own music. Music is a form of cultural transitions, but the next big fad was not what I was looking for.

*Music is 50 percent of a movie.*

*—George Lucas*

I focused on being a writer. I would always be a drummer, but it would have to be in some other way—as art—making my own secret and personal magick, no longer onstage with yelling fans and greedy managers. It was a painful sacrifice because I loved playing the drums, but I was also very glad to be away from it. The drummer's journey can take many unexpected turns.

Rhythm is life.

In a movie, when your pulse is pounding it's not because of the special effects, it's because of the music. If the scene *works,* many times it is because the music creates the mood. If a scene does not work, many times it is because the music is wrong. Think I'm kidding? Turn the sound off and watch an action/thriller movie and see how much it affects your mood. Not as much as when you hear the music.

The hero's journey is what the drum talks about. Before the movies, before the printing press, before shadow plays, before songs, there was the story accompanied by a drum. The drum is the oldest special effect in the world. It gives us the willies or gives us a good feeling. It makes us jump and it helps us to sleep. It makes us want to live life. It makes us willing to kill or die. It creates a healing world, and it's the only thing that can make a car alarm sound interesting.

My friends from the sixties tried to catch up later when they realized that they weren't going to get any gigs unless they wore skinny ties and played New Wave songs. They couldn't go all the way to Punk. It was too pessimistic for their mindset. I, on the other hand, was fascinated:

"Why would a person put a safety pin through their cheek?"

I came to understand that it was ritual. I didn't do it myself. Punk music showed me that I wasn't as angry as I thought I was, although I do like to play at 140 beats a minute. There is a live album I did with Tim Buckley in the early seventies where we are at that tempo. The album is called *Honeyman*, and it burns in some spots. That was a long time before safety pins and high-speed Punk music but it had some of the same energy.

Taking a sharp object into one's body is a cultural myth around the world. In Indonesia the kris or spiritual dagger is pointed at the dancer's own stomach and many times it draws blood, but it is all done in the spirit of killing the demons inside the dancer's soul. We must kill our own demons—no one can kill them for us. Christianity has some body piercing too. I'm not a big fan of it, but I am interested that it has gained such wide popularity. There is more need for ritual than ever before.

Body piercing is a way of creating a ritual, but our culture does not allow any spiritual significance to it, so it is just empty ritual and the pain that is suffered does not have a mystical quality to it. We sometimes need to have a greater cause than ourselves to suffer for if there is to be a meaning to life. The *self* is generally not heroic enough to suffer for. Something outside of our self many times is worth suffering for.

At the beginning of Punk music, the music industry rejected this new brutal music because they were tooled up to sell the Woodstock generation. A few independent record companies finally started to make money off the angry Punk music. It took the big corporations well over a decade to retool and sell the angry Punk thing back to the myth- and fashion-starved kids of the next "X" generation.

Woodstock became obsolete as a marketing tool. The real dream was still alive in people's hearts though. Peace, love, and music are three basic food groups for our souls. The sixties had only rediscovered that mystery once again.

Our culture possibly evolves through insults. If the culture insults you, you develop a way to avoid it or stop it. We don't always see the evolutionary trends talking to us until they have already taken over.

I'm not talking about fashion. I'm talking about the evolution of our souls. We are shedding our psychic skin quicker than ever before in the history of humanity. The drum gives us a way to reinterpret the new grooves in a safe way. The tempo of the Sex Pistols was faster, harder, angrier than the grooves of the Eagles. Times change.

The reason that Rock 'n' Roll has always resurrected itself is because of the beat. The chord changes are more or less the same. The grooves of the culture change and the beat changes to match the culture. We now are forced to match our own rhythms to a frantic culture that resembles a train racing out of control or a big rock rolling down a snake-filled cave, intent on crushing us, as in *Raiders of the Lost Ark*.

There is always a chance for redemption when we connect to a truth through basic drumming. Find a groove that is real for you and the world doesn't distract you anymore, but don't expect the same groove to always set you free. That is what the old Rock dinosaurs didn't get. They thought their grooves were always going to be the reigning grooves.

Our artists can either offend or enlighten us, that is their choice.

What the nonartist can do is talk about the moments in their own lives. Talk about the life they know. Storytelling with a drum has always been a way for us to feel the creative rush. Hit a drum . . . tell a story. Discover the magickal myths in your own life.

Your drumbeat will help you realize that your life is a huge, mythic, blockbuster of a hit.

Here is a *suspense* beat. It also swings bad when it's up to speed. It is also another study in subtraction. Start with the five-note pattern that we did in an earlier chapter. Play five notes, then pause before hitting the pattern again. Only the next time, subtract the last note. Then you will be ending on an upbeat. Wait, hit the pattern, again leaving off that fifth note. Ending on this upbeat creates a sense of expectation. It lifts the pattern and propels it through the silence. The accent note that we are now ending on is a worldwide upbeat. It is the key to many syncopated rhythms. If you want to play danceable rhythms, get familiar with this note. It is the last upbeat before the next downbeat. One, de, an, DA!

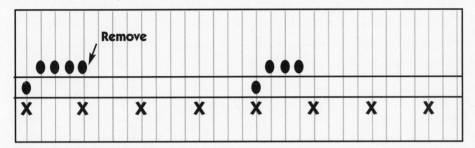

**Track 21: Remove last note.**

An upbeat is a danceable, clever accent that we are not always familiar with that will usually make us dance. Tap your foot (tambourine) on the "x"s, they are your downbeats. Pick up the tempo. The four quick notes can be counted as: one-de-an-**DA**. Then keep quiet. If that last note hits right, it lifts the whole groove and makes the silence swing all the way through the space until you repeat the four notes again. This is an example of building suspense using rhythm. Once you are up to speed, try it in a group and let each player solo over the open space for a bit, while the rest of the group hits that upbeat phrase. It smokes.

Your brain will be tempted to let that upbeat slide forward onto the next downbeat. It is habitually doing things like that; trying to make something correct according to an inappropriate assumption. The brain thinks the downbeats are the most important notes, so it tries to force you to hit this important note on a downbeat. The brain constantly tries to correct the body's instinctive acts of rhythmic courage. This ruins the cool syncopation that the body feels but the brain cannot yet comprehend. So feel the upbeat: watch out for your brain's attempts to subvert your funkiness into a safe, downbeat march.

The space will be calling out to you, asking to be filled with all your inspirational noodling. Resist that intellectual temptation as long as possible. Keep the suspense by adding little short bits of improvisation and letting the space swing.

Try this syncopated combination at your own tempo first, then speed it up if you get that accent going, and watch the excitement build. It is a vehicle to create suspense and also, maybe, even by accident, you too might get to the sacred chamber.

## The Sacred Chamber

When the heroic drummer plays from his or her heart, they are on a quest. If they are true to their nature, they will find the sacred chamber. It is like the hero suddenly discovering the place where power dwells; the hair stands up on your neck.

Goosebumps ripple up and down your skin like currents of electricity. You feel the presence of power.

It is a feeling of "Ah ha!"

But if you let it distract you, then you will lose your place and you will lose this connection. To find the sacred chamber with the drum is challenging; you must be good, have endurance, play lightly when needed, be constant in your soul and in your heart, willing to support the groove rather than just use it, and humble so that you don't get distracted by what appear to be your own great achievements.

Staying in the sacred chamber to drum in that space for a long period of time is more challenging than getting there. It requires a constant state of release, allowing the power to run through the player unimpeded by ego. That's why it is a surprise when you find the sacred chamber. You step from selfness to selflessness. It takes your breath away. The groove is so strong that you forget who you are. Your self is unimportant.

Our sense of discovery is a healing sensation. This sense of discovering a mystery is a rejuvenating rush of energy into our souls and our bodies. Endorphins are released. We are strong. We are capable.

When we get to the sacred chamber by accident, we discover the power of the groove and it takes us away. To try to get there by force of will doesn't work.

The Chinese word for this is *Wu Wei*, or "no forcing." It is allowing the thing to unfold on it's own, and the drummer is a witness but not the actual creator. The drummer is only a vessel of expression for something greater.

The labyrinth at Gaia Oasis, a neo-Pagan retreat in the California Sierras, is a symbol for our journey to the Sacred Chamber. Just follow the groove.

# 17

# GOING BACK TO THE WELL

Robert Christian Gandhi, the keyboard player in Bethlehem Asylum, used to say, "Goin' back to the Well." He said it when someone was trying to improve their craft. It meant that the player was going back to their source of inspiration to develop their art to the next level of understanding.

Notice I didn't say "get better." There was an implied mystical and spiritual pilgrimage to his term "Goin' back to the Well." It dates back to before the original Christian. It is a term that fits the most primitive of human endeavors—getting water. You get water at a source.

Water is the source of life and it is the source of joy. For me, as a drummer, "Goin' back to the Well" meant that I was going back to my own roots of my art, re-examining what I had learned in my life and how that applies to my music. I was not going to learn more licks or faster technique. According to Christian, that was a different phrase, which was "Goin' out to the Woodshed."

That was more work-oriented. That meant lots of practicing; running scales, practicing rudiments, studying different keys to play in, learning different kinds of music, listening to masters play and learning their improvising methods. "Woodshedding" meant learning more music and teaching your hands what you wanted them to do.

"Going back to the Well" is a term for rediscovering your inspirational source. Your personal source is like a wellspring that is pumping inspirational energy up through you. Our inspiration is visible if it comes out in some artform, but that is just one way it can be expressed. We can just *live in inspiration* and it is visible.

The Well is a source of dark Yin energy too. That is why it may be considered feminine energy, which might be difficult for some men to feel comfortable with. They are unsure about letting their feminine side surface. Don't worry about it. Your masculine side is still intact. With just a little bit of understanding of the creative, or feminine, qualities, men are more attractive to women, anyway. It's got nothing to do with sexual preference.

My high-school Rock 'n' Roll band was very popular. The girls came to the Surfer's Club to dance and to flirt with their favorite guys in Those Five. Their football-team boyfriends would not dance and wanted to kick my butt, mostly because they had to pay to get in the door and then watch their girlfriends stand at the foot of the stage and smile at us. There was a lot of smiling in those days. It was almost as good as sex. This was just before the sexual revolution. Just before the Pill. Just before a big change in that world's mindset.

Christian whispering in my very young ear about the deeper magick in the music and in our souls.

In high school, I was the only one with long hair. I didn't like having a high profile. It made me a target. After one of many cafeteria confrontations where the football team offered to mop up the floor with me and my long hair, a quiet guy approached me.

"You need to learn how to defend yourself," Richard said. He was a bookish type of kid with a short, nondescript haircut. Everyone had that kind of haircut then except me. I was the only guy bucking the dress code in my high school. The other members of Those Five were together in a rival high school, so I was also a traitor to my school. My hair was not long by today's standards. It didn't even hit the back of my collar very much, but the principal made me cut it before they would put my picture in the senior yearbook.

"It's not about the length of hair, sir," I tried to reason with the principal.

He was not into debating. The civics teacher's class put up a billboard at the edge of town that read: "Beautify America. Get a haircut."

We are talking about a mindset that saw itself as the dominant mindset in the world. It still does. Most dominant species think they are the baddest in the world.

On the other hand, Richard's presence was like a big, round solid stone. He resembled "Odd Job," the inscrutable martial-art bad guy in the early James Bond movies—the guy with the razor in the brim of his bowler hat. Richard was like that, only a high school version, non-Asian, and wearing a Sears shirt-jack. Someone had mentioned that he was into judo.

He invited me down to their *dojo*. The master *sensei* was a man of mixed heritage, French Vietnamese. We knew about Vietnam—that was where you went after you finished high school. Unless of course, you had injured yourself playing football or could buy your way into college. This was before the lottery. It was called "The Draft." If you were nineteen and passably fit—they wanted you. They came and got you, put a uniform on you, and dropped you into a very unfriendly jungle.

The culture had solved the problems of the world by using this method in the past. That was the way things had been done. Along with a whole lot of other kids lucky enough to be born in the United States, I tried to make sense out of it. According to the football coach, I was the guy with the bad attitude. The team had orders to take me out. So I went to Richard's dojo and learned to defend myself from the football team.

Richard wore a formal black *gi* in the martial art school. On the mat, in this quiet studio, Richard ceased to be a bookish, quiet, unassuming kid. He was now, suddenly, an authoritative, compassionate, ageless teacher, and a formidable opponent. It was a transformation that intrigued me.

I studied for quite a while, learning karate: the kicks, the blocks, the punches, and the *katas,* which are choreographed dances of death. It was a good discipline, and it got me in a little better shape. The guys in my band wanted me to show them how to defend themselves too. Every show we did had tough guys that were looking to take out a commie fag longhair. The political lines were being drawn. The American culture was splintering away from its Eisenhower-era mindset. The world was getting too complex for simple definitions of what was right and wrong. Things were changing quickly.

But in the dojo, everything was quiet—except for occasional yells and grunts. There was one small girl with long blonde pigtails who was very good. She was fast and she had the focus to deliver a punch with more power than most of the big guys. They didn't like fighting her. It was a hard mindset to understand. Hitting a girl was not right in their minds, unless it was *their* woman. I admit, I enjoyed watching her clean their clocks.

I didn't get much trouble from the high-school football team after that. There was a face-off with a defensive lineman once, but the water boy ran up and whispered in his ear that I'd been down at Richard's school.

"Yawll know karatay! No fair!" the meaty football player said petulantly. "I ain't fighting yew!"

Amazing what a little well-placed PR will do for one's survival.

John, another martial art teacher at the dojo, was very good. He was competitive and had the long legs and arms to be lethal at a distance. He could jump and kick like Barishnikov. It was amazing. He wanted me to excel and become competitive. He wanted me to get angry.

"Find your anger point and put it out there in front of you. Then hit it!"

"What's an anger point?" I asked.

He couldn't believe I didn't understand him.

"It's someone you hate. Someone you want to hit. Put an image of them out in front of you, then hit that. Focus all your hate into that point."

I realized that I didn't have quite the kind of killer instinct John wanted me to have. I was fast, but without that hate thing I was worthless as a competitor in his eyes. I also knew what John's anger point was—my lead singer. John's girlfriend was also a big fan.

Richard moved me into Jujitsu. I had learned to strike and kick, almost simultaneously because I was a drummer, but Jujitsu was different from karate. It was fluid. The movements imitated animals like the crane and the snake. This was a more poetic side to hurting people.

Soon, I was learning wrist throws. This is where the most puny of people can throw the biggest guy by just grabbing the bad guy's hand, hitting a nerve point, and twisting. Suddenly Mister Big ain't so big. The only problem was that my wrists were starting to make crackling sounds.

"That's just arthritis," the sensei said stoicly. "You will learn to live with it."

"I make my living playing the drums. Arthritis at seventeen is not an option."

My sensei shrugged, "You make your own life decisions."

I quit. It was hard because of the macho mindset that these kinds of activities engender in the participants. So, being a drummer saved me from a life of arthritis as well as being a tough guy. But don't be seduced or intimidated by guys who view drumming as a Warrior activity. That is a major dead end. Muscle tension, macho tension, a meat-headed attitude, all get in the way of really feeling a swinging groove. Stay loose, baby. Float like a butterfly. Sting like a bee.

The thing that I brought away from the teaching was something that had nothing to do with fighting:

Richard had been coaching me for many weeks, when he said, "Now it is time to become fast without hurrying."

"Fine," I said. I was a willing pupil. "Show me the technique."

He smiled. "No. I am talking about meditation. Zen meditation. You need to be quiet inside to be really fast."

He addressed the class. He had us sit on the mat, cross-legged, and do absolutely nothing. It was the hardest thing I had ever done. The cricket in the corner was driving me nuts. It was the only sound in my head. I tried to be empty but that cricket kept coming back to life just when I'd get into it.

Richard gave me an image that stuck: a calm lake. The calmness of the lake was an image that did work for me. I liked the idea of balanced effort. Not too much effort. Just enough effort for the task at hand. Then go back to the calm lake.

I approached Richard at high school.

"I'd like to learn as much as I can about Zen meditation. Are there books?"

He nodded with that secret smile. "Yes. There are books. "

I opened my notebook and poised pencil over paper free of cartoons. "Okay. I'm ready. Give me the titles."

He smiled and proceeded to give me a list of books available about Zen and meditation. The list included Alan Watts, and also *Zen Flesh Zen Bones*.

*"What is the sound of one hand clapping?"*

*—old Zen koan*

After I had scribbled furiously he said, "After you have bought all the books, put them in a pile and burn them."

I looked at him with shock and confusion. "But why?"

He finally laughed. "It's just a joke. Read them and you'll get the joke . . . hopefully."

The only time I knew of Richard actually fighting was when three rednecks were heckling him at a local baseball game. They made fun of his polyester Sears shirtjack. He was eating an ice cream cone when they came at him. He put them all on the ground and didn't drop the cone.

The Rolling Stones played in that same tiny baseball stadium on their first American tour a few weeks later. There was a riot. Too bad, the Stones didn't even get to end their show before the police shut the event down. Other shows had been successfully held in that stadium, but why did the Rolling Stones concert turn into a riot?

I think it's the beat, the Blues, and the booze. The Rolling Stones were playing a very energetic beat and they also were playing the Blues. Put those two things together with alcohol and a bunch of ignorant males, and you'll have a riot. That's why I stopped playing in nightclubs. It got to be as predictable as a chemistry experiment. Kick the tempo up, play some nasty-sounding Blues, and suddenly guys want to beat the crap out of each other, or me. A girl was usually the premise, but that was just an excuse to pound their chests and compare muscles. Dizzy Gillespie called alcohol "Ignorant Juice."

Male gorillas play that same Pata Pata rhythm on their own chest before they charge an unwanted visitor.

*I Can't Get No Satisfaction* was reputed to have been written by Mick and Keith in their hotel room, after that event in my high-school town. That hotel is now owned by a large science-fiction religious organization. Go figure. . . .

Here is a rhythmic combination. It can also be a combination punch if you need it to be.

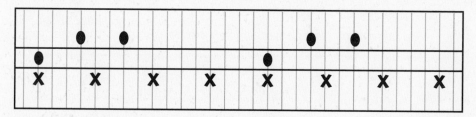

Track 22: **1** de an **da** 2 de **an** da 3 de an da 4 de an da.

Start this at a medium tempo to keep the momentum going. This is a very forceful rhythm and it is underneath much of the hot Salsa music that we hear. It is also part of the Clave—the sacred, magickal rhythms of the Caribbean.

The first note is on (1) the downbeat. The next note is on the "da" of one. The third note is on the "an" of the two-beat.

Subtracting all the unconscious "pata pata" notes that most people tend to play leaves you with a clear and forceful rhythm combination. Taking out notes is a challenge, but when you wake up to the unnecessary work that you are doing, this will bring you to a place of ease and fluidity where the least amount of notes carries the most power.

In your imagination, gaze out over a clear, calm lake while you drum. No need to think about hitting anything.

## Speeding Up to Slow Down

Even the best players speed up. It is a challenge to stay attentive to your own nervous energy which is making you speed up. The difference between *trance* drumming and other kinds of drumming is that the speed of the groove stays constant in trance drumming. Very constant, but it still has to be loose and open.

The reason this open trance drumming is so powerful is because everyone is cooperating, listening, not feeling anxious, not speeding up, maintaining a common, steady state of experience, and having fun—all at the same time. Our mind might settle on one thing and stay there. It may have nothing to do with keeping the beat steady. It may be the color of the person's hair across from you. The brain fixes on something as the groove struggles to be born. When you realize that your brain has fixated on something, you breathe out, release the tension that is generated when the brain fixates, and get back down into the groove.

We need to be aware in our particular cultural setting to avoid unconscious speeding up. In some other cultural settings, speeding up is not so epidemic. They have a different mindset. Here, we are discovering the art of constancy. I don't mean brutal, tense constancy; I'm talking about that graceful attention that is pleasurable. The drum can be a pleasurable way to meditate in a steady state of action.

People may not think they are speeding up. The speeding up is based on the culture. It insists that we go faster and faster. This mindless, driving force is at epidemic proportions in technological cultures. People are dropping from stress-related problems. The modern world has its foot to the floor. Computers are getting faster, people are trying to catch up to them.

In a drumming seminar, the healing energy of a constant force is important. The body and mind relax. The emergency hormones stop going into the blood stream, the metabolism steps down from possible war to possible peace.

The hardest thing to do on a drum is to play slowly. Many drummers don't want to do it—it can be nerve-wracking. You need to pay attention to every note, constantly monitoring your groove, and comparing it to the group to see if you're playing too fast, which you usually are. That is a very frustrating and intellectual way to play slowly.

Another way to play slowly is to feel the slow rhythms in a part of your body. Not the whole body—just one little part that doesn't take a lot of energy to keep going. That is your inner clock. It could be tapping a foot or chewing gum or humming, or a nervous tic or nodding head. The body finds its own ways of keeping time if you let it. Lionel Hampton grunted as he played the vibes. You can hear him on his Jazz records. That is not musical, but it was part of his music.

In body therapy, this could be seen as myofascial release; when the body is in a relaxed state it can release stored trauma. When you find a slow groove that settles into a steady state, the body shuts off its emergency functions and goes into a healing mode. Body workers get a release from their patients after they have gotten the patient to relax. The drum, in this slow, sacred pace, pulls our attention down into that relaxed state. The body then responds by healing. You give yourself a release by staying steady.

Senegalese drummers are poetically speedy drummers. They can push the beat and it still sounds relaxed. We don't quite have the same situation here. We are in a state of panic.

First things first. Before you can play anywhere close to what African drummers are doing and with their grace and taste, you have to feel. That is very simple to them, but to us, it is not so simple. "Feel" is not an intellectual term. It is an imperfect word that tries to describe a perfect physical and psychic state. The psychological distractions of our technological world interfere with feeling and healing. I'm not condemning technology, I'm interested in what it is doing to us.

The drum is technology. Use it.

## Tantric Groove #2

Here is a way to at least feel the sensation of relaxing, even if you don't know how to relax in your playing yet;

Start the basic simple pattern. The "x" is a tambourine or claves or cowbell or water jug to hit on the downbeats.

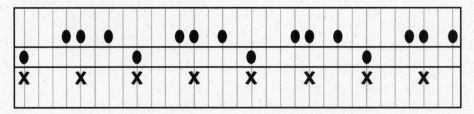

Track 23: Speed Up to Slow Down.

This groove is so vague that it can turn into a lot of different interesting things along the way. That is a different way of drumming than most folks are used to. Stay vague. The notes are not that important. They're just ego stuff anyway. Focus on the pulse that becomes repetitive. Usually, the downbeat or the first note will make that pulse. Keep that steady and don't worry about the little notes in between.

Now, speed up the groove slowly. Don't go too fast too soon; you'll hurt yourself. You'll notice that tension sets in. Your body goes into a low-level emergency mode; it's trying to catch up.

Try to settle in at a slightly faster pace. Try to keep it steady at this faster tempo for a while until it doesn't feel fast anymore. When you relax at this faster tempo, you can play with the same ease that you played at the slower tempo. It breaks the brain's habit of tensing up when we speed up. Ideally, everyone is listening to each other and watching. You have to watch to do this one. Remember not to play louder. That is a habit too.

After a bit, speed the group up again to a faster tempo—same beat, very little improvising. Settle in again at this higher tempo. Don't play loud. The tension will be strong now. Your body is in a higher priority catch-up mode. The tension tricks you to play louder. Instead, play softly—fast and soft. That starts to deprogram your habitual body and mind responses to stress.

So now that we are waling really fast and playing at a soft volume, we are going to do an unheard-of thing. We are going to slow down together as a group.

Now we are ready to slow down from the top speed that the group has been sustaining. Slow down to the next "notch" in the groove. Let it settle in at the slightly slower tempo. Let it settle in until it doesn't feel wobbly anymore. It will take on its own personality. Hold that groove for a while. Your body and mind will step down from that high-priority emergency mode. Hold that groove for a while, then drop the tempo down to the next slower groove. It will take a minute to stabilize everyone. This is an awkward time and the person playing the tambourine holds it together by hitting the downbeats.

After this slower groove has settled in and become stable again, you'll feel your body and mind shutting down from the emergency mode. It settles into normal. The body then gets the signal that everything is okay.

Keep the slow groove going, then drop it down to a slower groove. The downbeats will hold it together. Don't expect it to sound great. That's not the point. Now, the body and mind can go into a deeper healing state.

Keep this slower groove going. Stay here and release. Release trauma, release the bad day. Release hate. Release jealousy. Release resentment. Release greed. Release and then remember what it feels like to release. It is a sensation in your body. It is a chemical reaction in your brain.

*When you're young, you speed up to get things. When you're older, you slow down to get rid of them.*

What you release is not important. Feeling the release is the thing to pay attention to. End on a coherent, relaxed downbeat. Feel the emptiness, where previously there was tension.

The next groove your group gets into should be relaxed, back in the pocket, low volume, and will probably be a profoundly deep trance, as well as easier to play. Releasing is important for us. Otherwise we carry everything around with us that we don't need.

## Having a Vision

When we meditate on the drum, our attention focuses down to each note that we play. It is a tightening of our vision to an immediate point in time. That is where the power of the trance is created. If our attention or our vision gets distracted, we lose that immediate meditative connection to the groove and the magick goes away. The drumming gives us a psychic vision, too. When we get focused in the moment, our souls go out and get an overview of the Universal Consciousness.

People want to meditate and be *in the moment*, which is great, but we also need to meditate on the future. If we don't have a vision of our own future, someone else will come along and make a vision for us. Maybe that is not the future that we want. The hardest challenge for a drummer is to see the *long ball*. The future just doesn't seem that important when the immediate rush of creative inspiration is so overwhelming, but the distant future is where a lot of people are making plans for us and the drummer has access to that foresight, he or she just doesn't always use it. It seems unimportant.

Many times, drummers seem vague and scattered because they are so much in the moment. The drum brings us into the immediate moment, and that can be a trap. I try to keep in touch with where the world is going just to keep from falling into the meditative trap of always being in the moment. It may not be correct meditation practice, but our culture is pushing quickly into the future. We need to have a game plan for ourselves for what comes after this immediate moment, even if it is a great groove.

The drummer has access to a certain kind of vision about the future and it should be respected and used. It has to do with the dynamics of *keeping time.* Drummers manipulate time. The sense of time disappears when the groove is strong. If the drummer is aware of the opportunity, their consciousness can be free to see the future, when they are outside of time.

Al Green, the great Rhythm and Blues singer, went back to the Church after having a bunch of gold records. Why did one of the greatest romantic Soul singers go back to the Well? I figure he had to.

Maybe we all do at some point in our lives.

Al Jackson played drums behind Al Green. He was a mysterious drummer. I couldn't figure out how he got those smooth little clicks and upbeats on his HiHat. His tom toms had a special magickal tone. When that sound comes on the radio you know exactly who it is. *I'm So in Love with You, Tired of Being Alone.* He's playing a secret beat. He's in the groove so deep that you feel all kinds of things. You feel so funky that you believe you could have been born somewhere else and you could have felt a whole lot differently. That groove gives you possibilities with your life.

It's a slow groove. It's very sexy. It gets the "Butt Chakra" movin'. That kind of moving is what happens in sacred dance in India. The moves are carved on temples at what's left of Angkor Watt in Cambodia. Its traditional belly dancing moves appear in hieroglyphs at Geza, and in carvings at Palenque in Mexico. Were these body movements immortalized in different cultures by coincidence? Not likely. The most transcendental moments are when the dancer and the drummer are as one.

The Rumba was outlawed in Cuba. If somebody played it, especially if they were African, the police, acting under Spanish laws, would come and arrest them. They were performing ancient Yoruba sacred drum-dance ceremonies that were hundreds of years old. They were also having a good time. The Cuban law stated that if a conga drum was being used, then the law was being broken and the person playing the conga drum would be put in jail. So the drummers brought out wooden boxes and played them instead.

These were fish boxes or drawers to the dressers in their homes. The thin wooden veneer on a night stand dresser drawer is just the right thinness to get a tone and then change that sound with a slap and a muffled palm. There are lots of different notes if you sit with it between your legs and play it like a drum. This got around the law partly because it had a Spanish equivalent; the *cajon*, a Flamenco wooden box that looks similar to the traditional African version. Today we all dance to that Rumba which was illegal not that long ago.

I came across an unlabeled audiocassette tape in my nightstand drawer. I had no idea what it was, so I put it in the machine and hit "play." The most amazing sound hit my ear. I have one good ear. It's hereditary, I am told, and not from drumming. I was very careful about that. So one ear will have to be good enough for this drummer.

There was a recognizable voice on the tape. "Hello. This is the President of the United States of America."

Sure enough. It was Ronald Reagan. He was introducing a radio show to be broadcast in China; the first oldies Rock 'n' Roll radio show to be broadcast in Communist China. It all came back to me.

The guys putting this deal together had supposedly written a song that was a big hit in the sixties. This current deal had generated lots of anticipation over sponsor money. A huge soft drink company was involved. Ah, yes—the strange world of radio.

They asked me to write a radio show. They pulled the old trick of getting me into the recording studio to "cut a demo," and then they said something like. "No, we're not interested. We got someone else," and they used it anyway. Lots of hit records made money for record producers that way, while none of the money got to the artist. The recording engineer was a good guy. He must have sent me the finished product and I had just tossed it into the drawer with a lot of other unfinished songs and forgotten dreams.

"...And now, let the music begin!" President Reagan extolled at the end of the introduction on the cassette. The next sound is my nerdy little voice announcing Martha Reeves and the Vandellas singing *Dancing in the Streets*.

This deal had happened years ago. Someone in a recording studio had talked to a producer who was putting together a Chinese radio show and they needed a Rock 'n' Roll writer. I had written for *Creem* magazine and Wolfman Jack, so I qualified. The Hollywood Writers Guild was on strike. I wasn't a member so it didn't really apply to me. I did a demo for them. I also remember what had really bothered me about the whole deal.

I was sitting in this guy's office high atop a building overlooking the Pacific Ocean—expensive digs. But frantic. Everyone was running around answering phones that were sitting on the floor. Not enough desks. That should have tipped me off. There were posters of China and the U.S. shaking hands over a radio tower.

*"Hurry up, Let's go. They're playing the Rumba. Don't forget your cufflinks in the nightstand drawer!"*

"Two billion ears are listening," was their promotional one-liner. This guy was smiling too much.

"...And you'll stay at a really nice hotel by the radio station, just off of Tiananmen Square, outside of downtown Beijing. Great food in the hotel. Don't eat out. It's terrible everywhere else.

"Just show them which records to spin and what to say. They'll translate the Rock 'n' Roll jargon. You know. Generate the energy . . . Rock 'n' Roll! In China! It's great!"

I didn't like the smell of this one.

"Do you remember when they first played Rock 'n' Roll for the kids in New Jersey? Back in the 1950s?" I asked him.

He got bored immediately. "Yeah, Allan Freed was the DJ. Why?"

"The kids tore up the theater seats. They got so excited they couldn't contain themselves. Those sweet, God-fearing, middle-class kids went nuts. They'd been repressed for so long listening to the crooners from their parent's generation that when that Rock beat started they just lost it and tore up the theater. Rock 'n' Roll was outlawed in New Jersey and a few other places too. You do that in a culture that's as locked down as China and you're bound to have problems. Bad problems."

He looked at me with the smooth, confident poise he had just regained.

"Don't worry about it. We got that covered. The government will check the music. If it has a political overtone that they don't like, then we'll replace it with something that they approve of."

"I'm not talking about the words, man," I said impatiently.

He frowned. "What do you mean?"

"I'm talking about the beat. The beat is gonna drive them wild. What happens when they hear Little Richard playing *Good Golly, Miss Molly*? That's gonna knock them out. They'll tear up the theater seats, or worse."

"We're broadcasting one hour a day across all of China. No theaters. . . ."

"You're missing the point," I said. Blah, Blah, Blah. I ended up not doing the job.

I heard on the radio that the first person the Chinese Army shot during the Tiananmen Square massacre was the DJ at Radio Beijing.

It's like the warning on your radiator cap. "Caution. Contents under pressure."

In case you're interested, here is a simplification of what Little Richard knew all along. *Good Golly, Miss Molly!* Play it as a fast dance tune and feel the energy. Play it slow and fall in love. You can play this traditional American

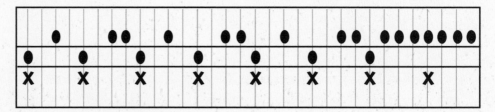

**Track 24: Rock 1 (Miss Molly).**

beat on an African dkembe too. The bass drum is a low note in the center of the drum and the snare drum note would be a high note at the edge.

Don't do anything stupid. It's just a drumbeat, but it's powerful stuff.

Don't worry about the little marks. Just glance at it and get the idea in your body. Don't let your mind dwell on the image of the notes too long. It will confuse you. You'll get locked up in your brain. Stay in your body.

Tap your foot on the "x", or have someone hit it with a tambourine. It's important. Get that going first. That is where the steady, repetitive downbeats are falling. On the first note, the downbeat hits together with the first bass note, but the accent jumps to the upbeat right away. That's the high note. It is like the crack of a loud snare drum on a drumset playing this good 'ole Rock 'n' Roll beat. The next deep note is like the bass drum hitting that solid downbeat. The next two high notes are again like the snare drum. It's a wild drive when it is played at a fast and *steady* pulse.

When it is played slowly, it still has power, but it is safer and deeper into the groove—more like Al Green's love songs. Either way, look out. This can generate just as much love as it can excitement.

Here is a variation:

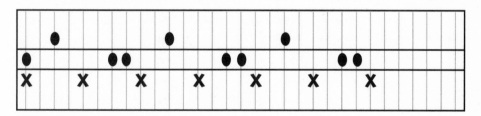

Track 25: Rock 2.

While you're at it, say a little prayer for the kids in Tiananmen Square, who didn't know what hit them.

A spontaneous healing groove can release tension and unite our hearts and souls, even at a preconcert soundcheck. Miami, 1971.

# 18

# TABOO MOVES

Certain body moves have been forbidden in our culture. They have been labeled "suggestive" because they disturb our established moral code, the religious/legal code woven into our society. We have revised our decency standards over the years, resulting in a healthier self-image of our bodies, but the residual hesitancy about our own body movements is a big source of tension.

Now, it is more legal to make fluid or suggestive movements. Women won't be put in the stocks like the dancing witches of Salem, but there is still fear from residual cultural taboos. It is also fear of the current mindset of men looking for sex. If a woman dances, some men mistake these movements as sexual invitations. This needs to be addressed in our culture. Men need to allow these sacred creative movements and protect them. It's a big step in the evolution of our culture and it is slowly happening. Men need to allow the sacred dance to unfold. It is not a sexual invitation. Let the Goddess dance, and we all benefit.

The moves may have been forbidden, but we still needed to do them. So, in popular dance sensual body moves were disguised just enough that one could feel the spirit in the dancing, but not suggestive enough to get arrested. This has been very confusing for our collective mind/body.

These sensual body moves are sacred. They are part of our human heritage and need to be expressed as sacred, not as profane moves. Thrusting hips is one movement that was not even allowed on the dance floor in contemporary America until recently. That move is invigorating and exciting. It can also throw your back out if you do it without a gradual loosening up.

Again: contents under pressure, open with care. By doing certain body movements you open up those energy channels and the rush of creative life energy is suddenly strong; like turning on a faucet too far. Gradual release is better, as in yoga.

Another move that is also frowned upon in our culture is thrusting your chest forward. This is where the person pushes their chest out into the world; making their presence known.

We have done this in our drumming group, once the women felt safe enough. I was thankful that we had a safe enough place in which they could thrust out their chests. It is difficult for women to do this. Men do this because it is a *male* thing to do. It is also a human thing to do.

In the Stella Adler school of acting where I studied for a bit, quite a long time ago, I didn't become a great actor, but I learned a little about how I affect the world with my personal being; my image, if you were to put it in Hollyweird terms. Everyone has an image. Sometimes it is not important, sometimes it's good to know how you affect the world with your image. Sometimes, you don't want to know how your image affects the world, and sometimes you wish that the world wasn't affected by your image at all.

In Stella's book there were simple little sketches of the human figure. Their different postures related to different types. For an actor to believably portray a character, he or she needed to know how that person would appear to the world. They had to assume the posture of their character. The posture that stood out the most was, of course, the assertive, confident, successful male. His chest was sticking out very far. Our body language tells the world what kind of person we are. The shy, vulnerable "victim" had a sunken chest, a stooping spine, and shoulders that drooped inward.

I'm not talking about good looks here. It has nothing to do with good looks. It has to do with the language in which you talk to yourself. Is it a good language? Is it a critical language? Most of us are self-critical and are kidding ourselves—that seems to be a human thing to do—but it's usually about the wrong things. Why be critical about your own creative energies? These inspirational energies can come out in a drum very easily when we get above our self-criticism and self-delusions. We also end up looking better because our self-image is better.

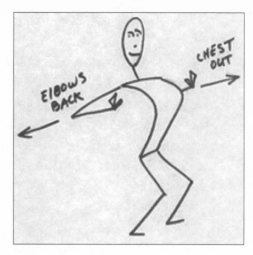

The thrust position.

Most people are kidding themselves. That is the nature of human insecurities. Even the assertive, confident Alpha personality may kid themself about some things. In some cases that type of personality might feel there is a great need to distract themselves away from an inner dialogue that could get self-critical and nonproductive. We protect ourselves from the harshness of the world and the harshness of our own inner voices by assuming a decisive, dominant attitude, but it is like acting; it's not really our personality. Alpha drummers are sometimes trying to ignore their own inner voices—and the voices of other drummers. If there is space in the groove, then we can hear our voices telling us things, maybe unpleasant, maybe needed, maybe joyous, about ourselves.

In a drumming group there is a dialogue between the drummers, but there is also an inner dialogue with yourself. Make sure that dialogue is an affirmative, confidence-building conversation. Say things like:

"I am doing this! It's great!"

"I have a good sense of rhythm!"

"I am a beautiful person, inside and outside."

"I am loved for what I already am."

"I love the world for what it is."

You get the idea.

What tends to happen are inner dialogues like:

"I can't do this."

People say this when they are actually finally *doing it.*

This could be called neurolinquistic programming or self-affirmations. Positive self-affirmations are very powerful in drumming. Our brain lobes interact with our hands. When both hands are involved with the same activity, such as passing a ball back and forth from one hand to the other or playing a drum, there is a conversation between both sides of the brain. It opens up a phone line to your soul.

When your hands are both doing the same thing on a drum and in life, you talk to your own soul. You'd better say something nice to yourself; otherwise you won't have any fun at all, no matter what you're doing with your hands.

Track 27: Thrust.

The "x"s are the downbeats. They can be played on a frame drum, a tambourine, cowbell, or even the slow steady clicking of your turn signal in your car. But don't thrust too hard if you're at a stop light.

You may have seen these thrusting moves in traditional African dance. Both thrusting of the hips and of the chest are joyous and beautiful moves. They need to be performed. Your body likes doing this stuff.

Elvis did these moves on the *Ed Sullivan Show* in the 1950s. I saw it. It was very weird. They put a black, diamond-shaped mask over Elvis' thrusting hips. You could see him from the chest up and the knees down but no swiveling hips were allowed on American TV.

Now, have we come a long way from there or what?

The other reason this move is so cool is that when we're drumming from a relaxed place, at a pause in the music, I can thrust my arms back, my chest pushes forward, and my spine will adjust itself with a whole series of pleasurable little pops.

I love it when that happens.

# Mahalia Jackson

When I was a kid, there was a woman who sang on the *Ed Sullivan Show* every once in a while, when Elvis wasn't around. She sang Gospel. She sang Black Spiritual Music. She was gifted and full of the Holy Spirit.

When someone asked Mahalia Jackson why she didn't go into the commercial market and sing Jazz, She said, "I don't want to sing the Blues."

The Blues and Black Gospel Spiritual music are a result of mixing sacred African ritual music with European church music here in the melting pot of the world. Check out the Blind Boys from Alabama to hear the real thing.

The Blues scale is an African scale originating partly in Mali and in other places. There are notes in the Blues scale that you cannot hit on a piano because they are in between the white and black keys. Piano players spend years developing ways to slide those two keys together to get Blues notes. The piano is a great piece of technology, but it still is tuned by the people who invented it. They want a Classical scale so all the pianos in the world are tuned to that same scale, but that's not the whole world of music.

Gospel music has the African scale as well as European notes, but it uses a different part of the African scale than the Blues. Those Blues notes were avoided by early Gospel piano players because it was too sinful or depressing, but when the Gospel piano player went to work on Saturday night at a juke joint, they certainly did play those Blues notes. That was a separation of where you have fun and where you pray—American style. It was out of respect to God.

The Blues scale leaves out a very happy part of the African scale, the part that makes people smile and laugh and dance and sing. The Blues is emotionally powerful and can get downright oppressive sometimes. The Blues has become the predominant scale from Africa here in America and the modern world, but there are other scales that are fun. We have gotten locked into the Blues scale and the Blues culture. It has become a rite of passage for musicians. Paying dues and playing the Blues is part of learning American music. I have seen a lot of kids from healthy childhoods get hooked on the Blues and live a life that is sort of depressing because they misunderstood the Blues and the heritage of that scale.

People are looking for other scales to sing and worship with; hence their interest in Celtic, Arabic, and Native American music. Using what comes naturally to you is difficult in our culture. We have been tricked into thinking that spiritual correctness must come from someone else.

Mahalia Jackson was a big woman with a huge smile. She sang for everybody. When they asked her why she didn't sing the Blues, she smiled and said, "I'm too thankful to sing the Blues."

## Rolls

The long note on a drum is called a *roll*. It is the only way a drum can sustain a note. You can blow a long note if it's a horn, flute, or reed instrument. You can bow a long note if it's a string instrument, or hold a long feedback note if you're playing an electric guitar and you're standing in front of an amplifier that is turned up to thirteen. But on a drum, there is only one way to play a long *held* note; that's by doing a roll.

Rolls are meditations in high gear. It's like you are driving a sports car and you just put your foot down to the floor. Your hands go really, really fast and the note sounds continuous. It never fails to get the audience going.

On a frame drum, you hit the mallet as fast as you can, staying relaxed, and the tone rings evenly. A hand drum roll is done with single strikes by each hand repeated so fast and smoothly that you can't hear the individual notes. This must be performed from relaxation, both mental and physical.

The roll can also be performed with sticks, bouncing two notes on each stick. The two notes on each stick are played so fast that it is a continuous buzz or roar, depending on how hard you are playing.

On a snare drum, there are many different rolls; five-stroke roll, seven-stroke roll, nine-stroke roll, and thirteen-stroke roll. The nine-stroke roll is interesting because it is handed down via an oral tradition. When playing the nine-stroke roll, the student says to him- or herself "Huckleberry pie," and the number of syllables corresponds to the number of pulses in the roll. This dates from the Revolutionary War.

Bouncing sticks is a delicate affair. To get an even roll you must have the right balance of relaxation and muscle-flexing tension. Breathing is important. Breathing out to release the tension is the basis for the drum-roll meditation.

On a hand drum, the single back-and-forth hand movements are simpler, but still induce tension. Breathing out to release tension is one of the great secrets of speed drumming.

One of the many interesting definitions of the Sanskrit word *Nirvana*, according to Alan Watts, is, "That state when we are breathing out." The act of releasing by breathing out the tension is a state of Nirvana.

Before trying fast rolls, warm up first. Play a few minutes in a comfortable groove so that your emergency functions shut off and you are nearing a relaxed state. Then try a medium speed roll; just back and forth with your hands. Pata Pata Pata. . . .

Start slowly. Don't jump ahead of yourself. We tend to do that in this culture—jump ahead before we do the work that is in front of us.

Start slowly, back and forth, then increase the speed, breathing out the tension. It's like putting your foot down on the accelerator, "Vrooommmmm!!"

Back off and settle back down into an idling, relaxed back-and-forth pattern. Then try it again.

"Vvvrrroooommmmm!"

Each time, go a little faster. Not a lot faster. Just a little faster. It is important to go gradually so as not to implant tension commands with the lesson. Always take it slowly when learning something new on the drum. Pushing the tempo will hurt your technique and possibly hurt your hands. If you learn with tension you will play with tension. We have enough tense drummers in the world. Play softly. Do not play loud and fast. That only makes things more difficult. Stay relaxed, play as softly as possible, and back off from the fast roll after you hit your speed limit. Go away from this exercise and do something else. When you come back to it, you will be able to do it faster. The body needs time to assimilate the lesson. This applies to a lot of things in life. Don't force it.

Your learning curve is yours—no one else's. Don't be hard on yourself. Keep smiling; it's supposed to be fun. Smiling releases the tension and gets you out into the world instead of into an internal dialogue that can get dark and dreary. Don't treat this as an exercise. Treat it like you are playing music for fun. Maybe pretend you are standing in front of thousands of people and you are playing a great drum solo, or imagine you are playing a drum inside a pyramid for sacred belly dancers. Pretend you are in the rain forest and you are playing a roll to entice an anaconda out of its deep cave. Anaconda skins make good drum heads.

Snakes and drums have always been connected. If you listen to a rattlesnake when it has been disturbed, you'll hear the rattle and hissing before it strikes. That is a very deeply imprinted sound that we know as danger.

It sounds a lot like a drum roll.

# 19

# PERSONAL MAGICK

I realized that I had to make the magick. I couldn't depend on anyone else to make magick. I couldn't wait until I learned what magick was. I had to make it up as I went along, following my instincts and listening for clues. Rediscovering our own magick is a mystery for each of us to solve.

I had the good fortune to meet an incredible woman in Atlanta, Georgia. Her name was Rebecca Stacy.

She was a beautiful, mature woman with an interesting and successful life. She was a hypnotherapist and regression therapist. She had also been a Miss America finalist in some forgotten year, probably in the fifties. She had also been the first woman executive at a major makeup corporation at a time when women were not executives.

A friend in Atlanta asked me if I would be interested in having a past-life session with Rebecca. L.A. had made me somewhat cynical of certain therapies, but this seemed like the right time in my life to take a look at what other lives had to say about this one.

Rebecca first asked me what questions I wanted to ask my other lives. What questions indeed! My life was in another state of flux and I was feeling unsure about my new calling: drumming seminars. I had left the corporate world of the film industry and had then redeemed myself by

179

finding a new line of inspiration—teaching drums again. Charlie, a successful musician and old partner, stopped by the store and jammed when he was passing through town with Hall and Oates. He predicted this crisis years earlier.

He had said, "Buddy, you're the freelance king. You can do anything in the film business. But . . . you're a drummer. You've always been a drummer. You'll always be a drummer. You're going to have to come to terms with that fact."

I finally admitted he was right. The drum came back into my life. I could see that people were hungry to drum and find a peaceful, exciting groove in their lives. Their brains just got in the way. There was no way to make money at helping people find their groove, but that didn't seem to matter. This drumming thing was part of a bigger picture; people were coming out of their psychic shellshock and moving forward. I knew that I too was changing once again. The drum was an obvious tool for helping me and other people through our next transition. A few friends who were wealthy from being in the music biz were perplexed by my decision to focus on drumming with people who had never hit a drum before. Kevin, a veteran drummer from Iron Butterfly, said that it was a "courageous" thing to do. I totally believed that everyone does have a sense of rhythm so it didn't seem that daunting. I was curious about how people needed to drum.

Jimi Hendrix scuffled to become the great artist that he was. When he started out, he had to sleep on the streets of Atlanta. Once, his only food was a candy bar and a cockroach ate it out of his pocket. That's paying dues. That was after Jimi had been a paratrooper in the 101st Airborne. He wasn't a bum. He was following his life path. Later, it took him to the heights of creativity and success. He changed the way the world hears music. His songs will live forever. Surviving our life paths is the challenge.

The price the artist pays for his or her creativity may seem small when compared to the contribution they give to the world. Just don't try to tell that to the struggling artist. Rags to riches is our cultural mindset for artistic endeavors, but there is a way to be an artist and not feel bad if you don't get rich from doing it. That is a pitfall where the inner critic gets us down. We feel the creative juices flowing when we drum, but the inner critic makes the assessment that we may not be good enough to get rich at drumming, so we give up. Creative drumming is a life-saving activity, with or without getting rich at it.

Getting rich can happen for the artist, but that doesn't mean the artist can forget about the rags. The poor times are usually where the inspiration originally comes from. I had been back and forth from Ragtown to Richville a few times, so that game had grown old for me. I thought I was after bigger game: wisdom. I just had to follow my instincts—if I still had any.

I was getting some esoteric kind of guidance, some higher direction, from people. They were telling me what they needed and I was giving them some help. I decided to give instead of take. It was my last recourse. The greed, power, ambition game was not holding my interest. After all, I was a drummer, wasn't I? Or was I? I had thrown a tantrum years back and decided that I wasn't going to drum anymore. I was going to deprive the world until something changed—in me. I hadn't considered the drum itself. I had always known that the drum was more than an inanimate object, but I had deprived myself of the power that it held for me. It was maybe an atonement for whatever imagined transgressions that I had committed. The reasons that I had stopped drumming were long forgotten, so I decided to reacquaint myself with the drum, not as a musical instrument, but now as a tool primarily for healing.

The drum insisted that I give the people help. It's the drum's fault that I decided to do this teaching thing. So what if it was making me poor. The drum insisted that all these people who want to play the drum find out how to do it—by me or somebody else. It didn't matter. Just get them to a drum and get them to hit it.

Early on, when I was first getting an inkling about people's need to drum, an American Indian woman strolled into the shop. When we talked about the few drums that I had, I mentioned that I was helping people who wanted to drum.

She turned and looked at me directly, which is very unusual for an Indian to do. She said, "Teach the white man to play the drum. That's a good thing."

But here I was in Atlanta with just a few very nice people showing up, but not enough to . . . what? Make money? The drum said that wasn't the reason I was being forced to do this. The drum didn't care if I was broke. It just said, "Everything will be all right. Just keep drumming."

So I did.

This seemed insane to me. I needed some outside help on this one.

I was ready to be regressed.

I went to Rebecca's apartment, north of Atlanta in Buckhead. She put me in her gentle trance and before long I was floating down the stream of consciousness in a small boat. It was dark, but then it opened up as if coming out of a stone tunnel.

*Above me soared buildings made of bricks, two and three stories tall. That was quite exciting. It was the first big city this young man had ever seen. He was entering Delft, Holland.*

*In Delft he worked as a tinsmith apprentice to his uncle. He wasn't that smart, but he was honest. Soon, he made his way to the New World and worked in the woods, clearing trees and planting crops with the help of local Indians and other early settlers. The problem was the soldiers.*

*There was a bridge.*

*The young man stood on the bridge with other people like himself, and with some Indians too. They faced the troops and were shot down. That young man died looking up at the tall green trees as the Hessian mercenaries marched over their bleeding bodies. His last thought was something like; "I don't understand what is happening here, but I think it is important."*

The "tin" thing is interesting. Tin art has been a lucrative form of expression for me. I have been making handcut tin/steel mobiles for years. It was a result of wanting an art form that was not technological. I was tired of the high-tech art. I had previously been a post-production supervisor at Lorimar for TV shows like *Falcon Crest, Knott's Landing*, and *Dallas*. I had done computer graphics in Hollywood. It was not fulfilling, and it was every stressful, but the most irritating thing was that I wasn't drumming. I wasn't happy about that.

Once I had changed life paths back to a personal creativity, the tin folk art seemed to hit a nerve with the buying public. My friend in Atlanta introduced me to R. A. Miller, an oldtimer folk artist living up north of Atlanta in the woods. His hand-cut tin art pieces are all over the world now, but he didn't care. He was inspiring to me because his creative energy wasn't impeded by the "bizness" or by overeducation. His love was keeping him alive. I had seen that same love of creativity saving other people too. I felt that I needed that kind of creative love in my life again.

> *". . . you're a drummer. You've always been a drummer. You'll always be a drummer. You're going to have to come to terms with that fact."*

I asked my partner Cathy what constituted folk art for Santa Monica, California, and she countered without hesitation, "Surfers, dude."

So I made Tin Surfers. I set the goal of making a thousand handcut, hand-painted surfers, all of them signed and numbered. It was a creative goal for my life. It had nothing to do with making it rich, or getting famous from doing it. It was a simple act, based on a personal desire. We sold them to our clientele in our store, Seasons on Montana, in Santa Monica, California and on the internet. Our mobiles became a form of magickal fetish portraits.

My past-life regression with Rebecca was fascinating, not only because this particular past life had tin work in it. I was getting a sense of resonance from past lives; what were issues and abilities in other lives would be issues and abilities in this life.

Rebecca took me through many lives, each with lessons for me to ponder for the rest of this life. The long-term effects were profound. I felt a sense of integration too.

One of my questions concerned my father and my mother. I wanted to be in a life with my father. In this life, he had died mysteriously when I was four and a half. Rebecca prompted me to go to an earlier life to meet my father from this life.

> *I looked up at a small stone castle in Denmark. I was astride a horse and wearing a long sword that my father, a baron, had given to me, along with the command to go to the Holy Lands and fight the Crusades. The dutiful son obeyed. He waved goodbye to his father and his mother, who were standing on the parapet. She was wearing a pointed hat with a scarf draped from the top point. I couldn't tell if she was weeping or not.*
>
> *I found myself in the Holy Land several years later. Defeated, disillusioned, and destitute, but full of curiosity about the sacred teachings of the Persian culture. I was living by a well in a small Bedouin community. No one spoke to me. A woman brought food by. I struggled to read and write about what I was learning from the sacred Arabic texts. I was shunned by everyone and did not hear my own voice for many, many years. I did not hear my own language ever again. I died quietly while writing; the quill pen slipped from my hand and that life faded away into the desert.*

Middle Eastern music has always been a part of me and I don't know why. I was currently on this trip from California to Atlanta, trying to drum up some business in the drum workshop business. As usual, I was too early. The scene hadn't arrived yet. No one showed up at my drumming events. I was losing money and I didn't really worry about it. This seemed important, even though not many were into it yet. I was on the trail of something.

A realization shook me. The drums I was carrying around to teach with were clay derbougas, like dombegs—village-crafted, with goatskin heads. They were very fragile, low-fire clay drums, but I took them with me anyway and played and sold them to people around the country. Women could play them easily, which seemed to be an important point in this process. Women drummers seemed to be a big part of this unfolding scenario. This didn't seem that unusual to me. When I was eight years old, my first drum teacher was a woman. She was a brilliant teacher. Women drummers have always been a part of my life.

The drum that most women could easily play were these derbougas. We got them from two solemn but very nice Muslim men who wrapped them in rugs and shipped them from Algeria to L.A.

This was the same drum that would have been played where the displaced Crusader had his crisis of faith in the Mideast. Hundreds of years later, I was using this drum to help people get to their own sacred well. I realized that now I was able to speak and that I should let my words spill out with the help of the drum. It was okay to speak now. I can thank Rebecca for that. She was a great healer. She touched many lives and she is sorely missed. She had a retreat in the Blue Ridge Mountains of North Georgia. I thank her for helping me to see other lives and to see this life more clearly.

When I returned to L.A., Antoine, a student in the ethnomusicology department at UCLA, came by our drumming workshops and sat in. From Lebanon, he plays all the Mediterranean instruments very well. He wanted me to learn some traditional songs on the dombeg while he played the flute. We rehearsed and he was surprised that I got the arrangements so quickly. There was a deep sense of familiarity, even though I play very untraditionally. I was just faking it, but it worked for him pretty well. I tried to explain about the regression session that I had just gone through in Atlanta, but then I thought better of it. I didn't want to make Antoine uncomfortable. We are from such different cultures and religions—I had no idea about his views on past lives. I just told him that I can fake just about anything, but don't expect it to be the real thing. He complimented me by saying that I played dombeg in the American style. That is a very gracious compliment from a classically trained Arabic musician.

The dombeg and derbouga are belly dancing drums. I have always played for the dance. I needed to do that again. I think that it is one of the most beautiful things in the world. It was why I couldn't put up with the Rock star thing. When I couldn't see the girls dancing anymore, I lost interest. That, and my partner was killed.

I needed to play for the dance again. It seemed more important than anything else; the expensive car, house, suit, wife, and film job in L.A. all faded away when the drum started. I was waking up from a long, fitful sleep and the first thing in my waking mind was the sound of the dombeg, the belly dancing drum.

Rebecca surprised me at the end of the last of our three separate past-life regression sessions. She started by asking me the usual; "What questions would you like me to ask your past lives?"

"How come I'm not more successful?"

So at the end of the session, while I was still in a deep trance, she prompted me to go to a *successful* life.

> *The lives slipped away like diaphanous layers of silk until there was a strange man standing next to a temple in Egypt. He wore a skull cap and his hand rested on the side of a temple to Isis.*
>
> *"What is your name?" she asked him.*
>
> *He replied, using my lips, "You cannot pronounce it."*
>
> *"What do you do?" she asked gently.*
>
> *"I turn numbers into buildings so they treat me as a god," he replied simply.*
>
> *"Describe where you are, please," Rebecca asked.*
>
> *"This is a temple to Isis. Huge stone blocks are supported by pillars. The stone slabs overhead are large enough to crush hundreds of people if they fall.*
>
> *"How did you lift the stones?" she asked, very intrigued.*

*"That is not important," he stated matter-of-factly.*

*"Are you from another planet?" she asked carefully.*

*"That is not important," he again stated matter-of-factly.*

*"I built the temple and I conduct the ceremonies. I am the priest and the administrator."*

*There was a strange intensity as his perceptions focused across time to this current life. He was perceiving this end of the time tunnel.*

*"I can see your life," he said, looking back at us from his place. "I am not impressed. You have problems with sex. We use sex for sacred ritual here."*

*Rebecca asked him to help in this life. He thought about it, then said, "Yes. I can do that."*

When I awoke it seemed like life was fresh and new. I was seeing through different eyes. I felt the closeness of this strange Egyptian architect priest.

Rebecca told me later that something had been bothering her about every one of our regression sessions. In every life, the person always described the buildings, even when they had been an inarticulate mercenary from the middle ages or a country bumpkin. They all spoke about the buildings with attention to detail. They described how stones were laid on top of each other. This final Egyptian architect made that clear to her. Architecture had been a college goal for me. I had built studios as well as movie sets. It was all too fascinating for both of us to comprehend.

Now, I had a very interesting partner riding along with me.

The oddest sensation hit me when I called Florida from Atlanta. I was going to go down and see my family. I had been too long away. My mom answered the phone.

"We're going to Egypt for a short vacation," she said. They were invited by my stepfather's daughter, a major in the Air Force. They were gone when I arrived. The house was empty. The newspapers were neatly stacked. On top was an article about a new tomb that had been discovered in Egypt. It had been made for a person who wasn't royalty. It was a smaller tomb for a manager of the building of the pyramids. It showed the workers and what they ate. A carved figure of the manager was sitting facing the new world as the diggers opened up the chamber.

The regression had been just a few days earlier and everything seemed a bit shaky. I was changing my point of view on a lot of things. There was a stream of illogical events that beckoned to me to keep following the mystery, to keep searching for the groove.

"The answer will surprise and please you," something said to me.

So I continued the quest. The drums were playing again in my heart. I felt the life force. It was a groove, but it was different than it had ever been before.

## Pachamama

Up in the Andes Mountains in Peru, the Indians have an old friend in the earth, the Pachamama. It eats the dark energy of the human spirit and sends it back down into the earth to be recycled. They carve stone figures to signify the Pachamama receptiveness to dark energy. Pachamama is always hungry and likes to eat our dark energy.

We have a culture that makes money from selling, but also denies that the dark energy exists; saying that it exists "out there" instead of "in here." That's always been the way things work. That's why it's called dark energy. It's scary business. We'd rather not have to deal with it or even look at it directly.

Our movies give us the dark energy, but it is often in an addictive manner, using special effects. We get a psychological hit from a scene that has dark energy in it. Scenes with killing, explosions, fights, screaming, horror, etc., are an addictive stimulant. I edited for a while in my sojourns around the film biz. Rock videos were just getting started. I could definitely do that.

The director for an Alabama video said, "Just cut it on the beat. Okay?"

"There are a lot of beats," I said. "Sit back and I'll show you a few."

He was glad he did. He got whatever awards they were giving out that year. Upbeat rhythm in the visual cutting made a big difference. It's everywhere now.

I realized that an editor holds the life of a film in his or her hands. Women seem to have the patience for this intense work. The director and editor know about addictive hits in the editing of a film or television show.

**Andean Indians of Peru believe that the Pachamama stone eats our dark energy.**

If a scene is slow, then it could be followed by a *jump cut* or *hard-butt* edit into another scene that jolts the viewer. The music can also be a jolt from silence to hard-edged bashing. It is all calculated to get the viewer addicted to that particular movie. The people doing the calculating are very good at what they do. The world of film editors is a realm of wizards. They make magick that affects our behavior.

Our culture is becoming so *virtual* now that the distinctions between what is real and what is not real have blurred. What is real and what has always been real is the dark energy. It is tangible energy that can be manipulated. That is why the most popular character in the *Star Wars* movies was the Dark Lord; Darth, baby. That part of the amazing Lucas success was somewhat unexpected. They had started with the best of intentions to create a Light Energy Hero, but the dark energy of that character was too dramatic to ignore. It makes good box office.

The brain works off stimulation. Without stimulation it shrivels, goes to sleep, and eventually dies. The science of film editing has evolved by studying the way the human brain reacts to visual and audio stimulus. The people who do it for a living do not consider what they do to be dark energy. They are well-intentioned people who make art for a living. The evolution of the commercial film-making system has created a worldwide business complex that generates more income than many countries in the world—and it is all illusion.

## Algorhythm

Our addiction to entertainment is getting more sophisticated by the day. Each new movie has a special effect that is a new mathematical computer program written in algorithm. Algorhythms are formulas that the computer uses to crunch numbers to create an effect. The "rhythm" part of algorithm is too abstract for me to understand, but it is there. It might have something to do with a repeated computation. We are creatures of rhythm, even if it is a computer program that runs at the speed of electrons. Music synthesizers also use algorhythms to make new sounds. We are living in the age of algorhythms and only a few people know what they are. They are driving us forward at an ever-increasing rate.

The drum is nondigital. It is a way for us to release ourselves from the computer program that we are stuck in. Organic drumming rhythms are not opposed to the digital world, but are just an escape and an antidote for the massive programming to which we are all subjected. Our psyches feel the fracturing of sound and image that is part of the digital entertainment world—it affects our sense of timing. We feel tense and we don't know why. Instead of the old-fashioned flow of images and sound at twenty-four frames a second, we now have bits of information at much faster rates. Our systems sense those tiny breaks and struggle to handle the jolts of information.

*"Life is just shadows on the wall," to crudely paraphrase Socrates.*

*Movies are better than just shadows on a wall, 'cuz there's popcorn.*

After a blockbuster movie has run its course in the theaters, the special-effects computer algorhythms that created the cinema illusions are then sold to a software company and those expensive computer effects, say dodging high-speed bullets, or turning someone into liquid chrome, become common domain for other less-highly financed movies or commercials to use. You then see a bunch of lesser movies with the same effects done at a lower cost. The cost goes down and so does the quality of the story. This lowering of sensibilities is a function of the marketplace—making cheaper movies and commercials, and never mind about quality.

What we need is quality in our lives. We don't need to be constantly cheating ourselves out of a real experience. I'm talking about finding the courage to turn off your television set and go out into the real world and live.

Our addiction to the media will only increase. It might be a good idea to unplug once in a while. "Media fasting" is a term that I have heard lately. What a concept for our times.

What happens when we unplug is amazing. It's called "living." Then our perception of the dark energy will change. The addiction will subside. Fear and panic might be less overwhelming without the technological media *hit* of constant dark energy. Anxiety will diminish too. Drumming is a way to disperse the anxiety of modern culture but the addiction is still surrounding us.

The dark energy that we can channel through the drum is healthy. It goes down into the earth because you send it there with your own work. Your hands and your feet and your life energy send it down into the earth, right out of the hole in the bottom of the drum. The earth eats it gladly. It is the Pachamama getting fed. You can be freed from it until it fills you up again, then you send it back down into the earth where it belongs.

Denying that we have dark impulses only sets us up to be ambushed by the same dark energy that we suppress. Better to admit that we have it and dispose of it in a healthy, nonaddictive way.

# 20
# NEW WAY

You might become a good drummer, but that doesn't really matter. What matters is the quality that you bring to your own life and the lives of others. The drum can be a tool to fashion your energies into a coherent, integrated, successful life. If you can play well, that is icing on the cake. Plenty of great drummers are walking psychological casualties. The drum has to be allowed to do its healing work on our spirit. This can't happen if one is *proving* something to the world. A lot of guys use the drum as an equalizer in a world they perceive as stacked against them. The drum becomes their weapon to disrupt the status quo. Their intensity is incompatible with a meditative groove. Their pain is the only thing that they can contribute and it sounds like egotistical anger instead of a healing groove. When they relax and become a member of the human race, their support of the groove is much better than their contributions as an angry victim.

Improving for the sake of your craft is fine. That is a different thing entirely. It's not bad to want to be excellent, but it can be a dead-end road if you use it to deny the dark energy that has to be dealt with in your soul.

The drum has at least two distinctly different roles to play. It is a musical instrument, but it is also a spiritual tool that is not a musical instrument. I think many people want to use the drum for a spirit tool but they are intimidated by the musical instrument. Their brain thinks being musical is the only way to play a drum.

One thing that always excited me over the years of searching for music and art was when people picked up instruments who had never learned any music. They were artists, or just regular people, but for some reason they decided to pick up a musical instrument and make some sounds. They let themselves do this and it was very rewarding. Many times that nonmusician can articulate life's energies better than a trained musician because they don't have the same blinders on their ears that trained players have. The novice comes up with unique ideas.

When the B-52s were a new band, record company execs could not figure out why the band sold so many records. *Rock Lobster* was not a particularly pleasant sound to their ears. Their music was not that *polished*. Their own record label didn't understand their sound but the public certainly did like that sound, in a big way. The B-52s approached their music like art instead of music, so they had a completely different set of needs and desires about what they played.

I constantly listen to the new players in a drumming group to hear what they are trying to play. Many times it is very cool, but they don't trust themselves enough to make it solid. I'll support them many times and they won't even realize that the group went to their rhythm. They just don't have much faith in their own creative ability, but I do. I love to explain afterward that I was following them. This may not be correct behavior for a drum facilitator, but so what.

Turn off your television set and start a band. It could be the best thing you ever did.

## Start a Band

A lot of people want to have a band or a musical group of some sort. It might be disguised as a corporation, a gang, a coven, a cult, a religion, or a school. It's still a band. It's where everyone shares the same arrangements, plays parts, and supports the tune. I grew up playing in many different bands and it is something that I look back on with fond memories.

Some of my fondest memories are of playing music with friends on stage in front of people—really saying something—and having the audience *right there* with you.

One of the participants in a Gaia Oasis drumming retreat in the California Sierras, in July 2000, was a woman drummer, Lynn Rank. She shared with us family pictures (below) of her musically inclined grandparents, Claude and Oliva Campbell, who had a "wine bottle orchestra," and presented other unique musical performances. See chapter 14 for a mention of the career of Lynn's great-grandfather, Moses Findley Campbell, a battlefield drummer in both the Civil War and World War I.

Even the wealthiest, most successful people in the world harbor a desire to make music. A number of entrepreneurs have gone back and learned how to play guitar after they became the richest men in the world. It has something to do with a shared ritual.

Claude and Oliva Campbell with their wine-bottle orchestra. Their granddaughter Lynn is also a drummer and very proud of her musical heritage.

It has been a culturally acceptable way for men to be creative together. Women always have had the ability to blend creatively, and having an all-girl band used to be unusual. Not anymore. This is a comingling of creative energies for the purpose of coming up with a tune. It is not sexual comingling, but it is very intimate, and the people doing the cocreating get a glimpse into each other's souls. It is music, but there is some naked truth about the people who made the music behind the hot licks.

Bands don't have to sound good. Great bands sometimes don't. I wouldn't dare list the bands that sound bad live, but I've heard bands play great one night and then sound terrible the next night, and the audience still got a lot out of it.

*Turn off your television set and start a band. It could be the best thing you ever did.*

A band generates some other kind of harmonious energy and the audience is transported to another realm. It doesn't matter if the band sucks. The point is that they are doing it. The group of people are making sounds together and it really works—at least for that moment. The experience is what lives on with the people who were there.

The truth of the matter is simple. Anyone can do this. It is too easy for us to shell out a hundred bucks to see the great dinosaur Rock groups instead of making our own music. The reason we can't make our own music is that we think too much.

Oh yeah, I suppose some talent is essential, but not always. I saw the Germs live in Los Angeles during the early Punk years—they were terrible, but they were great. Their energy was fresh and exciting. They took chances on stage. So many bands at the beginning of the New Wave Punk era were throwing out old definitions of what music should be. They made new sounds because they decided not to judge what they were playing. That kind of creativity has always been interesting to me. It is a liberating experience for both the audience and the players to break the rules. Sometimes I think it is as close as we can come to a religious experience.

Carlos Santana is going in a spiritual direction and it is a great benefit for everyone to experience the power of that music, but I am talking about a personal groove—a group of people who get together more than once and create sounds together.

"Hey, let's play that thing we played the last time we got together."

That phrase has been spoken in every language in the world since the very beginning of time. The act of making sounds together is as natural to us as eating together. It is nourishment. The artist eats the world and then puts it back out in his or her creativity. The trick is to not get confused about being "an artist." Don't be. Be something else, whatever it takes to free up your creative ideas; just play music together.

I use the term "music" very generously. It includes anything that doesn't even remotely sound like conventional music. So much the better if it doesn't, because creativity is a search. We're all searching for that kind of inspiration. The need to search together for inspiration will always be a part of humanity no matter if they hit a drum or a computer.

It's also better to put that kind of energy into a band than somewhere else. It can be negative and even destructive if channeled inappropriately. A gang of young, tough-looking boys has always been a scary scenario, but if they happen to turn out to be in a band together, then well, maybe they're not so dangerous as we first suspected. They might even be interesting, despite their fashion sense.

Right now, the *look* for kids is very tough out there on the street. Kids are being hit with a lot of negative images and they feel the need to adopt protective covering to hide their vulnerability. A band is a way for people to trust, drop their social facade, and let their feelings show. This is safe to do in a rehearsal, because no one else is allowed in. That's a big part of having a band; the sacred rituals are private.

## Band Members Only

Rule number one: no watchers or groupies during rehearsals until everybody in the band is comfortable with the idea. Performing for people is different than rehearsing by yourselves. The band forges a secret unity in which only they share membership. They learn the secrets of the Universe together. Later, the world can watch and listen to them do it. That kind of secret initiation is a safe thing for people. It is a rite of passage that our culture is lacking. Sometimes a band is the closest thing to a secret sect that we have. It is also safety in the real world. I have always felt safer in a band, even though we may have all been idiots.

The strangest talents can be appreciated in a band. A person may be a total catastrophe in everyday life, but when they get in their band, they come alive with a creative energy that can't be denied. I've seen it happen time and time again. The safe rehearsal space lets someone's deepest creativity well up, if the other players are supportive. Of course there can be a lot of drek, but there should be honest, good intentions. This is the magickal part of it. Intentions are important. Good intentions are best. Honesty has been the goal in all great music. Sometimes a band is the closest thing we have to a social counselor in this culture.

People learn social skills from watching television. That's scary when you see the people who create television shows; they're no more sane than the regular person. They're crazy. Better to learn social skills where they really have some relationship to reality. A band forces people to socially interact, debate even, all for the sake of the song. It is a selfless argument at best, but it can also get petty, with innuendoes and slurs being thrown back and forth. All that is forgotten when the song finally works.

It's nothing personal because the reason for the band's existence is greater than the individual egos. This is an ideal band of course, but it is the reason that bands stay together. They have a sense of mission and it's their secret, the source of their magick and their power.

There may be only one overriding rule in every band. Even the Beatles obeyed this rule: "Don't punch the singer in the mouth."

Everything else might be okay. Just kidding . . . play nice.

# 21
# ARTISTIC CONNECTIONS TO THE OTHER SIDE

**M**any different kinds of beings want to talk to us. They hover at the edges of our dimly aware consciousness, calling out to us. The artists on the other side try to give us things. It is up to us to find a way to take these gifts and make them real art in this realm.

I worked with the great singer/poet Tim Buckley in the seventies. He was murdered in 1975. It was a traumatic event for many people, including me.

It was a decisive event in my musical career. I became distrustful of the music business after I saw the bloodthirsty managers, lawyers, and record labels eat up the remains of this great, underappreciated artist.

Tim came through to me in my dreams. I heard his new melodies and tried to write them down, but I was in too much pain. The other guys in the band went on to become successful musicians and producers, but I took a turn away from the music business into a quest for understanding and peace in my soul. I went to art school and majored in performance art.

I paint and I am a sculptor, as well as a mystic and a musician. I consulted the *Egyptian Tarot Deck*, the I Ching, psychics, and spirit readers. I was using these arcane areas of study to find a meaning to ritual. I saw ritual in the performance art world and it intrigued me. It was as if people were hungry to have ritual in their lives, but they were afraid to have any spiritual content in the rituals. Spirituality was unfashionable in the art world. I attended a lot of interesting ritual art in San Francisco, L.A., and New York. I saw that there was a hunger for ritual in our lives, but there was fear in having sacred content. Much of the ritual was meaningless and boring. It was what modern art had become: pretense.

I still drummed, but now I was beginning to see the drum as a performance art tool instead of a musical instrument. I was finding ways to free myself from my old definitions of what drumming was. I knew there was some other way to use the drum instead of selling Pop music, but that meant going back to what the drum had been to me in the South—a tool for magick. I heard the Santería drums living in Coconut Grove, and the funky Swamp VooDoo style of drumming around New Orleans. I had played that kind of drumming, and I knew that it hit a deep chord in people's souls. I believed it was really magick, but I had made a decision not to use the magick in the drum. I didn't feel it was for making money. It was for connecting to God, but I was not finding a group who felt that funky mysticism. My drumming rituals were solitary but still deep, so I taught and I played, but there was no magick in it.

I was getting soul transmissions from the other side, not only from Tim but also from my father. He had been killed when I was four-and-a-half years old and it was something that I had not dealt with. I had not grieved for my father. He had been a beloved secret that my family never talked about, partly because of his intelligence business connections, but primarily because of shame about losing the man of the family. I realized that I missed my father immensely. It took many years for me to discover that he was with me all the time, but I had been too angry and afraid to talk with him or to listen to him.

The Card Precipitation really helped.

On a visit back to Florida, my sister introduced me to one of her psychic friends, Hoyt. I attended a seminar where he took a stack of white index cards and put them in a sealed woven basket with a bunch of colored pens. He closed this basket tightly to keep any light out. The energies at work needed only the essence of the pens, but they had to have total darkness to work.

Hoyt then did psychic readings on each of the two dozen people in the room. Everyone in the room got some things from those readings, even me. My grandmother, Lilly Helm, came to me. Chief Many Horns, a real Indian, was encouraging me to continue the drumming workshops. He said that it was helping to bring people up. There were other spirits clamoring to get through to me via Hoyt's amazing channeling, but the cards were even more amazing than the readings.

After an hour of readings, Hoyt opened the sealed basket and took out the stack of cards. Now, they were covered with the most beautiful images. Colorful, inspiring, mysterious artwork that could not have been done beforehand. This was proof that there were artists on the other side capable of giving us great art, if only we can accept it.

The more amazing part was when we each turned our cards over, our Spirit Guides' names were written on the back. My relative's names were also written on the back. Grandmother Lilly, Uncle Roy, and my father, as well as Chief Many Horns and Sister Mary Leucretia.

I searched the Internet later and found the facts on Chief Many Horns. He was an Indian delegate to Congress in 1850. He participated in Little Big Horn.

Hoyt saw that I was surrounded by Indians and they were encouraging me to continue with the drumming workshops. I had avoided using Indian rhythms. Out of respect, I didn't want to make bad energy with their rhythms. But I had played with American Indians. They seemed to get along with me okay. Now the Spirit Indians were saying that this was an important thing to do. It was helping people. That made it hard for me to stop doing the workshops. They also stated that it was just the beginning of my musical career. I didn't know if I liked that idea or not. The only reason I decided to continue these soul drumming workshops was because people got something out of them.

I am grateful for the sessions with Hoyt because he put me in touch with my people. They are a mixed bag. Not only relatives but spirits who have an interest in what I'm doing. They are giving me advice and I am taking that advice. That makes a big difference in my life.

This is the card produced for the author during the Card Precipitation segment of Hoyt's psychic seminar.

Roland Kirk made a great early recording called *I Talk with the Spirits.* I believed him. I have always wanted to do that. It recently dawned on me, once again, that they have been talking to me all along. I am just learning how to hear them.

The artwork on the Cards of Precipitation impressed me. There are many artists on the other side that want to make art. I don't get a chance to make art as often as I would like to and I am still breathing. Spirit artists must feel the same frustration on the other side.

Imagine a great artist with a God-given talent, but he or she dies. There must be a great sense of longing for the physical realm where art can be made tangible with oil paints and the stone and clay of sculpture, where there are watercolor paper and musical instruments waiting to be played. What frustration for great spirit artists who must watch us struggle just to survive. I would think that they look for humans to give art to. Maybe the quest for artistic spirits is to find a human who can receive their gifts of art.

This is where I might want to draw a line of warning though. Art is to some degree a spiritual endeavor, but it is also a work of suffering and self-growth.

Some people use art as a healing tool. It's a way for them to handle the trauma of their lives. Some artists are not all lightness; their art can be dark. The act of being an artist opens us up to all kinds of influences as well as our own demons.

We can use art to define our demons and grow beyond them to a fuller consciousness of the Universe inside of us. In that case the art is merely a stepping stone to an integrated whole spirit. There is also the suffering artist trying to make sense out of a confusing world. Spiritual artists talking to us from the other side may be trying to make sense out of their own world. Their attempts to give us art may not always be the best thing. It's up to us to decide what we can handle from the other side, based on our individual taste and courage.

A lot of art is based on suffering, whether through the learning process of mastering technique, or suffering through a painful life. It may be *great* art, and it may be seductive and inspiring. Then there is *Spiritual* art that might seem bland and lacking drama, many times because the artist is not trained or the concept is just too Cosmic for simple images. These people feel a rush of creative energy and they are compelled to be creative—training or no training, suffering or no suffering. So, we are faced with the question of, "What is good art?" I'll leave that to the folks who talk instead of drum.

In a drum, the art comes through in a vocabulary that is nonintellectual. It is full of wisdom and it is dramatic as well as insightful. It is up to us to get the amazing complexity and poetry being sent through us. It is up to us to let the really good Spirit drummers use us to make magick with the drums. When the drums open us up, all kinds of inspirational gifts come through. Sometimes we don't understand the download of inspiration until much later when we've figured out how to open the file. It was downloaded to our hearts.

## Drumming for the Future

We are discovering the rhythms for our future. Yes, there will be a future, despite what Hollywood has been telling us.

I get excited when I hear a person hit a drum for the first time. It is a miracle to me that we can play together. We are all so different in our personalities, but when we combine forces, something happens that is greater than the individual human elements.

When a person has never hit a drum before, they feel the urge of rhythm pushing up into their consciousness. It is a voice without words. They struggle for a moment, then realize that they are part of this flow and the music comes through. They then begin to articulate the rhythms for our future. In a way, this is evolutionary.

The artist has always had the thankless job of giving us a vision of the future. That is their personality type. I call them "Creatives." That's a word that other personality types understand, somewhat. It's a handy term in Tinsel Town where agent personality types and lawyer personality types and producer personality types are eager to nail you down into a pigeonhole in their Rollodex. "Creative" would come right after some other arbitrary designation like "computer programmer," with Bill Gates' home number written on that card.

We are all producing our own lives: This Ecstatic Drama, This Computer Program, This Virtual Reality Illusion. We are making the "Content." We are producing our own soundtrack. We decide the meaning of our own movie—yet we still think it's a mystery. It's our show, but where is the executive producer?

And why are there so many commercials?

## Too Many Notes

A young Japanese-American woman came in today and wanted to drum. She had come in before and had a good time drumming in our groups. She is highly motivated in everything she does. She is in great shape, but today she was feeling insecure and somewhat *beat up* by the musicians she tried to work with. They had criticized her playing and she needed a little clarification.

She said that the Brazilian guys she had tried to sit in with told her she should do this or that or some such thing, but basically, I realized, they were trying to tell her, "Don't play so many notes."

She is a very strong woman, she works out, she seems to be trying to compete in a "man's" world. I wanted to tell her that her creative feminine energy was what was needed, not more testosterone busyness that some people with too much bovine growth hormone think drumming is.

She had taught herself the bongo part to the *I Love Lucy* show when she was younger, and she could play that bongo part very well. She had developed the ability to go back and forth with her hands at a fast, even rate. That is a good first step, but it is important not to get stuck there. Many people do.

The steady "pata pata pata" is a way to get your hands going, but it is not drumming in the best sense of the word. You need to take out notes before it becomes good drumming. Most people just get to the busy notes and never start to subtract unneeded notes. That's a shame for them and the group. It is a symptom of our mental state—lots of meaningless data that covers the groove.

In any beat there is the downbeat and there are accents. The other notes are unimportant and generally in the way, but many people insist on playing all the possible notes because it is a way to feel that they are on the beat. It keeps them on tempo. I call those little notes "training wheels," because they keep you on the clock. Playing all the little notes is a way to stay steady, but it gets in the way of the real groove. Also, no one else can play with you. You are not sharing the space.

The hardest thing is to play fewer notes. Take off the training wheels.

Okay. I admit I play a lot of training wheel notes, *but* they are very, very soft. Sometimes I need them to set up a cool accent that hits on my weaker left hand. I still use the "pata pata" notes, but they are as quiet as I can possibly make them.

I showed the woman a simple pattern (p. 207) that had only four notes in it. She habitually tried to play all the busy notes but I gently stopped her and asked her to listen again. I was playing only four notes. It just sounded like a lot more. She got it pretty quickly. The hard part was to break the habit of this continuous "pata pata pata." Once she could just hit the four notes, a new world opened up. The world of the space in a groove. She started to realize that the space was more important. Not the notes.

Some people *think* that what they are playing sounds good but what they are really playing isn't that good, it's just busy. Their minds are enhancing what their hands are doing. What results is chaos, with everyone playing those busy "pata pata" notes and not addressing just the accents, so it sounds like a freight train instead of a bubbling brook. The busyness hinders the groove.

Many guys refuse to play less. They can't let go of the master/warrior mind-set. I'm here to tell you that women drummers are many times better than the men, but they don't always have the same level of confidence.

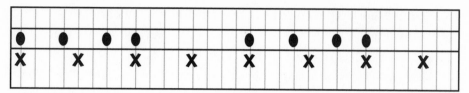

**Track 26: Four notes.**

By "better," I mean that women, and many men, too, can realize that they are playing too much. They start the mystical journey of subtraction from what they are playing and they arrive at an airy place where their few notes are crystal clear and perfectly adequate. They have no more anxiety about keeping up or keeping it up.

This young woman then asked me about the singer/songwriter she was trying to work with. He criticized her playing, but he couldn't tell her what was wrong. I said that would always be the case. They could tell you what they didn't like but they had no idea what the right part should be. She could deal with these guys by playing less and allowing them to have the breathing room to do their thing. They wanted the support of a drummer, but they didn't want the distraction of having one with a personality.

"Less is more," I repeated to her. Subtract notes until you are at the most basic pattern and that will probably be close to what the person wants to hear in their song.

As far as their bad taste goes, there is nothing you can do about that. You just are fulfilling the age-old job of being a drummer for someone else's ideas. That is fine. That is what a drummer does, but don't try to compete, it will only get you in trouble. Rather, serve them what they ordered, even if they don't know what it is. That is why Pop music is so simple. It leaves room for the star to do their thing and not feel crowded.

It was hard for this young woman to play only a few notes—it had been much easier for her to play a lot of notes. It is easy to play all the notes, but it is important to play only the necessary notes.

Here is a short, repeated phrase. That repetition is important to the trance, but let us look at the little notes or lines in between those numbers. I was taught to say, 1 de an da 2 de an da 1 de an da 2 de an da.

All those little notes are unnecessary to create a magickal trance. What is needed is just the *feel* of those little notes. The body and mind need the space in between the numbered downbeats for the magick to happen. This is also a big need in life. Space is needed in our lives and in our souls.

The first accent falls on "1" then the next accent falls on "da" and the next accent falls on the "an" of "2". Then the three accents repeat themselves.

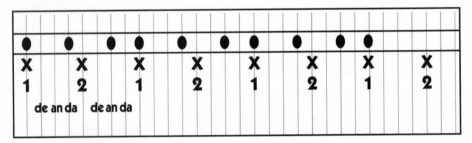

Track 28: Mambo? Maybe.

What happens with your hands is interesting. If you were to play all the notes, the second accent falls on your weaker hand (assuming that you started with your strong hand). When you hit the third accent, it will fall on your strong hand again. Then you start the sequence all over again. This is a way to develop your weaker hand. What matters here is the sequence of using both of your hands in an authoritative way.

Don't be hard on yourself. Just set up that pata pata (1 de an da 2 de an da 1 de an da 2 de an da) and let that become easy for you. Then start to think about accenting the notes I just described. First the downbeat, then that accent on your other hand, then back to your first hand. This alternating back and forth of your awareness is stimulating to your brain and it is also becoming a way to deprogram trauma in your soul. And you thought you were just learning to drum.

208

You will stumble and it will be awkward, but that's perfectly okay. It is on the road to enlightenment, so mistakes are minor events.

This subtraction of too many notes is important for people in order to work and live together, as well as play drums together. Some folks don't get it and think that drumming is hitting on all those notes and they don't have any concern for the space where other people might be able to fit in. Drumming can be a group experience that is transformational. Just don't fill up the space with notes. That is like covering the rain forest with a parking lot. The dancers need the space too.

Soloing is good in small amounts. Short fills are usually better than long drawn-out solos because the groove stays intact.

## Creatives

Calling myself a "Creative" was a form of self-defense. In this age of definitions, one's fate can be decided in the blink of an eye. I searched for a simple word that would convey who I was. If I didn't define myself first, then people would define me by their own yardstick, which was usually a few inches short.

When I said, "I am a Creative," to people in the movie biz in Hollywood, they nodded their head as if they had heard it a thousand times.

"You're a Creative? Sure. I heard of that. The question is, are you a Union Creative?"

What I was trying to convey to the person was a broad concept that had to be explained in the blink of an eye—otherwise, they would walk away and hire someone else.

Attention deficit was invented in Hollywood.

"Creative" implied that I was quick on my feet and had unique solutions. It meant that I could be versatile. It was better than the term "Artist," which had a negative connotation in people's minds: temperamental, moody, undependable. But my secret identity, as a "Drummer," was even more controversial than any other self-definition.

When certain film executives found out I was really a drummer, instead of a production manager, it made them nervous. They didn't think drummers were capable of doing anything but drumming. "Creative" was sort of vague. It means a lot of different things, so it didn't limit my own self-image too much. Most people define themselves and then stay right there within their own self-defined limitations. I wanted a self-image that was more inclusive of new procedures that all stemmed from the same place: the creative flow. None of the definitions mattered much, because underneath I always knew that I was a drummer. That was still a comfort while I was undercover as a Creative in the film biz.

One time, on the set of a TV shoot, I had to whip out a painting for a Polaroid commercial. Mariette Hartley would appear to be painting a landscape and Jim Garner would take a picture of her.

We bought a whole set of acrylic paints, with an easel and lots of brushes—the whole nine yards. We would *dress the scene* with as much art paraphernalia as possible. It was shot in the backyard of a big house in the Pacific Palisades. The distant hillside had been scorched in a recent brush fire. It didn't matter though. They would focus on the developing Polaroid photo with the landscape painting next to it.

I realized I had a choice. Either I could get very uptight about this and insist on being alone while I knocked out a landscape, or I could let the process happen on the set, with the crew working and the art director hovering nervously. Film crews are cynical—not a great crowd to paint in front of—but they also respect the ability to perform under pressure. They have to. That's why they get the big bucks.

I took a deep breath and put paint on the canvas, while forty-two people watched me out of the corner of their eyes as they worked. The art director immediately rolled his eyes and walked away in disgust. After a while the lighting director came over and very politely asked me what I was painting with. He was Ernesto Caparos, a very successful, older filmmaker from Cuba.

He had directed the first "talkie" in Cuba and had even dined with Batista at the Presidential Palace once, before Fidel came into power.

He had been part of this commercial director's team for many years. He was one reason their commercials always looked the best. He could see light and tell you how to shoot it to make it look good without using a light meter. He painted with light.

"Acrylics," I said as casually as I could. I was young and all these people were total pros. I had gone to art school, which had given me a somewhat self-conscious attitude toward art, but it had given me some technique too.

That is always a trade-off when being a Creative; either you *learn* how to do something, say it is drumming or writing or painting or weaving or whatever, but you also want to just *do it*, from a spontaneous place in your soul. That is always the pull in a personal creative moment. Balancing both creative methods seems to be the answer.

I tried to stay unself-conscious and focus on the painting, which was looking like a hideous landscape and would not work at all. I was being very critical in my unself-conscious approach. Ernesto noticed my dilemma, but didn't say anything directly. Instead, he offered a gracious solution.

"*Acrylicos . . .*" he said thoughtfully in his cultured Cuban accent. "Do you mind if I try them?"

"Sure," I nodded. "Go ahead."

He picked up a brush the way a wizard picks up their magick wand; with ease and confidence, like Toshiro Mifune picking up a samurai sword.

"Where can I test them?" the old man said innocently.

I gestured to the canvas. He nodded, gratefully acknowledging my deference to his age and grace.

He put brush to canvas with the lightest touch and a miracle appeared. It was as if his brush only thought about touching the canvas. A galloping horse appeared; its golden mane flowed in the breeze. Then with a quick touch he painted a beautiful woman riding bareback on the horse. It was in the lower right-hand corner, and it saved the whole canvas. I had never seen anyone paint with such ease and self-confidence.

"That's beautiful," I said.

"Thank you," he said, with his very Cuban politeness, and returned to his job of telling people where to hang lights and filters. I didn't touch the canvas. It was great. The art director came over and took a Polaroid picture and we watched it develop. He didn't like the color scheme so I painted the background until it looked okay, about ten shots later. It ended up with mostly primary colors, but that horse and rider always made the painting work, no matter what other crap I put on. It had a great energy of spirit, done with the proper amount of casual attention. I can do that on the drums, but painting is something else.

Paradiddle Cornfield: oil on canvas, 1987. Combines music and art in an autobiographical story that was part of the author's journey toward self-integration.

I tried for years to copy that sense of grace. I saw it again years later in the hills of northern Georgia. An old man, R. A. Miller, made tin folk art pieces and sold them in his front yard. He made whirligigs, and all sorts of plaques with sayings on them, adorned in his simple style with angels and devils, snakes and crosses. He was clever and had a great sense of humor. It was keeping him alive. I found out that he was almost blind, but that didn't matter, people came from all over. His work is in the House of Blues as well as in galleries in major cities. He is a real creative. He had lived in the same "holler" all his life (a holler is a wooded canyon sort of place) and he cut roofing tin with tin snips into the shapes of Elvis and devils and used house paint to embellish them. He had come to his art late in his life, but it was amazingly direct and honest. He had become famous and he couldn't care less. He just liked to meet people.

The creative flow is what keeps us alive.

When we can let it come through us without choking it off, it leaves something in its passing that we can cherish. That is like a blessing.

This energy can be strong. Sometimes people have not been able to handle the creative flow. It has been too strong for their minds or their bodies and their place in life. Energy management is the key to creative success. Drumming can give you evidence of this creative flow and you can manage it. It is a way to build a working model for letting the creative flow through your own life at a manageable rate. Drumming is adjusting the flow of creativity through your own soul.

In any kind of creativity there is ritual, whether it is addressing the four corners and thanking the Powers or cleaning your paint brushes. We seem to need ritual in our lives, although too many times we have empty ritual. With the drum, we can have a quick, meaningful ritual if need be, or a long-drawn-out, intense ritual.

I encourage some people to hit the drum when they come into our shop. They look like they need it. When they finally do hit the drum, no matter how soft or muffled, they get a charge out of it. They are the people that define the drums for the future. They are the ones who need it.

The heart seems to open up when the drum is played in this creative way.

The creative ritual can be one note on the drum or many notes. It can happen in a moment or it can come slowly, with great effort. The creative flow is its own master, but we can use it.

The creative flow in magickal rituals is what makes things happen. I'm not talking about Hollywood magick movies. I'm talking about deep, healing energy that is prayer. Magick and prayer are the same thing. There will be a time soon when the division of who can pray and who can conjure will be healed. The need for creative ritual magick is now. We need the drum to sing the songs that will heal the earth—songs we all can sing and pray to.

The interesting thing about being a creative is that you have a self-identity in most situations. Many people avoid going into new situations because they have no self-identity in that new realm. Being something as vague as a creative or as decisive as a drummer gave me enough self-confidence to try something new.

We are all creatives. Every one of us. Even the ones who say they aren't. Even the ones who insist that they don't want to be a creative. Creativity is a part of being human. We need ways for the creative energy to become evident in different types of people's lives. Drumming seems to work for that. Drumming works in the boardroom or the backroom, as well as in the woods or in the church.

## Quiet Drumming

People want to have a quiet moment with the drum—not just a loud moment. I have always been a proponent of quiet drumming. The first assumption by many people is that drumming has to be loud, fast, and busy. The opposite is also true.

Quiet drumming can be at the sound level of conversation. It *is* conversation. This kind of quiet drumming usually happens at the end of a loud drumming group when people still want to feel the good effects of drumming, but they are too tired to play hard. So they play softly. I prefer this. It would be nice to have that kind of drumming at the beginning of a drumming event, but most folks are too wound up to just play quietly. They want to use the drum to get rid of their anxiety and the frustrations of their daily lives.

Using a drum in that loud way is great fun, but it is also a crude way to use the tool. It's like using a Maserati for a pickup truck. The smooth, fast playing of a softer drumming group can be much more exhilarating than some of the loud groups I have been in. This is also where the magick lives—in a space where people can hear each other play. The exchange of Tantric energy between people who are listening and talking to each other is very uplifting. That isn't just an adrenaline rush, it is a soul rush.

A phrase came to me in a dream: "moral diffuser." In a sense, when we drum we can be a moral diffuser. We can fill the air with soul and life energy, like an aromatherapy diffuser sending healing aromas out into the air. I get the sensation of some type of energy rushing up and out of the drumming groups. It could be called auric energy or Tantric. I had my aura read and photographed after a drumming group and the chakras were very open and balanced. The woman reading the printout assumed I was a Reiki Master. I told her I was a drummer. She nodded with understanding. It seemed to make sense to her.

## Simplified Samba

Here is a part that can be played on a frame drum or a djembe. It is a simplified foundation Samba rhythm. This type of rhythm can be played underneath someone who wants to play a lot of notes. This pattern can be played slowly or faster depending on the mood. The person who is willing to play this simple part is very valuable and will hold the group together while others solo and play fast. The ones who play fast won't sound good unless a basic part such as this one is being played underneath. It will go on after the fast players have run out of energy.

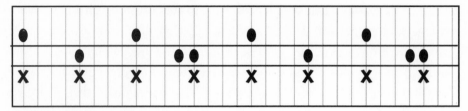

Track 29: Simple Samba.

The hardest drumming to do is quiet, steady drumming. If a person is willing to play the same drum pattern for ten minutes, they might be able to understand the real power of drumming. Most people cannot hold the same pattern of notes for ten minutes. It is an important meditation on the drum and leads one through the illusion of fast, busy playing to the enlightened playing of someone who uses only the cleanest notes to express the great mystery of life.

Repeat it as exactly as you can. Tap your foot if possible—it might help. Keep the basic pattern the same, but allow for subtle variations. Study the nuance of each beat as it comes around again and again. Study how it falls in relation to the downbeat and the groove. Each time it is slightly different because the rhythm is alive.

If it is boring to you, that could be a telling sign. You are probably living at a frantic pace and your mind is rejecting the concept of doing anything the same way for ten minutes. The body needs to slow down or risk a coronary, a nervous breakdown. Ten minutes can be an eternity when you try to do something like this but it is good for your mind and body to realize that ten minutes is a long time and a lot can be done.

We waste ten minutes in our lives quite often. This is something that will pull you into the present, into what is real, quicker than most meditations and with a better beat than most songs on the radio. You make the meditative groove and you get the benefit. It is a personal meditation that is a way to break through a lot of habits and assumptions about playing a drum and about being a person.

Do ten minutes of the same drum pattern, steady and quiet. When you can do that, then I bet you'll be able to solo better, too. It might have a positive effect in your life as well—better communication skills, social intercourse, and otherwise.

# My Favorite Things

This next pattern (p. 217) is a little shorter and has a more immediate feel. It has more drama in it because it has a quicker turn around. It can be counted in "3" if you need to give your brain something to do.

This might feel awkward, but when it gets up to speed, take out most of the downbeats, hitting only on the "One." It opens up into a lot of possibilities. In Jazz it is *My Favorite Things,* as performed by John Coltrane.

It is also an Eskimo Shaman rhythm and a Kachina Dance drumming pattern, a Mozart Waltz, and a Flamenco beat. It's an authentic earth beat.

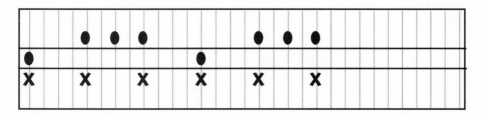

Track 30: Favorite.

# 22
# KEEP ROLLING

I was called in to play drums at a showcase for Rita's big debut in Hollywood. She had a great band of backup musicians. Some of the guys were from Muscle Shoals, Alabama; the place where Aretha Franklin cut those historic tracks like *Respect* and *Chain of Fools*. Roger Hawkins was playing drums on those tracks. They are historic events because he melded divergent cultural drumming styles into a great funky groove behind Aretha. Which means he was a white guy and he played drums on those great Soul tracks.

"He is a good ol' boy that took a left turn at the Blues," was the way Aretha Franklin's producer, Jerry Wexler, put it once.

Anybody from that part of the world is funky. I think it's the water. It was a real pleasure to play with this *phone band*. That's a group that is put together by telephone.

This showcase in Hollywood was a huge gay disco nightclub with a small club called Studio One in the "Back Lot" room. I flew into town to do the gig and had no idea what I was getting into.

The stage was black obsidian and as slick as glass. As we got into the music, the bass player standing next to me got excited and kicked over his beer. It spread into a slippery pool of foam under my drum stool. I was giving the count-off for *Put on Your Sailing Shoes*, a great song by Lowell George and Little Feet, when it happened.

Now, a count-off is the drummer's most important job. The drummer clicks his sticks together, then counts out loud, "One . . . two . . . three . . . four!"

Then hopefully the band starts the tune together. This count-off decides the fate of the song, and the future of the band. Without a good count off, the song flounders. The drummer is expected to know exactly what the correct tempo is supposed to be. If he counts it off too slow, the song dies a slow, horrible death. If the drummer counts it off too fast, the song explodes in nervous confusion and the singer sounds like a chipmunk. The band has implicit faith that the drummer will mysteriously know the exactly correct tempo for the song count-off. Don't ask me why. Maybe it's because the drummer doesn't have to know what key the song is in so he has extra brain room left over for at least remembering the right tempo. Maybe it is a reference back to an ancient trust in the village drummer to set the mood for ceremonial events.

As I was clicking my sticks together, and intoning those important numbers, everyone looked at me with great expectation. It was up to me.

"One . . . tw . . ."

My drum throne suddenly slipped out from underneath me on the wet glassy stage. I disappeared down behind my drum set, kicking a can of nails which hit a cymbal stand. The sound went straight into the mics, then out into the P.A. system, exploding into the nightclub like a ton of scrap metal being dumped onto the glittering crowd. I was flat on my back behind the drum set. My boots were sticking straight up in the air. Rita looked back at me in horror. Her big Hollywood debut was being ruined by . . . a drummer. She looked at me with that oldest of stage fright questions in her eyes,

"What do we do now?" she pleaded silently.

I twirled my fingers around each other in concentric circles in that ancient pantomime that all entertainers know. It means "Roll with it," or "Keep it rolling." Everyone knows what it means, even if they're not nightclub singers.

This gesture quite possibly started back in vaudeville or the circus, or before, when the most compelling moment in a show had arrived and the drummer was required to do a "roll."

The roll is the most attention-getting thing to do on a drum. It is a rush of notes played evenly and very, very fast. The two notes on each stick are actually played so quickly that it sounds like a solid buzzing. When a roll is played with a great deal of pressure and control it is called a "Buzz Roll" or a "Pressed Roll." This compelling event on a drum is used in the movies—when the soldiers start the attack, the president gives an executive order, or the hero makes a dire decision. That's the time the drums do a pressed roll.

The roll has always been a serious part of drumming. It is a no-nonsense kind of drumming. At the circus, the roll was used when the most dangerous of stunts was being attempted on the high wire act. In the military, the pressed roll is used to announce the presence of the highest ranking officers. It has always been equated with force; force applied in a massive way or threatening to be applied in a massive way. It is a very serious kind of drumming. In show business, a drummer was hired and fired on their ability to play a good pressed roll. Sometimes, they are required to play a pressed roll for a very long time.

Many times the announcer will say, "Ladies and gentlemen . . ." and then he will cue the drummer for a roll. The drummer starts the roll and cannot end the roll until the event has taken place and there is a cue for a climactic cymbal crash. Sometimes there is a hitch in the proceedings and the drummer is forced to play a long roll for a very, very, very, very, very long time. This is very hard on the drummer. The pressure in the fingers to force the roll to "buzz" intensely is very tiring because all the small muscles are tensed, allowing only the least bit of movement at a very fast rate.

Continuing the roll is imperative, because once the drummer has started the pressed roll, it is a signal to the audience that everything else must stop. Nothing is as important as a pressed roll. If the pressed roll stops and there is no special event, people get very upset. They are conditioned to respect a pressed roll—that is a worldwide phenomenon. So, the master of ceremonies keeps giving the signal for the drummer to keep it rolling . . . until the diva is dressed or the president gets his zipper up. Whatever the hitch, the drummer has to keep everyone focused on the impending momentous occasion—no matter how painful it is for their fingers and wrists. That's a drummer's job. This becomes a forced meditation. During the National Anthem at a football game, the drummers sometimes must play a roll for the length of the whole song—that's after they have been playing the pressed roll as an introduction to the song, getting everyone's attention in the football stadium. That can take a while.

It knocks me out that people want to be drummers and just wale without any sense of control. There is a discipline that most people are not interested in but that is a big part of drumming. I don't stress discipline but, as you have probably noticed, it is still there lurking underneath my good vibes and positive encouragements. I am glad that I went through this discipline. It gave me a working model for staying focused and willing to go past whatever limitations I might have set for myself. One worst-case scenario is marching with a heavy drum, and also rolling for a few miles while the baton twirlers do their thing under a hot sun. I am just making a point that there is a form of drumming that is very focused and strict but we do not have to have that mindset all the time. I would rather feel the groove and have fun, but I can still do a pressed roll if needed.

Meanwhile, back at the Back Lot, when Rita saw me give her that ancient symbol, she realized what she had to do. She had to improvise. After weeks of rehearsal, she had to do something unexpected. She had to roll with it. She turned to the audience and said, "Well, I guess I have to introduce my drummer now."

That got a big laugh. It saved her act. She laughed too. It broke the ice. From then on, our show was a piece of cake. We played looser and she sang better because the worst had already happened and we were still playing. It turned into a great show after all that tension was released. Sometimes we have to be really embarrassed before we do our best. Then we give up worrying about looking foolish and just play. I have been embarrassed too many times to let it slow me down much anymore.

Later on, in the dressing room, I was recovering from a little bit of chagrin when the door opened and Liberace came into the dressing room with his complete entourage. He was very nice to Rita, but then he came over to me and extended his bejeweled hand. There was a grand piano on his finger with a diamond candelabra on top of the piano. It was huge. He shook my hand.

"I just love your act," he said with a mischievous grin.

I was very surprised and sort of flattered. I thought I was invisible behind the drums. No one had ever mentioned "my act" before. I didn't think I had one, but here was Liberace telling me I had one, so I guess he ought to know.

He respected the ability to keep it rolling. He was an old trooper and he knew the value of being quick on your feet in a potentially embarrassing situation. Liberace also knew how hard it was to keep a pressed roll going for ten minutes and make it look easy.

After Liberace left, the Tuscaloosa, Alabama, organist in our band discreetly asked me to escort him to the men's room. He was too nervous to go in there alone. He said he needed someone to watch his back, otherwise "it wouldn't work." Good 'ol boys will still be good 'ol boys. I didn't mind watching his back at all. It was an honor. Some of the local boys from West Hollywood noticed what I was doing and had a good laugh about it.

## Witch Drum

I was invited to do a drumming event at a Pagan Halloween Samhain Sabat. It was great fun. We were in a dark old forest. There was a path through the woods that was lit by candles. We stayed close together as we tentatively moved through the darkness, wondering what was going to happen. Then, magically, candles appeared in the trees and we beheld a scene of fairy sprites and forest nymphs singing and swaying to an ethereal song. They were sensually luminescent in the moonlight as it filtered down through the dense ancient trees. It could have been any time in history. It was a timeless *Midsummer Night's Dream.*

Next we wandered down a hill and came to a low, boggy area where fog was settling over the gnarled tree roots. In the shadows, at the foot of an old oak tree, the fog parted and a figure rose up out of the leaves to reveal a marvelously terrifying tree/beast that groaned and lumbered toward us. It was so real that we screamed and ran on to the next vignette in the forest. There were several wonderfully magical events in the forest that made us wonder in awe at the imaginings of this gifted coven of devotees of the Craft.

Then for a finale, they burned a strawman hanging from a tree limb. It eventually fell in the water and floated down the creek. Everyone gathered on the rocks and lit a huge bonfire. This was the culmination of all their preparation. They were ready to dance around the fire and celebrate the Pagan High Holiday. I watched as the local drummers struggled to get going.

They generated a lot of noise. Everyone wanted to dance. Everyone knew they were supposed to dance, but the drumbeat was not danceable. It was not a dance rhythm at all. The guys who were drumming had no idea how to get the girls to dance. They just bashed away and the girls stood around and waited, all dressed up and with nowhere to go.

Finally, I requested that the leader, a nice, but stiff fellow on conga drums, take a break, and I would try something. He reluctantly acquiesced. I kept my eyes on the dancers, and suggested a beat. They started to respond a little bit. I coaxed it more in their direction. A drummer can tell what kind of beat will work if they pay attention to the dancers. If they dance, then you are on the right track. If they stop, you know you have lost them and you must simplify to a rhythm that they will like. Never mind about the authentic rhythms you learned from some video tape. Look at the girls' hips! If they are moving, then you are *right*. If they are not moving, then simplify and try something else. Usually, the drummers are playing too much. They are showing off. That is really the wrong way to go at this stuff.

This kind of dance is sacred. It must be supported by the drummers. It is not a time to show off. This is the most important ceremony for drummers and it must be geared for the dance. Otherwise there is no magick.

Can ceremonies be made more effective? Can important dance events have more power with joyous, sensual, evocative sacred dancing? The drum is there for the sacred dance. It is not intended to be a way for guys to just show off. That is our liability that we are working through in this culture. When we can free ourselves from this nagging self-consciousness, then the Universal magick can come through us. The drummer feels the energy and watches the dancers and pumps the rhythm through just as humbly as possible. Anything else is just show bizness.

The drummers got on the right groove and everything worked out fine, but the drummers needed prompting all the way through. That is one reason I am doing the drumming workshops—to get people to feel the beat enough so that they can create their own ceremony. That Halloween ceremony convinced me that we can do great and powerful things when we let the dance and the drum take us.

The drummer needs the dancer. The dancer completes the cycle of energy for the drummer. Otherwise it tends to get intellectual.

Every culture uses drums for magick. We have been separated from our magick rhythms but we are finding them again. It is not only Wicca, Celtic, Pagan, or Christian, or any one thing—it is a mix of all these things and more. It is the combining of the intellect with the heartbeat. It is a new, yet ancient way for us to worship.

Science is magick. Magick is science. A chip processor is magick. The primitive drum is science, but essentially the drum has always been a magickal tool.

The pulse is what carries the intent. Not a metronome type of pulse but a heart and body-feeling kind of pulse.

We are reconnecting to our intuitive sense of rhythm, and it's about time. We must listen to and play what the earth is telling us. This is important for our survival as Gaia—the world consciousness.

We are in a rhythmic state of shock though, so it is important to take it gradually. Too much too soon and people go crazy. Best to take it slowly. Stay in the pocket. Keep relaxed.

Dance beats are always relaxed—even if they are played fast. Relaxed beats mean playing back in the pocket, laid-back, behind the metronome, sloppy, late to the downbeat. It leaves room for the dancer to move. Without space in a rhythm, the dancer has no room to move. The dancer responds to the space, not the busy licks. A few well-placed licks may stimulate the groove, but sustained noodling will kill the groove and the dancers will falter. The drummer must integrate him- or herself with the dancers' needs. That is hard for some guys who want to be the top dog.

Magickal spells are grooves. They repeat and they go on for a long time. If the spells are grooves with real, deep feel, then you have real magickal power. The groove carries the spell. We need to discover the natural grooves in our souls. They tell us what magick is.

A magickal groove is a function of moving. If you can tap your foot and nod your head, then you're in the pocket. If you are not moving some part of your body, then you have to try something else. Just don't stop. When you try a new drumming groove, the Universe can change in an instant and become your friend. Suddenly the spell works when the groove works too.

Looking for the groove—getting to the groove—is what all the drumming is about. When you finally get to the groove, everyone should simplify their playing and not overplay. That happens when we get excited. We find a groove, then get excited and play too much and lose the groove. That is very much like sex. Remember to simplify when you arrive at the groove—no matter where it is. Don't get so excited that you blow the feel. Your partners, whether they are dancers or lovers, will respond to that thoughtfulness.

Relax; let everyone find a simple part that is easy to play for a long time. When this groove is open and stable, then the magick can begin.

The groove can step up a bit in intensity, but should not peak too quickly. The gradual building of emotional energy is a timed event. It should peak when all the people are grooving together. They don't have to be working hard—it's better if you're not working hard. It works when you just let it happen. Focused magickal intentions work like water does—it gets there in it's own time. Forcing it will clog the pipes.

When the sacred event takes place, the energy output should not be nervous or angry. It is the highest state of human consciousness—the closest we can get to Creation. We are linked to the Universal Mind. The drumming energy should not get lost at this point. It can be intense, but not necessarily loud. It can be done as softly as a cricket. The spell will still carry, sometimes better than playing loud.

Winding down is important. Coming down from a high plateau of consciousness can be very unstable sometimes. The drum makes reentry easier, so keep the drum going. If it is in rhythm, then the consciousness is welcomed back from its journey with a gentle homecoming. We should try to make these landings from another realm as soft as possible, so that the experience is not jarring.

*How do you keep a drummer in suspense?*

*Keep the beat going, and I'll tell you.*

The final integrating drumbeat at the end of the whole ceremony should be very comforting. Loud drumming is not always a good way to end a ceremony. It can initiate a psychotic break and should be avoided. We need to integrate our magickal experience with our earthly mindset in a harmonious way so that we can do it again.

## Events

Sacred events are important for the growth of new ceremony. We are looking for a ceremony that works for all of us. Something that connects us to the Divine, creative source of life. Drumming has been used in every religious practice so let's take a look at this eternal sideman; the drum.

By being a contributor to so many different kinds of ecstatic dances, the drum itself must have some wisdom. Being open enough to receive it is a challenge. The drum opens us up. To what?

To ourselves—both in a small way and a big way. In a small way by bringing the mind down into the body with a deep resonant pulse. This can become narcissistic and a self-centered way to drum. That can be appropriate at times but it diminishes the group if people go too far into themselves.

The drum opens you up in a big way to the inspired potential of creating your own Universe. By playing, you create. By playing with others you create something greater than the sum of the parts. Events happening in our future, when we get good at drumming together, can only be imagined. Focused drumming has always been a staple of indigenous cultures. When our civilized culture figures out how to do group drumming then I think there is great hope for all of us.

Creating a profound event is important for changing the minds of the people. Special events can be transcendent or they can be manipulated and only seem to be real. We need the real thing. Ceremonial drumming can be great bashing or intriguing light rhythms. The lighter rhythms hold people's attention in a different and dramatic way. Space defines the scope of the mystery in an event. Drums define the space. Subtle drums can create a large space just as well as loud drums do.

I read about Albert Speer when I was an impressionable teenager. Speer was Adolf Hitler's architect and event organizer. The pictures of the arenas he created were terrible and awesome. Banners rose high into the night sky, illuminated from below by huge searchlights shooting up into the darkness. The Swastika emblem that the Nazis used was stolen. I was told that the original emblem was that of Jain, which became Tibetan Buddhism; the oldest philosophy of peace in the world. The Nazis turned it around and used it for their own evil purposes. It flows in the other direction. Be very careful with symbols. They have power, even if they are reversed. Symbols and drums together are a very potent way to influence people's feelings.

We need events that are real, holy, and transcendent. There are too many fake events that use the drums to force us to feel something that we do not feel; like movies about Armageddon and phony heroes. That really scares me.

# Nine-Stroke Roll

Here is a roll that can either scare or inspire you, depending on when and where it is played. This important ceremonial drum roll is used in many different cultures. When it is done right, the hairs on the back of your neck will stand straight up.

Here, have a roll; a nine-stroke roll.

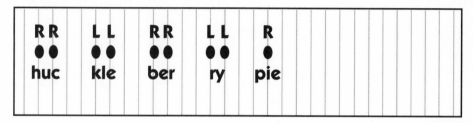

Track 31: Nine-stroke roll.

This is a roll done with two sticks, mallets, or pencils. Do NOT do this with just your hands. Hit the drumhead with two notes with each stick. Start very slowly. Bounce two notes on each hand. Say the word, using a syllable for each set of bounced notes: "Huckleberry Pie."

Now play it faster.

Let the bounce of the sticks create the two notes. Stay relaxed. Try it a bit faster. Let the drumhead bounce the sticks for you as you go faster. The faster you go, the more relaxed you need to be. Let the drumhead do the bouncing. When you can play it as fast as you can say it, then we're rolling!

# 23
# WHY WE'RE HERE

I don't know about you, but I have wondered about the meaning of life many times in my short span of years. Usually when something isn't going my way.

I tried past-life regression. I checked out some of the cults. I read Aleister Crowley; I studied Alan Watts, Gurdieff, and Colin Wilson. I read books on mysticism and Tantra. I studied the deep trances of indigenous cultures. I went to those really embarrassing seminars run by people in cheap suits that last for a week and they don't let you go to the bathroom.

I didn't want to do these things. People around me asked me to. They begged me to do something. I was not a happy camper. The friends that knew me were patient. I wasn't an alcoholic or a drug addict. I was just a drummer without a cause.

Christian Gandhi, the keyboard player in The Asylum, was born in Jaipur, India, and grew up in Harlem. He had one of the heaviest attitudes I have ever seen. He was also an accomplished Jazz musician on piano, flute, trombone, and percussion. His chordal voicings were so mysterious and indelible that I am still trying to figure them out, many years later. He was a very mystical person. He was also mysterious. No one really knew him, even though we lived and worked together for many years that were musically formative for me and the culture.

He showed me a lot of music. I say "showed" instead of "taught," because it is taking a lifetime to learn what he showed me. Drumming is like that. You don't ever figure it all out. There is always something else to discover. I have come back to it after seeking success and enlightenment in many other fields. And when I do come back, I know that I am coming "back to the Well," as Christian used to put it. It is a source of comfort for me.

He was a mystical teacher as well as a musical teacher. There is a great tradition of mystical musicians. I am just realizing that music is a way to gain some enlightenment. It is a source of wisdom. The lessons, and the teachers can be confusing sometimes, but each one of us can make sounds and share the creative spirit. That is a form of enlightenment. It is important to remember that it is a personal journey and that no one else can tell you what is right or wrong, although we must be humble to learn. People do not like to feel humbled, but when we study an inspirational art, an uncontrolled ego must learn restraint.

Christian sang percussion parts to me that I could not understand. He was patient, but would put up with absolutely no bullshit. His art was his life and he had little patience with anyone who was not as committed to their own inspiration.

Many years after we parted company, I was at a dinner party in Monterey, California. As I was returning from the dining room to the living room, a Gypsy psychic woman stopped me and said that I had someone behind me that was very powerful. She described him in great detail. He was a unique-looking person.

Then she asked me, "Is he alive? Or is he dead?"

I had no way to know. He was ineffable in death as well as in life.

He gave me insight into worlds that I would not have known otherwise. He gave me music that I would not have heard or played in my life. Music does that. It can be a great adventure for your spiritual growth. Its pathways are infinitely unique. That is why I try to encourage people to have a pleasurable experience with drumming and music. It opens us up to worlds that we do not know exist.

The simple act of hitting a drum puts us in touch with mystery and magic and wisdom. The hard part is letting ourselves do it. The journey afterward is to understand what the experience really meant. That can give us meaning in our lives.

## Where's the Melody?

We had a good group last night. I put a new flyer in the window explaining what we are doing as "Drumming Meditation Workshops."

That should confuse everybody.

I wanted to make a distinction between the over-the-top bashing that most groups end up with and the quiet grooves that we are discovering.

The group last night was an energetic crew: four women and two men. One father came in with his twenty-something daughter. The other man was a therapist and had been a regular for sometime. The grooves settled in quickly and we decided to maintain very long meditations. As the groove became more solid, people smiled and closed their eyes. They would nod in agreement like they were sharing a good story. The drums were not too loud, everyone could hear each other. The deep notes from the middle of the djembe heads made the downbeats strong, yet it was swinging because people were hearing the upbeats. I laugh at moments like that because everybody has their eyes closed and is deeply entrancing themselves. They were totally unself-conscious, like innocent babies.

People walked by on the street; it was a Friday night. They hung for a while and enjoyed the smooth, low-volume groove coming out of our little store. A couple gently came up to the open front door and listened for the longest time. Eventually they stepped in the front door and listened attentively. I could tell the guy wanted to drum, but he was restraining himself. He finally couldn't stand it any longer and started to do the "pata pata pata" on a conga drum that was standing in front of him. It didn't really fit and everybody came out of their trance, but the beat kept going.

I decided to get up and get a glass of water. I get up and walk away from the beat once in a while to make people carry the beat on their own. Sometimes they keep it going pretty good. This time, though, it finally ground to a halt.

The guy realized he had interrupted something, but he could not tell what it was. I explained briefly that we were just playing very simply. The guy and his wife smiled apologetically and left. I had to resolve myself to that. I was sorry that it had been embarrassing for them.

The next day the couple came in and said hello. They were very nice. I explained that it was a *meditation* kind of drumming where there wasn't a lot of soloing.

"That's what was so puzzling to me." he smiled. "It sounded great. There was a nice solid bass line and all this room in the groove. I wondered why there wasn't any melody on top."

I explained why there wasn't a "melody on top"; the melody can distract from the meditative groove. We are conditioned in this culture to expect a melody over a groove, that is a musical way to enjoy music, but a meditative drumming group is not necessarily playing "music". The trance is of course perfect for a melody; it can be entrancing but it can also keep the mind of the listener so entertained that the power of the magickal meditation is over-whelmed. I love melody. "No melody" is a hard concept to understand some-times, but he understood right away. His wife did too. She liked the supportive environment for the women. She was more lit up than he was, once they understood the process.

I didn't want to tell him that most of the soloing doesn't really fit that well anyway. Guys can be so delicate; they can turn morose if their ego is wounded. But so many can't even hold the basic pattern. Why in the world would their soloing be of any consequence if they can't do the basics?

I know this is brutal, but it's the truth. Most guys think that soloing is like dessert at their mother's dinner table. They forget they have to eat their vegetables first. I'm always searching for people who can really maintain a basic simple pattern. I will hold a pattern and most people will jump on the groove and take a free ride. Meanwhile I am waiting for someone to hold the basic pattern steady so that I can cut loose a little bit.

I do enjoy soloing, sometimes, but I don't *have* to do it. I had years of soloing. It doesn't hold the same mystique for me that it does for some. Usually the groove in other drumming groups is so boisterous that it is pointless for me to solo. I can't even hear it, so why bother.

I content myself with doing short little groove-based solo licks at the end of a phrase (a four-bar or eight-bar phrase) This serves two functions: I get to get my licks off, and it also gives the groove a little bump of excitement—just enough to keep it going and stay interesting. Not too much that would put it into the realm of self-centered showoff. This is a matter of taste, of course.

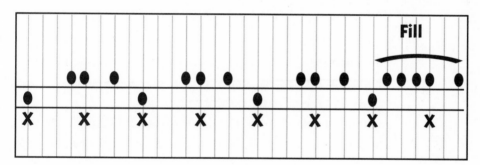

Track 32: Fills.

When we finished the drumming group last night, some of the people said that they heard melody wafting on top of our drumming grooves. The melodies are there, they are part of the fabric of reality. If we hit the groove just right, then music that has been played in that same groove will sympathetically vibrate. Music never dies, it goes on forever. Each person hears their own melodies. Sometimes we all hear the same melody.

When we understand that it is important to play simply and supportively, then the groove becomes powerfully seductive and very fun. The reality is that when we learn how to play this way, we become the good group drummers that we want to be. Then our soloing is great because it is appropriate.

## Two Different Worlds

There seems to be a fear among certain personality types about *surrendering* to the beat. They see it in terms of the individual versus community.

In a drumming group, people are gently introduced into the group consciousness. This can be scary because we are so inclined to be individuals. Our society is based on the rugged individual. Our history is about the unique heroes and heroines of our cultures.

Indigenous cultures see themselves as a tribe, a community where all are related to each other. In our culture we are not related—we are often at odds with some of our community members.

*What's the range of an electric bass guitar?*

*Twenty yards for most heavy metal drummers, if they unplug it first.*

The drumming group brings everyone into a group consciousness— out of their personal point of view into a larger perspective that might seem to obliterate the individual but in reality, makes the individual very strong. Everything is stronger if it knows that it is part of a greater whole.

Simultaneous drumming happens when the group becomes a community. People play exactly the same lick without even trying to do it. The group mind takes over.

Don't worry. When you are done, you can regain your individuality, but you have had the experience of sharing in a greater whole.

The drumming group can expand outward toward the Cosmos as a single entity, a single consciousness. Then it can accomplish whatever is desired. It can be a gentle blessing of rhythm, or a powerful thrashing of elemental forces, but it is done as a group. That group sensibility is what we are not used to and even fear, but it is something to cherish. It is where we can feel that we belong. We belong to a greater group than just ourselves. We are also mentally safer in that group.

The challenge is to make the group sound. Then translate that into life in a meaningful way. The drum provides a way to understand the energies with which we must live and work. The drums show us how to use the energies of the Universe for our own good intentions. The drum is a tool and a friend to both the rugged individualist and the members of the group. It is a tool that brings these two very different personalities together in a harmonious way.

The drum is a bridge between our hearts.

## One More Past Life

In one of my past-life regressions conducted by Rebecca Stacey, I was a fur trader, paddling a canoe along a clear river. I arrived at my favorite Indian encampment to trade for their fine furs. I was looking forward to seeing a young woman who was a member of the tribe. We had grown very close over the last few visits.

I had learned of a great danger. There was military activity being planned in the area. I urged the tribe to pick up their tents and move to a safer place but they could not. This was their land. I tried to persuade the young Indian maiden to leave with me. She would be safe and we would be together. She could not even imagine leaving her tribe. It was a hard concept for the trader to accept. She would rather perish with her own tribe than to be separated from them.

The remainder of this trader's life was spent pondering the great mystery of that sad lesson. Their tribal consciousness was the most important thing in their lives, like a big white cloud that they all shared. The trader was European in heritage and his individual identity had been very highly developed. He could not understand why she would not leave with him. He felt a great longing for her, but he also longed to understand that feeling of being included in a group consciousness.

Today, in the drumming workshops, I gently guide us into a a group consciousness. I respect our individuality, but we are also part of a great family of life. We are hungry to feel the Tribal Mind.

# 24
# LEAVING LAS VEGAS

This reminiscence was prompted by a visit from Michael, a nice young gentleman from Guatemala, who came into the store and wanted to say hello after reading my book, *Drumming the Spirit to Life*. He was returning to his home country after attending a drumming facilitator's retreat in Hawaii, and he was on fire with the passion of drumming.

He asked me questions and I tried to answer them, respecting his sincerity. Normally I'm not that interested in talking about myself.

But he asked me, "Was there a moment in your life when you 'got it'; when you became aware of something . . . special? When did you realize whatever you realized? Was it a unique moment?"

He seemed to be asking me if there had been a moment of enlightenment in my life. It caught me off guard. At first, all I said was, "The Mystic seems to be a personality type."

I could see the same questing nature in him, but it made me think about moments of enlightenment in our lives.

Drummers can always improve. That is what keeps it fresh. Life lessons can be shown on the drum so the drum is always a teacher. Many years ago, I did a Country-Western gig in Las Vegas for a few weeks, across the

239

street from Frank Sinatra's place, Caesar's Palace. I told the less than scintillating front man that he should, "Talk it up—make jokes. It's Las Vegas. The people want a show. Don't just stand there and play *On the Road Again* for the millionth time. Make it fresh."

"Well, if you want to talk so much . . . then here," He drawled.

He put the mic in front of me. That wasn't easy. I was sitting behind my drum set on a six-foot-tall drum riser platform. I finally got it situated between my legs the way I had seen Jerry Lee Lewis put the mic between his legs while he sang at the piano.

The bass player, Jan, had been in my high school Rock 'n' Roll band. Old musician friends are a treat to play with because you can see how their life has changed based on how their playing has changed. Our high-school Rock band had opened for Jerry Lee Lewis in Florida. He was incredible to watch; a torrent of joyous, libidinous, sexual energy blasting through that Southern Christian upbringing with his relentless pagan beat.

*"Moments of enlightenment can be like your in-laws. . . . They come when you're not expecting them and sometimes they never leave."*

—*The Legendary Psychic Cowboy*

I wasn't Jerry Lee, but it was Las Vegas, so I sang a few tunes anyway. *Act Naturally* was particularly rousing. I had blonde dyed hair with dark roots at the time. I had been in L.A., playing in punk bands, and had even done a movie. The dark roots were beginning to show through quite a bit.

I felt like I had the first punk haircut in Las Vegas; 1981. I had worked with this Country band a month earlier. The leader had assumed I was a real blonde then. He had just called and said to meet them in Las Vegas in two weeks. When he saw my two-tone punk hair, he took the ten-gallon cowboy hat off his head and gave it to me. "*You* wear the hat," he said.

A family from the Midwest was sitting at the next table, eating those famous Las Vegas $1.95 breakfasts. They actually said out loud, "That is the ugliest haircut I have *ever* seen!"

To me, it was just show bizness. Soon there would be many colorful hairdos here. It was a natural for Vegas. I just happened to be early. The movie I did a scene in was called *Jekyl and Hyde . . . Together Again*. I played the drummer in a punk band called The Shitty Rainbows. Now, that was a real piece of art.

Even in Las Vegas, the only thing that mattered was the music. We played great and had a good time.

When it came time for us to take a break, I kicked into the break song. I played this little Country Jazz shuffle beat, ala Bob Wills and the Texas Play-boys. My right stick was riding lightly on the Ride cymbal, playing that standard Jazz lick that everybody knows when they hear it.

My left hand was popping the snare drum on the upbeats, keeping the feel bouncing along. My right foot was just hitting the bass drum on the down-beat—nothing fancy. My left foot was stepping on the HiHat, shutting the two cymbals together every other upbeat—what the hell, I had to make it interesting for myself somehow.

Drumming in a Country-Western band is not the height of excitement sometimes, so I would hide my clever little drumming jokes inside the basic beat by playing around with the HiHat. I would play an official Country beat but underneath it was the merest hint of a Samba. It was my perverse sense of humor, I suppose.

The leader would turn around and look at me with fear. I would settle back into the basic Country beat and pretend that nothing was wrong. It was starting to get to him. Anyway, all this was going on and the band was playing our break tune, but . . . nobody was talking to the audience!

*We* had to inform the audience that *we* were leaving the stage for our union-ordained fifteen-minute break. The visitors from the Midwest were expecting to sit there and listen to more tunes before they went back to the slot machines. If we just walked off the stage it would be rude. The guys in this band were nice, but a little short on the "Entertainer" thing, so I started to talk on the microphone that was sticking up between my legs. "Okay! It's time. . . ."

That's when my life changed.

I froze up.

It was one of the few times that something had been impossible for me to do on the drums. I could not talk and drum at the same time.

I could sing, but I could not talk. It was a very strange sensation. I ended up speaking in broken syllables, "We-are-now-go-ing-to-take-a-lit-tle-break!"

Each time I hit the drum I could say a word but I could not speak when I wasn't hitting a drum. It was the most amazing sensation in my career. I realized that my mind was locked up to my hands in the wrong way for me to talk and play drums at the same time. Singing was okay, but talking and drumming did not work! Amazing!

Now I've had amazing experiences playing the drums. Once I almost choked myself to death on my own very long hair while chewing gum and playing a drum solo. But that's another story.

Anyway, here in Las Vegas, I was stopping each time I hit the drum and then talksing. The audience thought it was a bit odd.

Amazing! Something that I could not do. So . . . I quit show bizness.

That was nothing new. I had quit before. It was not that fulfilling anymore.

My life changed. I did anything but play music: film and TV production, computer graphics, archivist at the Playboy channel (it was a dirty job and I got to do it), teaching, writing, sculpture, retail, importing, the list went on and on, but in the back of my mind was this nagging fact that something was not working right. It had to do with drumming and it had to do with who I wanted to be.

Back in Las Vegas, I had decided to create a personality for the stage: "The Legendary Psychic Cowboy." It was actually a tribute to "The Legendary Stardust Cowboy" who is the most amazing Country-Western singer I have ever heard. You could maybe call his style "Transcendental Yodeling"; sort of like the sacred Persian singer Nusrat Fateh Ali Khan mixed with Kentucky Bluegrass or Johnny Cash's band on a bad night. I mean no disrespect to either style of music. Hearing the Legendary Stardust Cowboy's singing redefined Country-Western music for me.

The Legendary Psychic Cowboy could have been a hilarious *bit* as they say in Vaudeville. When I had the mic in front of me, I tried to be incorrigible, like other Vegas comedians, but my heart wasn't in it. Between the songs, I would get up the courage and pretend to get an emanation from people in the audience. I would then make up outrageous things about them. They could not deny it because they were in the audience—without the microphone.

Lenny Bruce had made that point clear decades earlier—whoever has the microphone has the power. When that microphone was put in front of me, I realized that I had to either put up or shut up. It beckoned to me like a great challenge deep in my soul.

"Go ahead," I heard a little voice say. "Go ahead and talk. You have the power."

The Legendary Psychic Cowboy seemed like a funny idea, but inside of it was a seed. What needed to be done with the drum was more than just backing up Willie Nelson songs, even though that is an honorable and very enjoyable profession. But there was something else, just this one thing, that prevented me from being the working drummer that I thought I was supposed to be; I couldn't talk and drum at the same time. That meant something to me, but I had no idea what.

*How many drummers does it take to screw in a lightbulb?*

*Twenty-one. One to screw it in and twenty to tell him that he's doing it wrong.*

I knew that my playing had changed over the years, it was a result of practice and learning but it was also mystical learning that had changed my drumming. The mystical side of drumming always had to take second chair, while the working drummer sat in the first chair position and made the decisions and the money. That is a Classical European approach to playing music.

The drum has always been a barometer of my soul. It has told me where I am, in this life. It shows me what I can do, based on what I have learned in this life—not just as a musician but as a human being.

Christian used to explain that a person's playing was the only truthful thing about them sometimes.

"People can talk a lot, but the truth comes out when they get up on the bandstand and play. You can't fake that."

243

Years passed on the calendar like so many old Ted Turner movies blowing in the wind. Then one day, about six months after we had returned from Bali, a gray-haired woman came into the store and said, "I want to play the drum . . . but I don't want to learn a lot."

A bell went off in my head. Of course! People want to play from their hearts, not just their minds. I knew there was a difference. I had discovered along the way that I too had a heart. I threw out all my years of Classical music training and showed her how to hit the drum. No technique, just play and feel. She got it immediately, and came back for several lessons in our backyard. She bought a set of clay derbougas from us.

They were pretty drums with Arabic designs on them, tied together with goatskin thread, and they had goatskin heads. They were Arabic bongos. She got good and played what she wanted to play. She started a women's drumming group of her own. One day we were quietly playing outside in the backyard and Phyllis said, "You should record this."

The shade from the old eucalyptus trees protected us from the bright California sun as we quietly drummed behind the store.

"Why do you say that?" I asked.

"You're talking while you're playing the drum. It's interesting."

I was dumbstruck. My whole life hiccuped in front of me. It was a quietly amazing event. We just kept playing.

"Why is it interesting?" I managed to say while I was slipping into the realization that I had been talking and drumming.

"The stories," she said, hitting the drum softly. "About the drum. They're interesting. . . . It helps."

I figured we had better record the lessons. I had no idea what was going on. She got to keep all those tapes. I just listened a little bit to check them. More importantly, I woke up to the rest of my life. It had taken many years for this mysterious, mystical drumming lesson to get through to me. I have a very hard head.

So recently, when Michael, the young man from Guatemala, asked me: "Was there a moment of enlightenment?" I can answer now.

I didn't get enlightened. I released something. I lightened the load I was carrying. I threw out a whole lot when Phyllis asked me to show her how to just hit the drum and nothing more.

I had been throwing off a lot of psychological baggage over the years, anyway, because I knew someday it would weigh me down too much, but it didn't really make a difference until I gave my *lightened* personality a chance to come alive when I was being unselfish. I gave something freely—something which I had previously thought was too precious to ever give up. When my heart opened, I was *lightened up*. When we give from our hearts we can become enlightened.

But I don't expect this kind of enlightenment to last. It is based on doing. When there is a flow of giving and also a receiving of love and respect, then there is a sense of light. That isn't always an easy state of mind to be in, but the meditative drumming helps. It puts me and the others into a state of mindfulness where we can let go of whatever is bothering us. It isn't angry or traumatic. It is a peaceful release, and I think that is the most powerful event on the drums for me. I have seen other people release the parts of their lives that have been weighing them down. I don't know the specifics of their past, and it doesn't matter. I have witnessed this release when the drumming groove is gently persuasive. That is why I am helping people get into the gentle grooves. If we can release our past, then we are free to make the future.

# 25

# OUR BODY TALKING TO US

**O**ur body is trying to find ways to talk to our brains. It is desperately trying to communicate its condition and needs, but seldom does the brain listen or care what the body is saying. That is a separation.

Muscle resistance is a fascinating way to listen to our bodies. It tells us whether a medication is good for us just by the resistance of our outstretched arm.

Our bodies are calling out to us and we're not listening. Dancing is a way to feel our body's needs. Drumming is a language that our body can use to tell our brain important information about our state of health, relaxation, and healing—if we can listen.

## The Future: Let the World Begin

The drumming that will happen in the future will be a celebration of our shared culture and our shared experiences here on our home planet as well as a celebration of the unique cultures we have. The drumming that we struggle with today will be our sacramental invocations for the future.

Just what kind of future is it going to be?

The Dark Ages are hopefully over. Civilization is just beginning. I know we all thought that civilization had already been here for quite a while, but I think that we are now just beginning to be civilized.

The various cultures around the world are struggling to survive. The world order is taking over, and the subtleties of many indigenous cultures are being eliminated. That isn't a good thing, That reduces the human experience. Indigenous cultures have a great secret to show the rest of the world, not only with their healing ways but with their ability to function as a community. Benjamin Franklin based the American Constitution on the Iroquois League's constitution.

Cultures are clashing because they do not want to lose their identity and do not want to adopt the mindset of a ruling group of businessmen. The world is shrinking and we are feeling the smallness of our planet.

The drum is a way for us to discover the new world community and to share in it. The isolated individual is now being absorbed into a world consciousness at a surprising rate. So when you play a drum, think of all the people that are also playing and feeling. The groove is our family.

What if, in the distant future, historians see our era as the last of the Dark Ages? What if we are finally seeing the beginning of civilization, after countless years of bloody antagonism? Can we handle this new world view? We must. Can we save ourselves and the planet from pollution and war? Yes. There may be people who refuse to accept a positive new world community for opposing reasons, but the truth is that we are being forced by evolution into a new mindset—a mindset that has never been a part of the human experience before. That is why I stress that we need to be flexible in our attitudes. Get ready for the next shift. That is what improvising is all about. Keep it rolling, baby.

In the beginning part of this book, I suggested a song, *Mother Earth We Sing, Let the World Begin.*

What if the world is just beginning? What if we are just waking up from a fitful sleep full of disturbing images, into a life that is a family? What if our

Dreamtime is now over? This family includes not only humans, but everything of the planet.

The Gaia consciousness is where we are headed. We are realizing that we are a functioning part of a large community, not only humans but everything that is alive. Our individual minds are feeding into a greater mind that is our planet. The thoughts that we create in our own minds are the reality that is created in our world. We are the makers of our own world. We are the protectors of our own world. Our thoughts make things real. The drums are very powerful tools that can turn thoughts into action.

Our internet is a model of the next world consciousness that is now upon us. We talk to people all over the planet. That is the beginning of civilization. When we sing , dance, and play our prayers to the Earth, we share in the Gaia Beat. We are the Gaia Tribe—the Gaia World/Beat.

The drum creates that sense of belonging and it becomes a song that we all can sing and play and dance to.

## About the CD

The lessons on the CD are short explanations of rhythm theories. It would be nice to have a CD where the grooves could last for twenty minutes, but for now, you will have to listen to the short samples and try the basic parts yourself, with your friends.

I have tried to avoid the intellectual traps of thinking too much about what you are learning and instead focusing on enjoying the learning process. This is only one way of learning to drum. There are many different ways to get to the same grooves and improvisational concepts. I hope this will illuminate the path for you as a drummer and a human being. Just don't be afraid, because there have been many other people like yourself on this path. It is a rewarding trip and a great adventure that will never end.

The grooves go on forever.

# Appendix 1

# INJURIES

ere are a few remedies or techniques for alleviating some of the typical injuries that people sustain while drumming:

The angled drumhead is important. The tone can come out the bottom. If you're interested in the drum stand, let me know. If you're interested in the leopard pants, talk to Kim.

*Chapped hands:* Use Sheabutter, if available. It is useful on the drum too; both on the wood and in small amounts on the head.

*Elbow soreness:* Tilt the drumhead away from you (left). This will change the angle at which your arms swing downward and will ease the strain on your wrists and elbows.

*Deafness and ringing ears:* Play softer, use earplugs. Ginko biloba sometimes helps tinnitis (ringing in the ears).

*Blood blisters on your hands:* You are playing too hard. Instead of hitting harder, try hitting quicker. You are using too much force to get a sound out of the drum; that kind of force muffles the sound. The harder you hit, the less sound comes out. Rather, hit it quickly, bring the sound up and out of the drum, but don't overgesture. Just raise your hands up enough to let the head vibrate. Stay close for the next note. This also gets the healing, vibrational energy into your hands from the drum itself while it is vibrating. Feel the resonance of the drum in your hands. Play by listening with your hands.

*Muscle soreness:* Try MSM (methylsulfonylmethane). It replaces the sulphur that is depleted in joints, tendons, and muscles.

*Stiffness in your back and shoulders:* This comes from focusing too tensely on what you are doing. Remember to laugh off the tension. Occasionally move your body if you're locked into one position. Maintain a good posture as in yoga (see below). Focus on full, deep, smooth breathing, using the exhalation to release tension.

## Apartment Drumming

Many people live in close proximity to other people. It is possible to play drums in that situation, but it must be very quiet, very meditative, and very soothing. That kind of energy will be more readily accepted in any situation than bombastic pummeling. Better drummers can play softer anyway. Playing at a whisper will open new possibilities, and your neighbors may not mind it so much.

It can be a prayer for everyone within listening distance of the drum. They may even like it.

# Appendix 2
# TUNING

Tuning an African style drum is not that hard, but putting on a new head can be a lot of work.

The Mali weaving on a djembe or ashiko is the best way to tune a goatskin head. It has evolved over hundreds of years and is very effective. The many vertical ropes pull the head down evenly around the shell, but still leave a small spring tension to give the drum nuance and subtlety when you play it.

Once the vertical ropes are pulled as tightly as possible, and the head is even around the edge of the shell, you start the horizontal weaving, the Mali weave. It is a beautiful knot that locks on itself when you pull it through. When you have completed one row of knots around the drum, skip over an extra vertical rope to start the next layer. That sets the weave off so that the diamond shape continues up the drum (see photo p. 254).

"Pulling diamonds" is a term used to describe the Mali weave.

Traditionally, the edge note of a djembe is very sharp and penetrating and the big note in the middle of the head is profoundly deep. Our culture many times does not need that incredibly piercing note at the edge, so sometimes the head may not be as tight as in Africa, but it is still a very beautiful-sounding drum. Many people prefer a mellower sound than that high piercing traditional note at the edge. It is all still good drum music. The heart and soul of what you play can be much more interesting than the drum itself—no matter how it is tuned.

There is also a middle tone on a djembe. Your hand hits the head, using all of your fingers and the meaty front portion of the palm. This note is a bit trickier to get, but it is a middle range note and is where much of the melody of a drum is played. It is not too difficult to get, but it takes a bit of playing to get comfortable with all three different notes on a djembe. I have avoided this kind of technique in order to get people past the major pitfall of thinking instead of feeling their playing. Once our feel is solid, then we can develop technique. Otherwise, learning technique first, without getting the feel, could make our playing intellectual and soulless. I encourage everyone to develop their own way of learning the drum, whatever your interests are—traditional or just for fun.

The author pulling the vertical ropes tighter on a standing ashiko. Try a more comfortable position to do this.

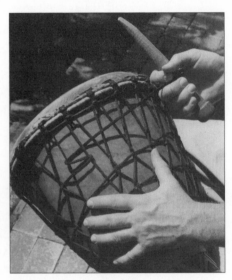

Detail of the knot technique. This is called "pulling diamonds."

# Illustration/Photo Credits

Page vii: Photo by Ron Sill

Page xv: Photo by Cathy Javier

Page xviii: Photos by Cathy Javier

Page xix: Photo by Cathy Javier

Page xxii: Photo by Chris Galfo

Page 14: Photo by Buddy Helm

Page 20: Photo by Buddy Helm

Page 24: Photo by Cathy Javier

Page 27: Photo by Cathy Javier

Page 35: Photo by Chris Galfo

Page 44: Photos by David Gallaher

Page 46: Poster, courtesy of Knott's Berry Farm

Page 61: Photo by Charlotte Wycoff

Page 68: Photo by Cathy Javier

Page 79: Photo by Marcia Galleher

Page 93: Photo by Cathy Javier

Page 100: Photo by Cathy Javier

Page 119: Photo by Marcia Galleher

Page 123: Illustration, *The Celtic Art Source Book*, by Courtney Davis. Blandford Press, London, 1989

Page 124: Photo by Cathy Javier

Page 127: Photo from Lynn Rank family archives

Page 134: Photos by Steve Karowe, courtesy of The Overseas Connection

Page 151: Photo by Buddy Helm

Page 154: Photo by Ron Sill

Page 170: Photo by Ron Sill

Page 173: Drawing by Buddy Helm

Page 189: Photo by Cathy Javier

Page 195: Photo from Lynn Rank family archives

Page 202: Card owned by author

Page 240: Photo by Cathy Javier

Page 242: Photos by Chris Galfo

Page 251: Photo by Cathy Javier

# ☽ REACH FOR THE MOON

*Llewellyn publishes hundreds of books on your favorite subjects! To get these exciting books, including the ones on the following pages, check your local bookstore or order them directly from Llewellyn.*

## Order by Phone
- Call toll-free within the U.S. and Canada, 1-800-THE MOON
- In Minnesota, call (651) 291-1970
- We accept VISA, MasterCard, and American Express

## Order by Mail
- Send the full price of your order (MN residents add 7% sales tax) in U.S. funds, plus postage & handling to:

  **Llewellyn Worldwide**
  **P.O. Box 64383, Dept. 0-7387-0159-9**
  **St. Paul, MN 55164–0383, U.S.A.**

## Postage & Handling
- **Standard** (U.S., Mexico, & Canada)

If your order is:
    $20.00 or under, add $5.00
    $20.01–$100.00, add $6.00
    Over $100, shipping is free
(Continental U.S. orders ship UPS. AK, HI, PR, & P.O. Boxes ship USPS 1st class. Mex. & Can. ship PMB.)

- **Second Day Air** (Continental U.S. only): $10.00 for one book + $1.00 per each additional book
- **Express** (AK, HI, & PR only) [Not available for P.O. Box delivery. For street address delivery only.]: $15.00 for one book + $1.00 per each additional book
- **International Surface Mail:** Add $1.00 per item
- **International Airmail:** Books—Add the retail price of each item; Non-book items—Add $5.00 per item

**Please allow 4–6 weeks for delivery on all orders.**
**Postage and handling rates subject to change.**

## Discounts
We offer a 20% discount to group leaders or agents. You must order a minimum of 5 copies of the same book to get our special quantity price.

### Free Catalog
Get a free copy of our color catalog, *New Worlds of Mind and Spirit*. Subscribe for just $10.00 in the United States and Canada ($30.00 overseas, airmail).

**Visit our website at www.llewellyn.com for more information.**

## Drumming the Spirit to Life
### *Let the Goddess Dance*

**Russell Buddy Helm**

Beat a drum and feel the rhythm down in your body. Release your inhibitions! Feel confident enough to let loose with a couple of hot licks. After using the methods in this book, you won't be able to help yourself. Through drumming, you can release your trauma and fears. Anything seems possible when this type of drumming dawns in your soul.

*Drumming the Spirit to Life* is a rhythmic workbook that discusses the psychological and physical effects of drumming as a tool for healing and joy. It is an autobiographical exploration of how drumming has been a tool for understanding and growth as well as a career and an art form for the author, Buddy Helm. It is the only book that combines the actual experience of drumming with the active process of meditation.

*Includes audio CD with six cuts that demonstrate techniques from the book*

1-56718-432-4, 192 pp., 7½ x 9⅛                                      **$19.95**

# Destiny of Souls
## *New Case Studies of Life Between Lives*

### Michael Newton, Ph.D.

A pioneer in uncovering the secrets of life, internationally recognized spiritual hypnotherapist Dr. Michael Newton takes you once again into the heart of the spirit world. His groundbreaking research was first published in the best-selling *Journey of Souls,* the definitive study on the afterlife. Now, in *Destiny of Souls*, the saga continues with seventy case histories of real people who were regressed into their lives between lives. Dr. Newton answers the requests of the thousands of readers of the first book who wanted more details about various aspects of life on the other side. *Destiny of Souls* is also designed for the enjoyment of first-time readers who haven't read *Journey of Souls.*

Hear the stories of people in deep hypnosis as they tell about:

- Why we are on earth
- Spiritual settings where souls go after death
- Ways spirits connect with and comfort the living
- Spirit guides and the council of wise beings who interview us after each life
- Who is a soulmate and linkages between soul groups and human families
- Soul recreation and travel between lives
- The soul-brain connection and why we choose certain bodies

1-56718-499-5, 384 pp., 6 x 9, illus.                    $14.95

**TO ORDER BY PHONE, CALL 1-800 THE MOON**
Prices subject to change without notice

## Practical Guide to
## Past-Life Memories
### *Twelve Proven Methods*

### Richard Webster

*Heal your current life by remembering your past lives*

Past life memories can provide valuable clues as to why we behave the way we do. They can shed light on our purpose in life, and they can help us heal our current wounds. Now you can recall your past lives on your own, without the aid of a hypnotist.

This book includes only the most successful and beneficial methods used in the author's classes. Since one method does not work for everyone, you can experiment with twelve different straightforward techniques to find the best one for you.

This book also answers many questions, such as "Do I have a soul mate?", "Does everyone have a past life?", "Is it dangerous?", and "What about déjà vu?"

- No other book covers as many methods for recalling past lives

- For the first time in print: how to return to a previous incarnation with your spirit guide

- Filled with case studies that illustrate each method

- Features only the most successful methods from the author's own classes

0-7387-0077-0, 264 pp., 5³⁄₁₆ x 8                                   **$9.95**

**TO ORDER BY PHONE, CALL 1-800 THE MOON**
Prices subject to change without notice

# Dreams
## Working Interactive
### with Software for Journaling & Interpretation

**Stephanie Jean Clement, Ph.D., and Terry Rosen**

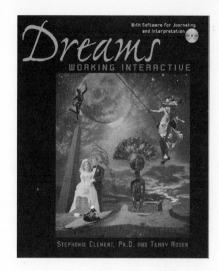

*Dreams* is the only complete and interactive system for helping you determine the unique, personal meaning of your dreams. What does it mean to dream of the house you grew up in? Why do certain people appear in your dreams again and again? How can you tell if a dream is revealing the future? Together, the book and software program provide everything necessary to effectively record and analyze whatever message your subconscious throws your way.

Absent in *Dreams* is the psychological jargon that makes many dream books so difficult. Examples of dreams illustrate the various types of dreams, and each chapter gives information about how to identify and work with dream symbols. The software program gives you the capacity to print out your dreams, incorporating the symbol definitions you select. What's more, the program will facilitate further exploration of your dreams with suggestions and questions.

*With the PC-compatible Interactive Dream Software you can:*

- Record your dreams, visions or waking experiences

- Get an immediate listing of your dream symbols that are included in the electronic dictionary

- Add your own new definitions to the database

- Answer questions to facilitate more in-depth exploration of your dreams

**1-56718-145-7, 240 pp., 7½ x 9⅛,**
**CD-ROM software program for PC format with Windows**                **$24.95**

**TO ORDER BY PHONE, CALL 1-800 THE MOON**
Prices subject to change without notice

## Pagans & Christians
### *The Personal Spiritual Experience*

### Gus diZerega, Ph.D.

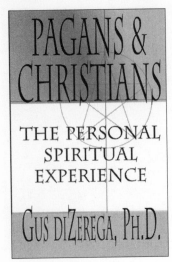

*Pagans and Christians* have been polarized within the spiritual landscape for two millennia. Recent media reports even talk of efforts by the Christian Right to boycott the U.S. Army for allowing Wiccan soldiers to practice their religion. There is no better time for Western civilization's most prominent religion and humanity's oldest religion to enter into intelligent and respectful dialogue.

Providing something for Pagans and Christians alike, Dr. diZerega presents an important and original contribution for contemporary interfaith understanding. For Pagans, his book deepens the discussion of Paganism's theological and philosophical implications, penetrating its inner truths and examining the reasons for its modern growth. For Christians, it demystifies Paganism, offering respectful answers to the most common criticisms levelled at Pagan beliefs and practices.

*This explicit comparison and discussion of the differences between the two religions includes:*

- The eight distinguishing characteristics of Pagan spirituality

- Wiccan spiritual outlooks, what it is like to encounter a Deity, the sacralization of the year in Wiccan practice, and the sacred role of sexuality

- A Pagan perspective of evil, Satan, and suffering

- Claims of biblical inerrancy, the value of revealed scripture compared to personal spiritual experience, the differences between Wiccan and Christian clergy

- How nature religion can help Christians appreciate elements of their own heritage

1-56718-228-3, 264 pp., 6 x 9, illus.                                    $14.95

**TO ORDER BY PHONE, CALL 1-800 THE MOON**
Prices subject to change without notice

The compact disk accompanying this book is a production of
Buddy Helm Music BMI. All rights reserved.

# The Way of the Drum

by

Russell S. Buddy Helm

All songs composed, performed, recorded by Russell Buddy Helm

Flute by Charlie Dechant

Background vocals by Brandy Ethridge

Total running time 1:13:26


For bookings, workshops, and lessons, contact:

Website: buddyhelm.com      email: buddy@buddyhelm.com


track  1: Downbeat  6:15  chapter one

track  2: Mother Earth Chant  1:40  (Chapter 1)

track  3: Mother Earth Samba  3:52  (Chapter 2)

track  4: Tripolet Intro  1:01  (Chapter 3)

track  5: Tripolet 1:  1.29  (Chapter 3)

track  6: Tripolet 2:  1:30  (Chapter 3)

track  7: Tripolets 3 & 4  1:53  (Chapter 3)

track  8: Elephant Walk  1:34  (Chapter 7)

track  9: 6 against 4  1:09  (Chapter 7)

track 10: StopTime  4:39  (Chapter 8)

track 11: Blues Shuffle  2:08  (Chapter 9)

track 12: 5 minus 1  0:45  (Chapter 9)

track 13: 5 minus 1 stretched out  0:57  (Chapter 9)

track 14: Invocation  5:09  (Chapter 10)

track 15: Soul  1:02  (Chapter 11)

track 16: Bo Diddley  2:09  (Chapter 13)

track 17: Marvin  2:00  (Chapter 13)

track 18: Celtic  2:03  (Chapter 14)

track 19: Funeral  1:42  (Chapter 14)

track 20: Gospel  1:14  (Chapter 16)

track 21: Remove last note  1:53  (Chapter 16)

track 22: 3 note combo  2:00  (Chapter 17)

track 23: Speed up 2 Slo down  6:32  (Chapter 17)

track 24: Rock 1 (Miss Molly)  1:11  (Chapter 13)

track 25: Rock 2  0:58  (Chapter 17)

track 26: 4 notes  2:13  (Chapter 21)

track 27: Thrust  0:53  (Chapter 18)

track 28: Mambo  3:00  (Chapter 21)

track 29: Simple Samba  2.11  (Chapter 21)1

track 30: Favorite  2:40  (Chapter 21)

track 31: 9 stroke roll  1.16  (Chapter 22)

track 32: Fills  3:02  (Chapter 23)

track: 33 Hit the Road  1:34  (Chapter 12)

Instrumentation: Djembe, Congas, shakere, claves, agogo, talking drum, Madal (Persian), Gretch Drum set, 12-string acoustical guitar, Yamaha keyboards, large and small Chinese gongs, Ting Sha, Bell Tree, Gwa Gwa, Djun Djun (African Bass Drum), spoons, Vibra Slap, Flex-a-tone, rain stick, fishskin Dombeq.

Insect, bird and animal sounds recorded in Palengue Jungle. Surf sounds recorded at Passa Grille Beach at midnight under a balmy summer New Moon.